Cambridge
Collections

Outsiders

a collection of fiction and non-fiction

Edited by Roy Blatchford
Series editor: Michael Marland

CAMBRIDGE
UNIVERSITY PRESS

CAMBRIDGE UNIVERSITY PRESS

Cambridge, New York, Melbourne, Madrid, Cape Town, Singapore, São Paulo, Delhi

Cambridge University Press
The Edinburgh Building, Cambridge CB2 8RU, UK

www.cambridge.org
Information on this title: www.cambridge.org/9780521703253

First published 2007

Printed in the United Kingdom at the University Press, Cambridge

A catalogue record for this publication is available from the British Library

ISBN 978-0-521-70325-3 paperback

Cover image: Punchstock/fstop

Cover design by Smith

Illustrations by Tom Sperling/Bright Agency

Picture research by Sandie Huskinson-Rolfe of PHOTOSEEKERS

Contents

Acknowledgements

The volume editor wishes to thank Sue Quainton, librarian, for her research and recommendations in the writing of this book.

The volume editor and publishers acknowledge the following sources of copyright material and are grateful for the permissions granted. While every effort has been made, it has not always been possible to identify the sources of all the material used, or to trace all copyright holders. If any omissions are brought to our notice, we will be happy to include the appropriate acknowledgements on reprinting.

p.2 *Why the Whales Came* by Michael Morpurgo © 1985 Michael Morpurgo. Published by Egmont UK Ltd London and used with permission; p.13 *The Highwayman* by Alfred Noyes. Reproduced by permission of the Society of Authors as the Literary Representative of the Estate of Alfred Noyes; p.18 *The Pied Piper of Hamelin* by Robert Browning (1812–1889). This version appeared in *Poems for Pleasure*, published by Cambridge University Press, 1961; p.29 *The Third Man* by Graham Greene, from *The Third Man and the Fallen Idol*. Published by Penguin Books. © Copyright 1971. Reproduced by permission of David Higham Associates on behalf of the author; p.36 *To Kill a Mockingbird* by Harper Lee. Copyright © 1960 Harper Lee, renewed © 1988 Harper Lee. Foreword copyright © 1993 by Harper Lee. Published by William Heinemann Ltd. Reprinted by permission of The Random House Group Ltd and HarperCollins Publishers (Canadian print rights). Electronic rights reproduced by permission of Aitken Alexander Associates on behalf of the author; p.46 *The Man Who Planted Trees* by Jean Giono. Copyright © 1989 Jean Giono. Reproduced by permission of Peter Owen Ltd, London; p.51 *A Christmas Carol* by Charles Dickens (1812–1870). This version appeared in *A Christmas Carol* published by Longman, 1994; p.60 *Silas Marner* by George Eliot (1819–1880). This version appeared in *Silas Marner* published by Longman, 1994; p.78 *Heroic Failures* by Stephen Pile, from *The Heroic Book of Failures*. First published in 1979 by Routledge. Copyright © 1979 Stephen Pile. Reproduced by permission of the author c/o Rogers, Coleridge & White Ltd., 20 Powis Mews, London W11 1JN; p.80 *Blind Spanish Woman Makes Television History* by Julian Coman from the *Sunday Telegraph*, 11 June 2000. Reproduced by permission of Telegraph Media Group Limited; p.83 *Marla Runyan (the Blind Olympian)* by Peter Sheridan from *The Mail on Sunday*, 23 July 2000. Reproduced by permission of Solo Syndication Limited; p.88 *Touching the Void* by Conn and Hal Iggulden from *The Dangerous Book for Boys*. Copyright © Conn and Hal Iggulden 2006. Print rights reprinted by permission of HarperCollins Publishers Ltd. Electronic rights reproduced by permission of A.M. Heath & Co Ltd on behalf of the authors; p.94 from *On Being John McEnroe* by Tim Adams. Published by Yellow Jersey Press. Reprinted by permission of The Random House Group Ltd; p.103 *The Madness of Man* by Andrew Alderson from *The Sunday Telegraph*, 11 June 2000. Reproduced by permission of Telegraph Media Group Limited; p.109 *It's Not About the Bike* by Lance Armstrong. Copyright © Lance Armstrong. Published by Yellow Jersey Press. Print rights reproduced by permission of The Random House Group Ltd and G P Putnam's Sons, a division of Penguin Group (USA) Inc. Electronic rights reproduced by permission of G P Putnam's Sons, a division of Penguin Group (USA) Inc; p.117 *Moondust* by Andrew Smith. Copyright © Andrew Smith 2005. Print rights reproduced by permission of Bloomsbury

Publishing and Rogers, Coleridge & White. Electronic rights reproduced by permission of Andrew Smith, c/o Rogers, Coleridge & White Ltd, 20 Powis Mews, London W11 1JN; p.134 *Coming to England* by Floella Benjamin. Copyright © Floella Benjamin 1997. Reproduced by permission of Benjamin-Taylor Associates on behalf of the author; p.138 *Refugee Boy* by Benjamin Zephaniah. Copyright © 2001 Benjamin Zephaniah. Reproduced by permission of Bloomsbury Publishing; p.144 *What's Your Problem?* By Bali Rai. Copyright © 2003 Bali Rai. Published by permission of Barrington Stoke Ltd; p.149 *A Boy Called 'Grenade'* by Fergal Keane from *Letters Home*. Copyright © 1999 Fergal Keane. Print rights reproduced by permission of Penguin Books Ltd. Electronic rights reproduced by permission of David Godwin Associates on behalf of the author; p.153 *Mirad, a Boy from Bosnia* by Ad de Bont. © Ad de Bont and Verlag der Autoren, Frankfurt am Main 1994. © Marian Buijs 1994 for English translation; p.164 *Zlata's Diary* by Zlata Filipovic from *Zlata's Diary, A Child's Life in Sarajevo*. Translated by Christina Pribichevich-Zoric. Viking 1994. First published in France as '*Le Journal de Zlata*' by Fixot et editions Robert Laffont 1993. Copyright © Fixot et editions Robert Laffont, 1993. Print rights reproduced by permission of Penguin Books Ltd. Electronic rights reproduced by permission of Susanna Lea Associates on behalf of the author; p.171 *Shooting an Elephant* by George Orwell from *Shooting an Elephant and Other Essays*. Copyright © 1936 George Orwell. Reproduced by permission of Bill Hamilton as the Literary Executor of the Estate of the Late Sonia Brownell Orwell and Secker & Warburg Ltd; p.180 *A Stranger's Eye* by Fergal Keane, from *A Stranger's Eye: A Foreign Correspondent's View of Britain*. Published by Viking 2000. Copyright © Fergal Keane 2000. Print rights reproduced by permission of Penguin Books Ltd. Electronic rights reproduced by permission of David Godwin Associates on behalf of the author; p.200 *The Rebel* by D. J. Enright. Copyright © 1974. Reproduced by permission of Watson, Little Ltd as licensing Agents; p.202 *Less Able* by Gervase Phinn from *Classroom Creatures*. Copyright © 1996. Reproduced by kind permission of the author; p.203 *Dear Aunty* by Patricia Borlenghi. Copyright © 2001 Patricia Borlenghi. Reproduced by permission of Bloomsbury Publishing; p.207 *Face* by Benjamin Zephaniah. Copyright © 2001 Benjamin Zephaniah. Reproduced by permission of Bloomsbury Publishing; p.214 *The Rescue of Karen Arscott* by Gene Kemp. Reproduced by permission of Pollinger Limited and Gene Kemp; p.220 *Red Sky in the Morning* by Elizabeth Laird. Copyright © 2001 Elizabeth Laird. Reproduced by permission of Macmillan Children's Books, London, UK; p.229 *The Curious Incident of the Dog in the Night-time* by Mark Haddon. Published by David Fickling / Jonathan Cape. Print rights reproduced by permission of The Random House Group Ltd and Gillon Aitken Associates. Electronic rights reproduced by permission of Gillon Aitken Associates on behalf of the author; p.236 *The Fifth Child* by Doris Lessing. Copyright © 1988 Doris Lessing. Reprinted by kind permission of Jonathan Clowes Ltd., London on behalf of Doris Lessing; p.244 *The Bus People* by Rachel Anderson. Copyright © 1993 Rachel Anderson. Reprinted by permission of Oxford University Press.

The publishers would like to thank the following for permission to reproduce photographs and illustrations: 48, Woodcut by Michael McCurdy, from *The Man who Planted Trees* by Jean Giono, Peter Owen publishers, London; 80, © epa; 88, John Cleare / Mountain Picture Library; 103, Clive Challinor Motorsport Photography; 151, 'Interrogation' by Ricky Romain, Oil on canvas 172 x 169cm 2005; 173, © Dallas and John Heaton / Free Agents Limited / CORBIS; 200, The Kobal Collection / Warner Bros; 265, Illustration © Mark Haddon.

General introduction

What do you think of when you read or hear the word 'outsider'? *Pause* for a moment . . . and gather some words in your head which you associate with 'outsider'.

Do your thoughts turn to someone you know who is a little bit different, perhaps on the outside of a group of friends? Or do you think of people who have moved from one country to another and feel that they don't quite belong to where they are now living?

Do you think even about individuals who lead particularly unusual lives or achieve things which most of us can only dream of – those whose experiences are beyond the everyday? Or you might call to mind characters in books you have read or plays that you have seen, who live on in your memory because their actions set them apart from those around them.

On the following pages you will read about 'outsiders' in fiction and non-fiction who come in many shapes and guises: from the asylum seeker to the cycling hero, from the highwayman to the moonwalker, from Charles Dickens' Scrooge to George Eliot's Silas Marner, from the severely disabled child to the intrepid mountaineer. This collection will help you think afresh about how you might interpret and re-interpret the word 'outsider'.

The collection is arranged in four sections, with the more difficult extracts placed at the end of each section, and with occasional illustrations to stimulate reactions and ideas.

To support your reading, less familiar words in the text are explained in brief at the foot of the pages where they occur. Ideas for further reading also accompany each text, and notes about the authors can be found at the end of the anthology.

Each section concludes with a range of reading, writing, speaking and listening activities to help you explore and enjoy the writers' ideas, opinions, styles, use of language and techniques.

There is great variety in the following pages. Enjoy what these writers have to say, and challenge some of your own assumptions about what it is to be thought of as an 'outsider'.

Roy Blatchford

# 1 Fictional outsiders

This section introduces a number of celebrated fictional characters who, in their different ways, are on the outside of their communities. For example, you will meet here Michael Morpurgo's Birdman, who has been isolated by the island people around him but who arrives to save their very community. In strong contrast is Graham Greene's wonderful creation, the Third Man, whose very name sets him apart in the novel he haunts.

Activities

1   Think about novels, poems and stories you have read in which 'outsiders' in some shape or form are an important ingredient. Make brief notes on how they are presented as characters, and the actions they take.

2   Now think about television programmes and films you have seen which feature 'outsiders'. Talk about them in your groups. Are there common ways in which 'outsiders' are presented in fiction, both in books and on the screen?

3   Look at the titles of the texts in this section, listed on the contents page. In groups, choose three titles and brainstorm what you think these texts might be about. When you work on these texts later, you can see how your original ideas compare. Discuss which of these titles would most prompt you to read on, and why.

Why the Whales Came

by Michael Morpurgo

The book from which this extract is taken is set on the Isles of Scilly, a scattering of tiny islands kicked out into the Atlantic by the boot of England. The date is April 1914 and the story is told through the eyes of ten-year-old Gracie Jenkins. The book is drawing to a conclusion and here we discover the power of the Birdman, who has been treated as an outsider by his fellow islanders for many years.

We did all we could to discourage the whales from coming in too close to the shore. Shouting and screaming at the water's edge, we hurled stones and driftwood at them but most fell far short and those few that did hit them did not seem to deter them. The Birdman's flock of gulls wheeled noisily overhead, but the whales took no notice of them either. All the time they were drifting closer and closer to the beach and disaster. Every faint whistle from the stranded whale seemed to drive the others out in the bay to distraction, sending them rolling and plunging in amongst each other and precipitating a chorus of thunderous

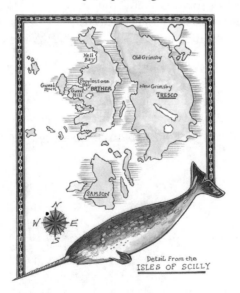

Detail From the
ISLES OF SCILLY

snorting and whistling that subsided only when the whale lay still and silent again on the sand. But each furious flurry of activity left them that much nearer the shore and there seemed nothing we could do now to stop them beaching themselves.

'Gracie,' said the Birdman, 'you go back to the whale and try to keep her happy. Stroke her, Gracie. Talk to her, sing to her, anything so's she doesn't call out.' And he took off his sou'wester¹ and handed it to me. 'It won't do to let her get too dry either, Gracie. You can use this for a bucket.'

So I went back and forth from the water's edge to the whale with the Birdman's sou'wester full of water. I began at her head, pouring the water all over her eyes and mouth. She seemed to relish it, blinking and rolling her head from side to side as the water ran down over her skin and into the sand, and all the while I talked to her quietly. I remember thinking as I looked into her eyes that she could understand me, that she could understand every word I said.

I was kneeling in the sand beside her head, stroking her behind the blowhole above her eyes, when I saw them coming back. They were hurrying along the path under Gweal Hill, Big Tim running out in front. It looked as if he had brought most of the island with him. Everyone had a weapon of some kind in his hand, a fork, an axe, a hoe or a scythe; and Daniel's father carried a harpoon over his shoulder. I looked for Mother amongst them but could not pick her out. The Vicar was there, his cassock tucked up into his trousers, and Mr Wellbeloved was there too, striding out with his stick along-side Daniel's father.

'Stay where you are, Gracie,' the Birdman told me, 'and keep her quiet if you can.' By the time they reached the beach, the Birdman, Daniel and Prince stood between them and the stranded whale. No one spoke for a moment. They all stood looking incredulously at the Birdman and the whale, at Daniel and me, whispering anxiously amongst themselves. It was only

---

¹**sou'wester**   waterproof hat

when they noticed the rolling black backs breaking the water out in the bay that they began to talk aloud.

'See,' Big Tim shouted in triumph, pointing his machete. 'Didn't I tell you? Didn't I tell you? There's dozens of them out there. I said there was.'

'It's a narwhal,' said Mr Wellbeloved. 'Yes, I do believe it's a narwhal. Well I never. Only the males have tusks, you know. He's a long way from home. That's the kind of whale that the Eskimos hunt off Greenland. Quite what he's doing here I cannot imagine. If I might take a closer look . . . ' As he stepped towards us Prince began to growl, his lip curling back above his teeth, his neck tense with fury. Mr Wellbeloved stopped where he stood.

'Look here, Mr Woodcock,' Daniel's father said, taking Mr Wellbeloved's arm and pulling him back, 'we don't much care what this thing is. Whale, narwhal, it doesn't matter to us. All that matters is that there's meat on it and ivory too by the look of it. That's money to us, Mr Woodcock. Anything washed up on our beaches is ours by right, always has been, Mr Woodcock; you know that.' The Birdman said nothing but looked along the ranks of islanders that faced him. 'And as for you, Daniel Pender,' Daniel's father went on, pointing at Daniel, 'you can come right back over here, else I'll take a strap to you right here and now in front of all these people. You've no business to be here with this man. You've been told time and time again.' Daniel stayed where he was alongside the Birdman.

'You can strap me all you want, Father,' he said, 'but you got to listen to Mr Woodcock. You got to listen to him. If you don't, then we're done for, all of us. You got to do what he says, Father.'

'Mr Woodcock,' Daniel's father said, his patience fast vanishing, 'are you going to move that dog or am I? Now I don't want anyone to get hurt . . . '

'He can't hear you, Father,' Daniel said. 'He's deaf. Gracie and me, we're the only ones he can understand.'

'Deaf?' said Daniel's father, and he was clearly taken aback. 'All right then, you tell him for us, Daniel. You tell him that the whale belongs to all of us and we aim to kill it and those out there in Popplestones as well. They're ours by right and he can't stop us. Tell him to stand aside.'

Daniel interpreted quietly and the Birdman nodded his understanding, putting his hand on Daniel's shoulder. He straightened up and faced Daniel's father. 'Then you will have to kill me first,' he said. 'This whale must go back to the sea where she belongs. Then we must drive them all back out to sea. If just one of them dies, the curse that fell on Samson when I was a boy will fall on you, and Bryher[2] will be cursed forever. You must help me before it's too late.'

'Oh come on,' said Big Tim pushing his way through. 'We don't have to listen to this old fool. Those whales out there could turn round any minute and head back out to sea and we'd lose the lot of them.' And the crowd began to move slowly in towards us.

'Stand aside, Mr Woodcock,' said Daniel's father. 'You know we're within our rights. Out of the way now.' At once Prince was on his feet and the growl had turned to a snarl. Those just in front of him fell back, but the rest kept coming until we were almost surrounded. At that moment the whale must have sensed danger for she raised her head and whistled again, twisting and turning and thrashing the ground behind her. Popplestones Bay suddenly boiled with life.

'Don't do it, please Father,' cried Daniel backing down towards me. 'Don't do it. Listen to him. He's telling the truth. I know he is.' But I could see from the hardness in the faces around me that they were ignoring him, that they were no longer even listening as they closed in around us.

'Wait!' It was a voice from the back of the crowd, a voice I knew well. 'Wait!' Everyone looked round. They hushed instantly, and then stood to one side as my mother came forward, Aunty Mildred beside her. Mother looked first at me and

[2]**Samson** and **Bryher**   two of the Scilly islands

then at the Birdman. 'You were up early this morning, Gracie,' she said. 'I wondered where you'd got to.'

'Had to go, Mother,' I said, standing up. 'I had to. Daniel came for me. Big Tim and all of them, they were going to attack the Birdman's cottage. Daniel heard them planning it, so we had to warn him, didn't we?'

'Were they indeed?' said Mother, looking around her. There was a hard edge to her voice I had never heard before. 'Did you know that, Mr Pender?' she asked, and Daniel's father looked hard at Big Tim.

'Well he deserved it,' said Big Tim. 'He was signalling to German submarines, I know he was. We seen him, didn't we?' But none of his friends supported him now.

Mother walked across to Big Tim and looked him in the eye. 'You know nothing, Tim Pender; because you don't think, you never have. You know only what you want to know. You're a bully and a coward and you should be ashamed of yourself.' And she turned and spoke to the crowd. 'This old man helped me and Gracie. He left honey and milk and bread on my doorstep when we needed it most. Just like you, I've known him all my life and never spoken to him, but in all that time I've never known him harm anyone. Yes, every one of us is frightened of him and we tell our children to keep out of his way; but what has he ever really done to harm any one of us?' There was silence. Mother came over to me and took me by the hand. 'I don't know what Gracie and Daniel have been up to, and I don't know why Mr Woodcock wants to save these creatures. I do know we owe it to him and to the two children at least to listen to them, to hear them out. If after that you still want to kill the whales, then you can. They'll still be here.' She did not wait for approval, she assumed it. She turned to Daniel. 'Tell us, Daniel. Tell us all about it.' And not a word was raised against her.

I wondered at the time that she was able to command such instant obedience. On reflection I think everyone was as shocked as I was at the sudden transformation in her. I certainly had never seen her so authoritative and passionate. All I know is that without a murmur, even from Big Tim, they all backed away and waited shamefaced for Daniel to begin.

Daniel turned to Mr Woodcock. 'Shall I tell them?' he asked, and the old man nodded.

'Tell them,' he said, 'tell them everything. But hurry, Daniel, hurry. There's no time to lose.'

They listened intently as Daniel told them of how the Birdman and his mother had witnessed the massacre of the whales on Samson all those years ago, how they had tried to stop it and failed, that it was the islanders' greed and cruelty that had brought the curse down on Samson. He told them the whole terrible story of the death of Samson, of the ghostship, of the starvation and disease that followed, of all the ships drawn to their destruction on the rocks off Samson, of the dogs the people had to eat to survive.

As the truth behind the age-old rumours came out, the islanders listened all the more closely. They heard how the people left one by one until finally the well had dried up and forced the Birdman and his mother off the island.

For some time no one said anything. They looked at each other uneasily, and then it was Big Tim that spoke up. 'So what? We don't know that any of it's true, do we? He could be making it all up, couldn't he? Where's the proof?'

'The proof's on Samson,' Daniel said. 'I've seen it – and Gracie's seen it too. We've seen the horn, haven't we, Gracie? In Mr Woodcock's cottage on Samson it was, hanging above the stove. Just like that one, it is,' he said, pointing at the whale.

'You been over there, Gracie?' Mother asked me. 'You been over to Samson?'

'We couldn't help it, Mother,' I said. 'It was that night we went out fishing and the fog came down. Never told you before 'cos I knew you'd be angry. Didn't know where we were, Mother, honest. Couldn't see a thing. Then we saw this light and rowed towards it. We thought it was Bryher at first, but it turned out it was the Birdman's fire on Samson. He lights a fire on Samson whenever there's bad weather. It's to keep the ships away from the rocks.'

Suddenly Mother was beside me. Hands on hips, she faced the crowd. 'Well?' she said. 'What are you waiting for? If we don't hurry, every one of those whales will be on the beach and then we'll never be able to get them off. We need a sail to roll her onto and we need ropes. We'll need a horse, or a donkey, both maybe to haul her back into the sea. Hurry now.' This time there were no arguments. On the contrary there was a sudden stir of excitement. Somehow, Mother had galvanised[3] the whole island into action. The Vicar and Aunty Mildred organised every spare man, woman and child into an extended line at the water's edge. There must have been a hundred people there advancing into the sea to keep the whales from coming in. Waist high in the water they were whistling and shouting and splashing, whilst behind them the rescue began.

It was Daniel's father who directed the delicate task of engineering the stranded whale back into the sea. 'Got to launch her gently, just like she was a boat,' he said. They dug a deep trench to one side of her and when the sail came they laid it in the bottom. Then they dug away the side of the ditch she was lying in and eased her sideways, rocking her gently until she slid down onto the sail. It took twelve men pushing, the Birdman, Mr Wellbeloved and Daniel's father amongst them, before the whale was finally in place.

All through the rescue I stayed by the whale's head whilst an endless relay of children with buckets, Big Tim and his friends mostly, fetched and carried water to keep the whale's skin wet. She was tiring quickly now. Her flourishes were less and less frequent and she had fallen almost silent. She moved quietly from time to time, her tiny eyes often closing for minutes on end so that sometimes I thought she might be dead. A bucket of water poured gently over her head seemed to revive her, but each time it took longer. She would open her wedge-shaped mouth under the horn and allow the water to trickle in through her teeth. I talked to her all the while, reassuring her as well as I

---

[3]**galvanised**   stirred

could that it would not be long now before she was back with
her friends and out at sea again. I could feel her breath on my
fingers as I stroked the top of her head around her blowhole.
She was breathing less often now and more deeply, almost as if
she were going to sleep. Or was she dying slowly?

Friend and another donkey were hitched up already to the
sail. At first it looked as if they would not be strong enough for
the task. Their feet sank deep into the sand as they pulled and
the whale did not move. What the Birdman said into Friend's
ear no one knows, but whatever it was was enough, for they
were soon hauling the whale down across the wet sand towards
the sea. There were a dozen men or more straining at the sail at
each side, so that the whale was returned to the water cradled in
a kind of hammock. I stood back and watched with the others
as the waves washed over her and she gradually came back to
life. On the Birdman's advice we left her there wallowing in the
shallows for some time, giving her time to regain her strength,
to feel her buoyancy. Then to our delight she began to heave
and thrash again and she let out a long wailing whistle. That
seemed enough to satisfy the Birdman and we gathered around
her and pushed her through the water towards the others that
lay waiting for her out in the bay. There was a flurry out in the
middle when she joined them and much rolling and groaning
and whistling, an exultant chorus of joy at their reunion. Then
she became one of them, and I was never sure which she was
after that.

I thought, as everyone thought, that the job was done then,
that once reunited they would turn for the open sea; but for
some reason they seemed reluctant to leave the bay in spite of
all we did to frighten them away. Big Tim it was who suggested
that banging on tin trays and corrugated iron might do the
trick, so we children were all sent home to fetch back any bit of
sheet metal we could find that would serve as a drum. It was a
good idea and the first time we all thundered on our makeshift
drums it seemed to have an effect, for they turned and swam
away; but then they stopped at the mouth of the bay and turned

back again setting up such a row of whistling, whooping and snorting so that you would almost have thought they were talking back to our drums. Far from driving them away, the drumming only seemed to interest them and excite them.

All day long the islanders sustained this frantic effort. Everyone took turns in the water now, for it was too cold to stay there long. Hot soup and bread were brought out to the beach and kept warm over a fire in one corner of the beach, so that a ready supply of food was on hand all day. We had one brief taste of success when a pair of the whales was spotted swimming out to sea, past Gweal Rock. However the others did not follow, so that by nightfall most of the whales were still trapped in Popplestones, unable or unwilling to find their way out.

The Birdman, Daniel and I were sitting drinking our soup by the fire when the Birdman had the idea. His face was ashen with cold and exhaustion, but suddenly there was an urgency in his voice. 'Look where they are,' he said, getting to his feet and pointing out into the bay. 'Look at them.' The whales were lying together in a pack in the dark waters on the far side of Popplestones. 'It's the fire,' he said. 'It's the fire. They're as far from the fire as they can be. They don't like fire.'

Flaming torches, oil lamps, piles of burning brushwood and driftwood, we used anything, anything that would burn. We lit fires all along the rocks around the bay; and then the Birdman, with a long line of islanders on either side of him waving their torches above their heads, waded out into the sea towards the whales. We children were told to stay on the beach. It was too dangerous now, out in the dark water with the whales' flailing tails and the sea whipped up into a frenzy by a fresh offshore wind. So we stayed and watched the line of torches as they moved out into the bay.

Only minutes later they brought the Birdman back, Daniel's father and the Vicar carrying him out of the sea. A wave had knocked the breath out of him, Daniel's father said as they laid him down by the fire beside us.

'I'll be all right,' the Birdman said, struggling onto his elbows. 'Let me get out there. We need everyone out there.'

'I think you've done enough, Mr Woodcock,' said the Vicar. 'They're going, they're turning. We can manage without you now. You nearly drowned out there. You stay here and rest.' And much against his will, he did. Mother put a blanket around him and Daniel and I huddled close to him, and Prince came to lie down at our feet. 'Maybe it'll be all right, children,' the Birdman said.

'Maybe it will be, after all.'

It was the line of flaming torches that at last made the whales leave for the open sea; for with a final flourish of triumphant whistling and snorting, and shooting great fountains into the air, they swam out past Gweal Island and left us in the gathering dark. A great cheer went up all around the bay, but beside us the Birdman was still not happy. He was on his feet again by now. He made everyone build beacons all along the beach to be sure they did not come back during the night; and even when almost everyone had left Popplestones for home he still would not go.

Mother asked him to come home with us. She begged him to come. 'Tell him it's a cold night, Daniel, and he can't sleep in a house with no windows. He's soaked to the skin. Tell him he must come home with us.'

Daniel told him and the Birdman smiled and shook his head. 'I'll be warm enough by the fire,' he said. 'I shall stay here and Prince will stay with me to keep me company, won't you, Prince? Maybe later when it gets light I'll take the boat out. I want to be sure they've gone – got to be sure they don't come back. You take those two children of mine home before they catch cold.' And as we were leaving, he called out without turning round, 'It's over now, children. The curse of Samson is redeemed, finished. All will be well now, I promise you. You'll see.'

So we left him there in the glow of the fire with Prince sitting beside him. As we went we saw the gulls settling on the beach all around him and from nowhere his one-legged kitti-wake[4] flew up and landed on his shoulder.

No one ever saw the Birdman again. They found his sou'wester washed up on Hell Bay some days later, but his boat was never found. I have always thought that he knew he might not be coming back because otherwise he would never have left Prince behind on the beach, and because of the remnants of a shell message we found the next morning in the sand beside the dog. The shells were scattered but we could still make out the letters 'Z.W.'.[5]

Further reading

If you've enjoyed this story, you might like to try reading some other stories written by Michael Morpurgo. Particularly recommended are *The White Horse of Zennor* (Egmont Books, 1982), *Kensuke's Kingdom* (Egmont Books, 1999) and *The Wreck of the Zanzibar* (Mammoth Books, 1995).

---

[4]**kittiwake**   small seagull
[5]**Z.W.**   the Birdman's initials

The Highwayman

by Alfred Noyes

The poet Alfred Noyes lived from 1880 to 1958. He wrote a number of poems about patriotism and war heroes.

This poem, written in 1906, is often voted as one of the most popular poems written in English, probably stemming from the fact that many, many adults learned the poem off by heart when they were at school. It is, first and foremost, a poem to be read aloud.

The wind was a torrent of darkness among the gusty trees,
The moon was a ghostly galleon tossed upon cloudy seas,
The road was a ribbon of moonlight over the purple moor,
And the highwayman came riding –
    Riding – riding –
The highwayman came riding, up to the old inn-door.

He'd a French cocked-hat on his forehead, a bunch of lace at
    his chin,
A coat of claret velvet, and breeches of brown doe-skin;

They fitted with never a wrinkle: his boots were up to the thigh!
And he rode with a jewelled twinkle,
    His pistol butts a-twinkle,
His rapier[1] hilt a-twinkle, under the jewelled sky.

Over the cobbles he clattered and clashed in the dark inn-yard,
And he tapped with his whip on the shutters, but all was
    locked and barred;
He whistled a tune to the window, and who should be waiting
    there
But the landlord's black-eyed daughter,
    Bess, the landlord's daughter,
Plaiting a dark red love-knot into her long black hair.

And dark in the old inn-yard a stable-wicket creaked
Where Tim the ostler[2] listened; his face was white and peaked;
His eyes were hollows of madness, his hair like mouldy hay,
But he loved the landlord's daughter,
    The landlord's red-lipped daughter;
Dumb as a dog he listened, and he heard the robber say –

'One kiss, my bonny sweetheart, I'm after a prize to-night,
But I shall be back with the yellow gold before the morning light;
Yet, if they press me sharply, and harry me through the day,
Then look for me by moonlight,
    Watch for me by moonlight,
I'll come to thee by moonlight, though hell should bar the way.'

He rose upright in the stirrups; he scarce could reach her hand,
But she loosened her hair i' the casement! His face burnt like a
    brand
As the black cascade of perfume came tumbling over his breast;
And he kissed its waves in the moonlight,
    (Oh, sweet black waves in the moonlight!)

---

[1] **rapier** sword
[2] **ostler** stableman

Then he tugged at his rein in the moonlight, and galloped
    away to the west.

He did not come in the dawning; he did not come at noon;
And out o' the tawny sunset, before the rise o' the moon,
When the road was a gipsy's ribbon, looping the purple moor,
A red-coat troop came marching –
    Marching – marching –
King George's men came marching, up to the old inn-door.

They said no word to the landlord, they drank his ale instead,
But they gagged his daughter and bound her to the foot of her
    narrow bed;
Two of them knelt at her casement, with muskets at their side!
There was death at every window;
    And hell at one dark window;
For Bess could see, through her casement, the road that *he*
    would ride.

They had tied her up to attention, with many a sniggering jest;
They had bound a musket beside her, with the barrel beneath
    her breast!
'Now keep good watch!' and they kissed her.
    She heard the dead man say –
Look for me by moonlight;
    Watch for me by moonlight;
I'll come to thee by moonlight, though hell should bar the way!

She twisted her hands behind her; but all the knots held good!
She writhed her hands till her fingers were wet with sweat or
    blood!
They stretched and strained in the darkness, and the hours
    crawled by like years,
Till, now, on the stroke of midnight,
    Cold, on the stroke of midnight,
The tip of one finger touched it! The trigger at least was hers!

The tip of one finger touched it; she strove no more for the rest!
Up, she stood to attention, with the barrel beneath her breast,
She would not risk their hearing; she would not strive again;
For the road lay bare in the moonlight;
    Blank and bare in the moonlight;
And the blood of her veins in the moonlight throbbed to her
    love's refrain.

Tlot-tlot; tlot-tlot! Had they heard it? The horse-hoofs ringing
    clear;
Tlot-tlot; tlot-tlot, in the distance? Were they deaf that they did
    not hear?
Down the ribbon of moonlight, over the brow of the hill,
The highwayman came riding,
    Riding, riding!
The red-coats looked to their priming! She stood up, straight
    and still!

Tlot-tlot, in the frosty silence! *tlot-tlot*, in the echoing night!
Nearer he came and nearer! Her face was like a light!
Her eyes grew wide for a moment; she drew one last deep
    breath,
Then her finger moved in the moonlight,
    Her musket shattered the moonlight,
Shattered her breast in the moonlight and warned him – with
    her death.

He turned; he spurred to the westward; he did not know who
    stood
Bowed, with her head o'er the musket, drenched with her own
    red blood!
Not till the dawn he heard it, and slowly blanched[3] to hear
How Bess, the landlord's daughter,
    The landlord's black-eyed daughter,

---

[3]**blanched**   went pale

Had watched for her love in the moonlight, and died in the
    darkness there.

Back, he spurred like a madman, shrieking a curse to the sky,
With the white road smoking behind him and his rapier bran-
    dished[4] high!
Blood-red were his spurs i' the golden noon; wine-red was his
    velvet coat;
When they shot him down on the highway,
    Down like a dog on the highway,
And he lay in his blood on the highway, with the bunch of lace
    at his throat.

And still of a winter's night, they say, when the wind is in the trees,
When the moon is a ghostly galleon tossed upon cloudy seas,
When the road is a ribbon of moonlight over the purple moor,
A highwayman comes riding –
    Riding – riding –
A highwayman comes riding, up to the old inn-door.

Over the cobbles he clatters and clangs in the dark inn-yard
And he taps with his whip on the shutters, but all is locked and barred;
He whistles a tune to the window, and who should be waiting there
But the landlord's black-eyed daughter,
    Bess, the landlord's daughter,
Plaiting a dark red love-knot into her long black hair.

Further reading

You might like to look up Alfred Noyes on Wikipedia to find out some
information on his writing and his life. Many other popular poems you
might enjoy are included in *The Nation's Favourite Poems* (published by
BBC Worldwide Books in 1996).

---

[4]**brandished**   being waved

The Pied Piper of Hamelin

by Robert Browning

Robert Browning is one of England's finest poets from the 19th century, and this is probably his best-known narrative poem. He lived from 1812 to 1889 and you will find his tomb in Poets' Corner in Westminster Abbey, London. Again, this is a poem for reading aloud.

I

    Hamelin Town's in Brunswick,
By famous Hanover city;
    The river Weser, deep and wide,
    Washes its wall on the southern side;
    A pleasanter spot you never spied;
But, when begins my ditty,
    Almost five hundred years ago,
    To see the townsfolk suffer so
      From vermin, was a pity.

II

    Rats!
They fought the dogs, and killed the cats,
    And bit the babies in the cradles,
And ate the cheeses out of the vats,
    And licked the soup from the cooks' own ladles,
Split open the kegs of salted sprats,
Made nests inside men's Sunday hats,
And even spoiled the women's chats,
    By drowning their speaking
    With shrieking and squeaking
In fifty different sharps and flats.

III

At last the people in a body
    To the Town Hall came flocking:
' 'Tis clear,' cried they, 'our Mayor's a noddy;
    And as for our Corporation - shocking
To think we buy gowns lined with ermine[1]
For dolts that can't or won't determine
What's best to rid us of our vermin!
You hope, because you're old and obese,
To find in the furry civic robe ease?
Rouse up, Sirs! Give your brains a racking
To find the remedy we're lacking,
Or, sure as fate, we'll send you packing!'
At this the Mayor and Corporation
Quaked with a mighty consternation.

IV

An hour they sate in council,
    At length the Mayor broke silence:
'For a guilder I'd my ermine gown sell;
    I wish I were a mile hence!
It's easy to bid one rack one's brain -
I'm sure my poor head aches again
I've scratched it so, and all in vain.
Oh for a trap, a trap, a trap!'
Just as he said this, what should hap
At the chamber door but a gentle tap?
'Bless us,' cried the Mayor, 'what's that?'
(With the Corporation as he sat,
Looking little though wondrous fat;
Nor brighter was his eye, nor moister
Than a too-long-opened oyster,
Save when at noon his paunch grew mutinous

---

[1]**ermine** fur

For a plate of turtle green and glutinous.)[2]
'Only a scraping of shoes on the mat?
Anything like the sound of a rat
Makes my heart go pit-a-pat!'

V

'Come in!' – the Mayor cried, looking bigger:
And in did come the strangest figure!
His queer long coat from heel to head
Was half of yellow and half of red;
And he himself was tall and thin,
With sharp blue eyes, each like a pin,
And light loose hair, yet swarthy skin,
No tuft on cheek nor beard on chin,
But lips where smiles went out and in –
There was no guessing his kith and kin!
And nobody could enough admire
The tall man and his quaint attire:
Quoth one: 'It's as my great-grandsire,
Starting up at the Trump of Doom's tone,
Had walked this way from his painted tomb-stone!'

VI

He advanced to the council-table:
And, 'Please your honours,' said he, 'I'm able,
By means of a secret charm, to draw
All creatures living beneath the sun,
That creep or swim or fly or run,
After me so as you never saw!
And I chiefly use my charm
On creatures that do people harm,
The mole and toad and newt and viper;
And people call me the Pied Piper.'
(And here they noticed round his neck

---

[2] **glutinous**   sticky

A scarf of red and yellow stripe,
To match with his coat of the self-same cheque;
And at the scarf's end hung a pipe;
And his fingers, they noticed, were ever straying
As if impatient to be playing
Upon this pipe, as low it dangled
Over his vesture³ so old-fangled.)
'Yet,' said he, 'poor piper as I am,
In Tartary I freed the Cham,
Last June, from his huge swarms of gnats;
I eased in Asia the Nizam
Of a monstrous brood of vampyre bats:
And as for what your brain bewilders,
If I can rid your town of rats
Will you give me a thousand guilders?'
'One? fifty thousand!' – was the exclamation
Of the astonished Mayor and Corporation.

---

³**vesture**   clothing

VII

Into the street the Piper stept,
    Smiling first a little smile,
As if he knew what magic slept
    In his quiet pipe the while;
Then, like a musical adept,
To blow the pipe his lips he wrinkled,
And green and blue his sharp eyes twinkled
Like a candle-flame where salt is sprinkled;
And ere three shrill notes the pipe uttered,
You heard as if an army muttered;
And the muttering grew to a grumbling;
And the grumbling grew to a mighty rumbling;
And out of the houses the rats came tumbling.
Great rats, small rats, lean rats, brawny rats,
Brown rats, black rats, grey rats, tawny rats,
Grave old plodders, gay young friskers,
    Fathers, mothers, uncles, cousins,
Cocking tails and pricking whiskers,
    Families by tens and dozens,
Brothers, sisters, husbands, wives –
Followed the Piper for their lives.
From street to street he piped advancing,
And step for step they followed dancing,
Until they came to the river Weser
Wherein all plunged and perished!
– Save one who, stout as Julius Caesar,
Swam across and lived to carry
(As he, the manuscript he cherished)
To Rat-land home his commentary:
Which was, 'At the first shrill notes of the pipe,
I heard a sound as of scraping tripe,
And putting apples, wondrous ripe,
Into a cider-press's gripe:
And a moving away of pickle-tub-boards,
And a leaving ajar of conserve-cupboards,

And a drawing the corks of train-oil-flasks,
And a breaking the hoops of butter-casks;
And it seemed as if a voice
(Sweeter far than by harp or by psaltery[4]
Is breathed) called out, Oh rats, rejoice!
The world is grown to one vast drysaltery![5]
So, munch on, crunch on, take your nuncheon,[6]
Breakfast, supper, dinner, luncheon!
And just as a bulky sugar-puncheon,
All ready staved, like a great sun shone
Glorious scarce an inch before me,
Just as methought it said, Come, bore me!
– I found the Weser rolling o'er me.'

VIII
You should have heard the Hamelin people
Ringing the bells till they rocked the steeple.
'Go,' cried the Mayor, 'and get long poles!
Poke out the nests and block up the holes!
Consult with carpenters and builders,
And leave in our town not even a trace
Of the rats!' – when suddenly, up the face
Of the Piper perked in the market-place,
With a 'First, if you please, my thousand guilders!'

IX
A thousand guilders! The Mayor looked blue;
So did the Corporation too.
For council dinners made rare havoc
With Claret, Moselle, Vin-de-Grave, Hock;
And half the money would replenish
Their cellar's biggest butt with Rhenish.[7]

---

[4]**psaltery**   stringed instrument
[5]**drysaltery**   a place where food is preserved, such as by pickling
[6]**nuncheon**   a light meal
[7]**Claret, Moselle, Vin-de-Grave, Hock, Rhenish**   wines

To pay this sum to a wandering fellow
With a gipsy coat of red and yellow!
'Beside,' quoth the Mayor with a knowing wink,
'Our business was done at the river's brink;
We saw with our eyes the vermin sink,
And what's dead can't come to life, I think.
So, friend, we're not the folks to shrink
From the duty of giving you something for drink,
And a matter of money to put in your poke;
But as for the guilders, what we spoke
Of them, as you very well know, was in joke.
Beside, our losses have made us thrifty.
A thousand guilders! Come, take fifty!'

X
The piper's face fell, and he cried,
'No trifling! I can't wait, beside!
I've promised to visit by dinner-time
Bagdad, and accept the prime
Of the Head-Cook's pottage, all he's rich in,
For having left, in the Caliph's kitchen,
Of a nest of scorpions no survivor –
With him I proved no bargain-driver,
With you, don't think I'll bate a stiver![8]
And folks who put me in a passion
May find me pipe to another fashion.'

XI
'How?' cried the Mayor, 'd'ye think I'll brook
Being worse treated than a Cook?
Insulted by a lazy ribald
With idle pipe and vesture piebald?
You threaten us, fellow? Do your worst,
Blow your pipe there till you burst!'

---

[8]**stiver**   a small sum

XII

Once more he stept into the street;
    And to his lips again
    Laid his long pipe of smooth straight cane;
And ere he blew three notes (such sweet
Soft notes as yet musician's cunning
Never gave the enraptured air)
There was a rustling, that seemed like a bustling
Of merry crowds justling at pitching and hustling,
Small feet were pattering, wooden shoes clattering,
Little hands clapping and little tongues chattering,
And, like fowls in a farm-yard when barley is scattering,
Out came the children running.
All the little boys and girls,
With rosy cheeks and flaxen curls,
And sparkling eyes and teeth like pearls,
Tripping and skipping, ran merrily after
The wonderful music with shouting and laughter.

XIII

The Mayor was dumb, and the Council stood
As if they were changed into blocks of wood,
Unable to move a step, or cry
To the children merrily skipping by –
And could only follow with the eye
That joyous crowd at the Piper's back.
But how the Mayor was on the rack,
And the wretched Council's bosoms beat,
As the Piper turned from the High Street
To where the Weser rolled its waters
Right in the way of their sons and daughters!
However he turned from South to West,
And to Koppelberg Hill his steps addressed,
And after him the children pressed;
Great was the joy in every breast.
'He never can cross that mighty top!

He's forced to let the piping drop,
And we shall see our children stop!'
When, lo, as they reached the mountain's side,
A wondrous portal opened wide,
As if a cavern had suddenly hollowed;
And the Piper advanced and the children followed,
And when all were in to the very last,
The door in the mountain-side shut fast.
Did I say all? No! One was lame,
And could not dance the whole of the way;
And in after years, if you would blame
His sadness, he was used to say, –
'It's dull in our town since my playmates left!
I can't forget that I'm bereft
Of all the pleasant sights they see,
Which the Piper also promised me.
For he led us, he said, to a joyous land,
Joining the town and just at hand,
Where waters gushed and fruit-trees grew,
And flowers put forth a fairer hue,
And everything was strange and new;
The sparrows were brighter than peacocks here,
And their dogs outran our fallow deer,
And honey-bees had lost their stings,
And horses were born with eagles' wings:
And just as I became assured
My lame foot would be speedily cured,
The music stopped and I stood still,
And found myself outside the Hill,
Left alone against my will,
To go now limping as before,
And never hear of that country more!'

XIV

Alas, alas for Hamelin!
> There came into many a burgher's pate[9]
> A text which says, that Heaven's Gate
> Opes to the Rich at as easy rate
As the needle's eye takes the camel in!
The Mayor sent East, West, North and South,
To offer the Piper, by word of mouth,
> Wherever it was men's lot to find him,
Silver and gold to his heart's content,
> If he'd only return the way he went,
And bring the children behind him.
But when they saw 'twas a lost endeavour,
And Piper and dancers were gone for ever,
They made a decree that lawyers never
> Should think their records dated duly
If, after the day of the month and year,
These words did not as well appear,
'And so long after what happened here
> On the Twenty-second of July,
Thirteen hundred and seventy-six':
And better in memory to fix
The place of the children's last retreat,
They called it the Pied Piper's Street –
Where any one playing on pipe or tabor[10]
Was sure for the future to lose his labour.
Nor suffered they hostelry or tavern
> To shock with mirth a street so solemn;
But opposite the place of the cavern
> They wrote the story on a column,
And on the great Church Window painted
The same, to make the world acquainted
How their children were stolen away;

---

[9]**pate**   head
[10]**tabor**   drum

And there it stands to this very day.
And I must not omit to say
That in Transylvania there's a tribe
Of alien people that ascribe
The outlandish ways and dress
On which their neighbours lay such stress,
To their fathers and mothers having risen
Out of some subterraneous prison
Into which they were trepanned[11]
Long time ago in a mighty band
Out of Hamelin town in Brunswick land,
But how or why, they don't understand.

XV
So, Willy, let me and you be wipers
Of scores out with all men – especially pipers:
And, whether they pipe us free from rats or from mice,
If we've promised them aught, let us keep our promise.

Further reading

Look up Robert Browning on Wikipedia, for information about his life
and times. If you liked the themes explored in *The Pied Piper* you could
try reading *The Ratcatcher* – a short story by Roald Dahl, included in
The Collected Short Stories of Roald Dahl (Michael Joseph Ltd., 1991).

---

[11]**trepanned**   snared

The Third Man

by Graham Greene

The Third Man is one of Graham Greene's most celebrated novels, set in a devastated, divided Vienna just after the World War II (1939–1945). Rollo Martins is invited by his school-friend and hero, Harry Lime, to spend some time with him. Martins quickly discovers that Harry is involved in crime as a penicillin racketeer (illegally selling poor quality versions of a medicine). Martins agrees to help a policeman, Calloway, (the narrator) trap Harry.

It only remained then to bait the trap. After studying the map of the sewer system I came to the conclusion that a café anywhere near the main entrance of the great sewer, which was placed like all the others in an advertisement kiosk, would be the most likely spot to tempt Lime. He had only to rise once again through the ground, walk fifty yards, bring Martins back with him, and sink again into the obscurity of the sewers. He had no idea that this method of evasion was known to us: he probably knew that one patrol of the sewer police ended before midnight, and the next did not start till two, and so at midnight Martins sat in the little cold café in sight of the kiosk, drinking coffee after coffee. I had lent him a revolver: I had men posted as close to the kiosk as I could, and the sewer police were ready when zero hour struck to close the manholes and start sweeping the sewers inwards from the edge of the city. But I intended, if I could, to catch him before he went underground again. It would save trouble – and risk to Martins. So there, as I say, in the café Martins sat.

The wind had risen again, but it had brought no snow; it came icily off the Danube and in the little grassy square by the café it whipped up the snow like the surf on top of a wave. There was no heating in the café, and Martins sat warming each hand in turn on a cup of ersatz[1] coffee – innumerable cups. There was usually one of my men in the café with him, but I changed them every twenty minutes or so irregularly. More than an hour passed. Martins had long given up hope and so had I, where I waited at the end of a phone several streets away, with a party of the sewer police ready to go down if it became necessary. We were luckier than Martins because we were warm in our great boots up to the thighs and our reefer jackets. One man had a small searchlight about half as big again as a car headlight strapped to his breast, and another man carried a brace of Roman candles. The telephone rang. It was Martins. He said, 'I'm perishing with cold. It's a quarter past one. Is there any point in going on with this?'

'You shouldn't telephone. You must stay in sight.'

'I've drunk seven cups of this filthy coffee. My stomach won't stand much more.'

'He can't delay much longer if he's coming. He won't want to run into the two o'clock patrol. Stick it another quarter of an hour, but keep away from the telephone.'

Martins' voice said suddenly, 'Christ, he's here! He's – ' and then the telephone went dead. I said to my assistant, 'Give the signal to guard all manholes,' and to my sewer police, 'We are going down.'

What had happened was this. Martins was still on the telephone to me when Harry Lime came into the café. I don't know what he heard, if he heard anything. The mere sight of a man wanted by the police and without friends in Vienna speaking on the telephone would have been enough to warn him. He was out of the café again before Martins had put down the receiver. It was one of those rare moments when none of my men was in the café. One had just left and another was on the pavement about to come in. Harry Lime brushed by him and made for the kiosk. Martins came out of the café and saw my man. If he had called out then it would have been an easy shot, but I suppose

---

[1]**ersatz**   substitute, usually a poor substitute for the real thing

it was not Lime, the penicillin racketeer, who was escaping down the street; it was Harry. Martins hesitated just long enough for Lime to put the kiosk between them; then he called out 'That's him,' but Lime had already gone to ground.

What a strange world unknown to most of us lies under our feet: we live above a cavernous land of waterfalls and rushing rivers, where tides ebb and flow as in the world above. If you have ever read the adventures of Allan Quatermain[2] and the account of his voyage along the underground river to the city of Milosis, you will be able to picture the scene of Lime's last stand. The main sewer, half as wide as the Thames, rushes by under a huge arch, fed by tributary streams: these streams have fallen in waterfalls from higher levels and have been purified in their fall, so that only in these side channels is the air foul. The main stream smells sweet and fresh with a faint tang of ozone, and everywhere in the darkness is the sound of falling and rushing water. It was just past high tide when Martins and the policeman reached the river: first the curving iron staircase, then a short passage so low they had to stoop, and then the shallow edge of the water lapped at their feet. My man shone his torch along the edge of the current and said, 'He's gone that way,' for just as a deep stream when it shallows at the rim leaves an accumulation of debris, so the sewer left in the quiet water against the wall a scum of orange peel, old cigarette cartons, and the like, and in this scum Lime had left his trail as unmistakably as if he had walked in mud. My policeman shone his torch ahead with his left hand, and carried his gun in his right. He said to Martins, 'Keep behind me, sir, the bastard may shoot.'

'Then why the hell should you be in front?'

'It's my job, sir.'

The water came half-way up their legs as they walked: the policeman kept his torch pointing down and ahead at the disturbed trail at the sewer's edge. He said, 'The silly thing is the bastard doesn't stand a chance. The manholes are all guarded

---

[2]**Allan Quatermain**   a big game hunter in Africa

and we've cordoned off the way into the Russian zone. All our chaps have to do now is to sweep inwards down the side passages from the manholes.' He took a whistle out of his pocket and blew, and very far away, here and again there, came the notes of a reply. He said, 'They are all down here now. The sewer police, I mean. They know this place just as I know the Tottenham Court Road. I wish my old woman could see me now,' he said, lifting his torch for a moment to shine it ahead, and at that moment the shot came. The torch flew out of his hand and fell in the stream. He said, 'God blast the bastard!'

'Are you hurt?'

'Scraped my hand, that's all. A week off work. Here, take this other torch, sir, while I tie my hand up. Don't shine it. He's in one of the side passages.' For a long time the sound of the shot went on reverberating: when the last echo died a whistle blew ahead of them, and Martins' companion blew an answer.

Martins said, 'It's an odd thing – I don't even know your name.'

'Bates, sir.' He gave a low laugh in the darkness. 'This isn't my usual beat. Do you know the Horseshoe, sir?'

'Yes.'

'And the Duke of Grafton?'

'Yes.'

'Well, it takes a lot to make a world.'

Martins said, 'Let me come in front. I don't think he'll shoot at me, and I want to talk to him.'

'I had orders to look after you, sir. Careful.'

'That's all right.' He edged round Bates, plunging a foot deeper in the stream as he went. When he was in front he called out, 'Harry,' and the name sent up an echo, 'Harry, Harry, Harry!' that travelled down the stream and woke a whole chorus of whistles in the darkness. He called again, 'Harry. Come out. It's no use.'

A voice startlingly close made them hug the wall. 'Is that you, old man?' it called. 'What do you want me to do?'

'Come out. And put your hands above your head.'

'I haven't a torch, old man. I can't see a thing.'

'Be careful, sir,' Bates said.

'Get flat against the wall. He won't shoot at me,' Martins said. He called, 'Harry, I'm going to shine the torch. Play fair and come out. You haven't got a chance.' He flashed the torch on, and twenty feet away, at the edge of the light and the water. Harry stepped into view. 'Hands above the head, Harry.' Harry raised his hand and fired. The shot ricocheted against the wall a foot from Martins' head, and he heard Bates cry out. At the same moment a searchlight from fifty yards away lit the whole channel, caught Harry in its beams, then Martins, then the staring eyes of Bates slumped at the water's edge with the sewage washing to his waist. An empty cigarette carton wedged into his armpit and stayed. My party had reached the scene.

Martins stood dithering there above Bates's body, with Harry Lime half-way between us. We couldn't shoot for fear of hitting Martins, and the light of the searchlight dazzled Lime. We moved slowly on, our revolvers trained for a chance, and Lime turned this way and that way like a rabbit dazzled by headlights; then suddenly he took a flying jump into the deep central rushing stream. When we turned the searchlight after him he was submerged, and the current of the sewer carried him rapidly on, past the body of Bates, out of the range of the searchlight into the dark. What makes a man, without hope, cling to a few more minutes of existence? Is it a good quality or a bad one? I have no idea.

Martins stood at the outer edge of the searchlight beam, staring downstream. He had his gun in his hand now, and he was the only one of us who could fire with safety. I thought I saw a movement and called out to him, 'There. There. Shoot.' He lifted his gun and fired, just as he had fired at the same command all those years ago on Brickworth Common, fired, as he did then, inaccurately. A cry of pain came tearing back like calico[3] down the cavern: a reproach, an entreaty. 'Well done,' I called and halted by Bates's body. He was dead. His eyes

---

[3]**calico**   cotton cloth

remained blankly open as we turned the searchlight on him; somebody stooped and dislodged the carton and threw it in the river, which whirled it on – a scrap of yellow Gold Flake: he was certainly a long way from the Tottenham Court Road.

I looked up and Martins was out of sight in the darkness. I called his name and it was lost in a confusion of echoes, in the rush and the roar of the underground river. Then I heard a third shot.

Martins told me later, 'I walked downstream to find Harry, but I must have missed him in the dark. I was afraid to lift the torch: I didn't want to tempt him to shoot again. He must have been struck by my bullet just at the entrance of a side passage. Then I suppose he crawled up the passage to the foot of the iron stairs. Thirty feet above his head was the manhole, but he wouldn't have had the strength to lift it, and even if he had succeeded the police were waiting above. He must have known all that, but he was in great pain, and just as an animal creeps into the dark to die, so I suppose a man makes for the light. He wants to die at home, and the darkness is never home to *us*. He began to pull himself up the stairs, but then the pain took him and he couldn't go on. What made him whistle that absurd scrap of a tune I'd been fool enough to believe he had written himself? Was he trying to attract attention, did he want a friend with him, even the friend who had trapped him, or was he delirious and had he no purpose at all? Anyway I heard his whistle and came back along the edge of the stream, and felt where the wall ended and found my way up the passage where he lay. I said, "Harry," and the whistling stopped, just above my head. I put my hand on an iron hand-rail, and climbed. I was still afraid he might shoot. Then, only three steps up, my foot stamped down on his hand, and he was there. I shone my torch on him: he hadn't got a gun; he must have dropped it when my bullet hit him. For a moment I thought he was dead, but then he whimpered with pain. I said, "Harry," and he swivelled his eyes with a great effort to my face. He was trying to speak, and I bent down to listen. "Bloody fool," he said – that was all. I don't know whether he meant that for himself – some sort of act of contrition,[4] however inadequate (he was a Catholic) – or was it for me – with my thousand a year taxed and my imaginary cattle-rustlers who couldn't even shoot a rabbit clean? Then he began to whimper again. I couldn't bear it any more and I put a bullet through him.'

'We'll forget that bit,' I said.

Martins said, 'I never shall.'

Further reading

This book was made into a memorable film, starring Orson Welles as Harry Lime. If you'd like to try other stories by Graham Greene, *The Fallen Idol* (Penguin, 1989), *The Tenth Man* (Penguin, 1986) and *Short Stories of Graham Greene* (Penguin, 1987) are all worth a go.

---

[4]**contrition**   remorse

To Kill a Mockingbird

by Harper Lee

To Kill a Mockingbird is a novel set in Maycomb, in the Deep South of America, during the 1930s. Tom Robinson is a black man falsely charged with the rape of a white girl. Atticus Finch is the local lawyer who comes forward to defend him. The events are seen through the eyes of his children, Jem and Scout. In this scene they are joined by their friend Dill, and are witness to an attempt by a group of local men to take the law into their own hands at the jail.

I caught Atticus coming in the door, and he said that they'd moved Tom Robinson to the Maycomb jail. He also said, more to himself than to me, that if they'd kept him there in the first place there wouldn't have been any fuss. I watched him take his seat on the third row from the front, and I heard him rumble, 'Nearer my God to Thee,' some notes behind the rest of us. He never sat with Aunty, Jem and me. He liked to be by himself in church.

The fake peace that prevailed on Sundays was made more irritating by Aunt Alexandra's presence. Atticus would flee to his office directly after dinner, where if we sometimes looked in on him, we would find him sitting back in his swivel chair reading. Aunt Alexandra composed herself for a two-hour nap and dared us to make any noise in the yard, the neighbourhood was resting. Jem in his old age had taken to his room with a stack of football magazines. So Dill and I spent our Sundays creeping around in Deer's Pasture.

Shooting on Sundays was prohibited, so Dill and I kicked Jem's football around the pasture for a while, which was no fun. Dill asked if I'd like to have a poke at Boo Radley. I said I didn't think it'd be nice to bother him, and spent the rest of the afternoon filling Dill in on last winter's events. He was considerably impressed.

We parted at supper-time, and after our meal Jem and I were settling down to a routine evening, when Atticus did something that interested us: he came into the living-room carrying a long electrical extension cord. There was a light bulb on the end.

'I'm going out for a while,' he said. 'You folks'll be in bed when I come back, so I'll say good night now.'

With that, he put his hat on and went out of the back door. 'He's takin' the car,' said Jem.

Our father had a few peculiarities: one was, he never ate desserts; another was that he liked to walk. As far back as I could remember, there was always a Chevrolet in excellent condition in the car-house, and Atticus put many miles on it in business trips, but in Maycomb he walked to and from his office four times a day, covering about two miles. He said his only exercise was walking. In Maycomb, if one went for a walk with no definite purpose in mind, it was correct to believe one's mind incapable of definite purpose.

Later on, I bade my aunt and brother good night and was well into a book when I heard Jem rattling around in his room. His go-to-bed noises were so familiar to me that I knocked on his door: 'Why ain't you going to bed?'

'I'm goin' downtown for a while.' He was changing his pants.

'Why? It's almost ten o'clock, Jem.'

He knew it, but he was going anyway.

'Then I'm goin' with you. If you say no you're not, I'm goin' anyway, hear?' Jem saw that he would have to fight me to keep me home, and I suppose he thought a fight would antagonize Aunty, so he gave in with little grace.

I dressed quickly. We waited until Aunty's light went out, and we walked quietly down the back steps. There was no moon tonight.

'Dill'll wanta come,' I whispered.

'So he will,' said Jem gloomily.

We leaped over the drive-wall, cut through Miss Rachel's side yard and went to Dill's window. Jem whistled bob-white. Dill's face appeared at the screen, disappeared, and five minutes later he unhooked the screen and crawled out. An old campaigner, he did not speak until we were on the sidewalk. 'What's up?'

'Jem's got the look-arounds,' an affliction Calpurnia said all boys caught at his age.

'I've just got this feeling,' Jem said, 'just this feeling.'

We went by Mrs Dubose's house, standing empty and shuttered, her camellias grown up in weeds and johnson grass. There were eight more houses to the post-office corner.

The south side of the square was deserted. Giant monkey-puzzle bushes bristled on each corner, and between them an iron hitching rail glistened under the street lights. A light shone in the county toilet, otherwise that side of the court-house was dark. A larger square of stores surrounded the court-house square; dim lights burned from deep within them.

Atticus's office was in the court-house when he began his law practice, but after several years of it he moved to quieter quarters in the Maycomb Bank building. When we rounded the corner of the square, we saw the car parked in front of the bank. 'He's in there,' said Jem.

But he wasn't. His office was reached by a long hallway. Looking down the hall, we should have seen *Atticus Finch, Attorney-at-Law* in small sober letters against the light from behind his door. It was dark.

Jem peered in the bank door to make sure. He turned the knob. The door was locked. 'Let's go up the street. Maybe he's visitin' Mr Underwood.'

Mr Underwood not only ran the *Maycomb Tribune* office, he lived in it. That is, above it. He covered the court-house and jail-house news simply by looking out his upstairs window. The office building was on the north-west corner of the square, and to reach it we had to pass the jail.

The Maycomb jail was the most venerable[1] and hideous of the county's buildings. Atticus said it was like something

---

[1]**venerable**   respected

Cousin Joshua St Clair might have designed. It was certainly someone's dream. Starkly out of place in a town of square-faced stores and steep-roofed houses, the Maycomb jail was a miniature Gothic joke one cell wide and two cells high, complete with tiny battlements and flying buttresses. Its fantasy was heightened by its red brick façade and the thick steel bars at its ecclesiastical[2] windows. It stood on no lonely hill, but was wedged between Tyndal's Hardware Store and the *Maycomb Tribune* office. The jail was Maycomb's only conversation piece: its detractors[3] said it looked like a Victorian privy;[4] its supporters said it gave the town a good solid respectable look, and no stranger would ever suspect that it was full of niggers.

As we walked up the sidewalk, we saw a solitary light burning in the distance. 'That's funny,' said Jem, 'jail doesn't have an outside light.'

'Looks like it's over the door,' said Dill.

A long extension cord ran between the bars of a second-floor window and down the side of the building. In the light from its bare bulb, Atticus was sitting propped against the front door. He was sitting in one of his office chairs, and he was reading, oblivious of the nightbugs dancing over his head.

I made to run, but Jem caught me. 'Don't go to him,' he said, 'he might not like it. He's all right, let's go home. I just wanted to see where he was.'

We were taking a short cut across the square when four dusty cars came in from the Meridian highway, moving slowly in a line. They went around the square, passed the bank building, and stopped in front of the jail.

Nobody got out. We saw Atticus look up from his newspaper. He closed it, folded it deliberately, dropped it in his lap, and pushed his hat to the back of his head. He seemed to be expecting them.

---

[2]**ecclesiastical**   church-like
[3]**detractors**   critics
[4]**privy**   outside toilet

'Come on,' whispered Jem. We sneaked across the square, across the street, until we were in the shelter of the Jitney Jungle door. Jem peeked up the sidewalk. 'We can get closer,' he said. We ran to Tyndal's Hardware door – near enough, at the same time discreet.

In ones and twos, men got out of the cars. Shadows became substance as light revealed solid shapes moving towards the jail door. Atticus remained where he was. The men hid him from view.

'He in there, Mr Finch?' a man said.

'He is,' we heard Atticus answer, 'and he's asleep. Don't wake him up.'

In obedience to my father, there followed what I later realized was a sickeningly comic aspect of an unfunny situation: the men talked in near-whispers.

'You know what we want,' another man said. 'Get aside from the door, Mr Finch.'

'You can turn around and go home again, Walter,' Atticus said pleasantly. 'Heck Tate's around somewhere.'

'The hell he is,' said another man. 'Heck's bunch's so deep in the woods they won't get out till mornin'.'

'Indeed? Why so?'

'Called 'em off on a snipe hunt,' was the succinct answer. 'Didn't you think a'that, Mr Finch?'

'Thought about it, but didn't believe it. Well, then,' my father's voice was still the same, 'that changes things, doesn't it?'

'It do,' another deep voice said. Its owner was a shadow.

'Do you really think so?'

This was the second time I heard Atticus ask that question in two days, and it meant somebody's man would get jumped. This was too good to miss. I broke away from Jem and ran as fast as I could to Atticus.

Jem shrieked and tried to catch me, but I had a lead on him and Dill. I pushed my way through dark smelly bodies and burst into the circle of light.

'H-ey, Atticus?'

I thought he would have a fine surprise, but his face killed my joy. A flash of plain fear was going out of his eyes, but returned when Dill and Jem wriggled into the light.

There was a smell of stale whisky and pig-pen about, and when I glanced around I discovered that these men were strangers. They were not the people I saw last night. Hot embarrassment shot through me: I had leaped triumphantly into a ring of people I had never seen before.

Atticus got up from his chair, but he was moving slowly, like an old man. He put the newspaper down very carefully, adjusting its creases with lingering fingers. They were trembling a little.

'Go home, Jem,' he said. 'Take Scout and Dill home.'

We were accustomed to prompt, if not always cheerful acquiescence⁵ to Atticus's instructions, but from the way he stood Jem was not thinking of budging.

'Go home, I said.'

Jem shook his head. As Atticus's fists went to his hips, so did Jem's, and as they faced each other I could see little resemblance between them: Jem's soft brown hair and eyes, his oval face and snug-fitting ears were our mother's, contrasting oddly with Atticus's greying black hair and square-cut features, but they were somehow alike. Mutual defiance made them alike.

'Son, I said go home.'

Jem shook his head.

'I'll send him home,' a burly man said, and grabbed Jem roughly by the collar. He yanked Jem nearly off his feet.

'Don't you touch him!' I kicked the man swiftly. Barefooted, I was surprised to see him fall back in real pain. I intended to kick his shin, but aimed too high.

'That'll do, Scout.' Atticus put his hand on my shoulder. 'Don't kick folks. No – ' he said, as I was pleading justification.

'Ain't nobody gonna do Jem that way,' I said.

---

⁵**acquiescence**   agreement

'All right, Mr Finch, get 'em outa here,' someone growled. 'You got fifteen seconds to get 'em outa here.'

In the midst of this strange assembly, Atticus stood trying to make Jem mind him. 'I ain't going,' was his steady answer to Atticus's threats, requests, and finally, 'Please Jem, take them home.'

I was getting a bit tired of that, but felt Jem had his own reasons for doing as he did, in view of his prospects once Atticus did get home. I looked around the crowd. It was a summer's night, but the men were dressed, most of them, in overalls and denim shirts buttoned up to the collars. I thought they must be cold-natured, as their sleeves were unrolled and buttoned at the cuffs. Some wore hats pulled firmly down over their ears. They were sullen-looking, sleepy-eyed men who seemed unused to late hours. I sought once more for a familiar face, and at the centre of the semi-circle I found one.

'Hey, Mr Cunningham.'

The man did not hear me, it seemed.

'Hey, Mr Cunningham. How's your entailment[6] gettin' along?'

Mr Walter Cunningham's legal affairs were well known to me; Atticus had once described them at length. The big man blinked and hooked his thumbs in his overall straps. He seemed uncomfortable; he cleared his throat and looked away. My friendly overture had fallen flat.

Mr Cunningham wore no hat, and the top half of his fore-head was white in contrast to his sun-scorched face, which led me to believe that he wore one most days. He shifted his feet, clad in heavy work shoes.

'Don't you remember me, Mr Cunningham? I'm Jean Louise Finch. You brought us some hickory nuts one time, remember?' I began to sense the futility one feels when unac-knowledged by a chance acquaintance.

---

[6]**entailment**   legal proceedings for inheriting land

'I go to school with Walter,' I began again. 'He's your boy, ain't he? Ain't he, sir?'

Mr Cunningham was moved to a faint nod. He did know me, after all.

'He's in my grade,' I said, 'and he does right well. He's a good boy,' I added, 'a real nice boy. We brought him home for dinner one time. Maybe he told you about me, I beat him up one time but he was real nice about it. Tell him hey for me, won't you?'

Atticus had said it was the polite thing to talk to people about what they were interested in, not about what you were interested in. Mr Cunningham displayed no interest in his son, so I tackled his entailment once more in a last-ditch effort to make him feel at home.

'Entailments are bad,' I was advising him, when I slowly awoke to the fact that I was addressing the entire aggregation.[7] The men were all looking at me, some had their mouths half-open. Atticus had stopped poking at Jem: they were standing together beside Dill. Their attention amounted to fascination. Atticus's mouth, even, was half-open, an attitude he had once described as uncouth. Our eyes met and he shut it.

'Well, Atticus, I was just sayin' to Mr Cunningham that entailments are bad an' all that, but you said not to worry, it takes a long time sometimes . . . that you all'd ride it out together . . . ' I was slowly drying up, wondering what idiocy I had committed. Entailments seemed all right enough for living-room talk.

I began to feel sweat gathering at the edges of my hair; I could stand anything but a bunch of people looking at me. They were quite still.

'What's the matter?' I asked.

Atticus said nothing. I looked around and up at Mr Cunningham, whose face was equally impassive. Then he did a peculiar thing. He squatted down and took me by both shoulders.

---

[7]**aggregation**   crowd

'I'll tell him you said hey, little lady,' he said.

Then he straightened up and waved a big paw. 'Let's clear out,' he called. 'Let's get going, boys.'

As they had come, in ones and twos the men shuffled back to their ramshackle cars. Doors slammed, engines coughed, and they were gone.

I turned to Atticus, but Atticus had gone to the jail and was leaning against it with his face to the wall. I went to him and pulled his sleeve. 'Can we go home now?' He nodded, produced his handkerchief, gave his face a going-over and blew his nose violently.

'Mr Finch?'

A soft husky voice came from the darkness above: 'They gone?'

Atticus stepped back and looked up. 'They've gone,' he said. 'Get some sleep, Tom. They won't bother you any more.'

From a different direction, another voice cut crisply through the night: 'You're damn tootin' they won't. Had you covered all the time, Atticus.'

Mr Underwood and a double-barrelled shotgun were leaning out his window above the *Maycomb Tribune* office.

It was long past my bedtime and I was growing quite tired; it seemed that Atticus and Mr Underwood would talk for the rest of the night, Mr Underwood out of the window and Atticus up at him. Finally Atticus returned, switched off the light above the jail door, and picked up his chair.

'Can I carry it for you, Mr Finch?' asked Dill. He had not said a word the whole time.

'Why, thank you, son.'

Walking towards the office, Dill and I fell into step behind Atticus and Jem. Dill was encumbered by the chair, and his pace was slower. Atticus and Jem were well ahead of us, and I assumed that Atticus was giving him hell for not going home, but I was wrong. As they passed under a street light, Atticus reached out and massaged Jem's hair, his one gesture of affection.

Further reading

If you enjoyed this and you're interested in some of the issues it explores, try reading *The Other Side of Truth* (2000) and *Journey to Jo'burg* (1985) by Beverley Naidoo, both published by HarperCollins. The film of *To Kill a Mockingbird*, featuring Gregory Peck as Atticus Finch, is well worth seeing.

The Man Who Planted Trees

by Jean Giono

This is the first part of a simple, short tale about a man called Elzéard Bouffier. It is set in the south of France.

For a human character to reveal truly exceptional qualities, one must have the good fortune to be able to observe its performance over many years. If this performance is devoid of all egoism,[1] if its guiding motive is unparalleled generosity, if it is absolutely certain that there is no thought of recompense and that, in addition, it has left its visible mark upon the earth, then there can be no mistake.

About forty years ago I was taking a long trip on foot over mountain heights quite unknown to tourists, in that ancient region where the Alps thrust down into Provence. All this, at the time I embarked upon my long walk through these deserted regions, was barren and colourless land. Nothing grew there but wild lavender.

I was crossing the area at its widest point, and after three days' walking, found myself in the midst of unparalleled desolation. I camped near the vestiges[2] of an abandoned village. I had run out of water the day before, and had to find some. These clustered houses, although in ruins, like an old wasps' nest, suggested that there must once have been a spring or well here. There was indeed a spring, but it was dry. The five or six houses, roofless, gnawed by wind and rain, the tiny chapel with its crumbling steeple, stood about like the houses and chapels in living villages, but all life had vanished.

It was a fine June day, brilliant with sunlight, but over this unsheltered land, high in the sky, the wind blew with unendurable ferocity. It growled over the carcasses of the houses like a lion disturbed at its meal. I had to move my camp.

---

[1]**egoism**   selfishness
[2]**vestiges**   remains

After five hours' walking I had still not found water and there was nothing to give me any hope of finding any. All about me was the same dryness, the same coarse grasses. I thought I glimpsed in the distance a small black silhouette, upright, and took it for the trunk of a solitary tree. In any case I started towards it. It was a shepherd. Thirty sheep were lying about him on the baking earth.

He gave me a drink from his water-gourd and, a little later, took me to his cottage in a fold of the plain. He drew his water – excellent water – from a very deep natural well above which he had constructed a primitive winch.

The man spoke little. This is the way of those who live alone, but one felt that he was sure of himself, and confident in his assurance. That was unexpected in this barren country. He lived, not in a cabin, but in a real house built of stone that bore plain evidence of how his own efforts had reclaimed the ruin he had found there on his arrival. His roof was strong and sound. The wind on its tiles made the sound of the sea upon its shore.

The place was in order, the dishes washed, the floor swept, his rifle oiled; his soup was boiling over the fire. I noticed then that he was cleanly shaved, that all his buttons were firmly sewn on, that his clothing had been mended with the meticulous care that makes the mending invisible. He shared his soup with me and afterwards, when I offered my tobacco pouch, he told me that he did not smoke. His dog, as silent as himself, was friendly without being servile.[3]

It was understood from the first that I should spend the night there; the nearest village was still more than a day and a half away. And besides I was perfectly familiar with the nature of the rare villages in that region. There were four or five of them scattered well apart from each other on these mountain slopes, among white oak thickets, at the extreme end of the wagon roads. They were inhabited by charcoalburners, and the living was bad. Families, crowded together in a climate that is excessively harsh both in winter and in summer, found no

---

[3]**servile**   begging for attention

escape from the unceasing conflict of personalities. Irrational ambition reached inordinate[4] proportions in the continual desire for escape. The men took their wagonloads of charcoal to the town, then returned. The soundest characters broke under the perpetual grind. The women nursed their grievances. There was rivalry in everything, over the price of charcoal as over a pew in the church, over warring virtues as over warring vices as well as over the ceaseless combat between virtue and vice. And over all there was the wind, also ceaseless, to rasp upon the nerves. There were epidemics of suicide and frequent cases of insanity, usually homicidal.

The shepherd went to fetch a small sack and poured out a heap of acorns on the table. He began to inspect them, one by one, with great concentration, separating the good from the bad. I smoked my pipe. I did offer to help him. He told me that it was his job. And in fact, seeing the care he devoted to the task, I did not insist. That was the whole of our conversation. When he had set aside a large enough pile of good acorns he counted them out by tens, meanwhile eliminating the small ones or

---

[4]**inordinate**   excessive

those which were slightly cracked, for now he examined them more closely. When he had thus selected one hundred perfect acorns he stopped and we went to bed.

There was peace in being with this man. The next day I asked if I might rest here for a day. He found it quite natural – or, to be more exact, he gave me the impression that nothing could startle him. The rest was not absolutely necessary, but I was interested and wished to know more about him. He opened the pen and led his flock to pasture. Before leaving, he plunged his sack of carefully selected and counted acorns into a pail of water.

I noticed that he carried for a stick an iron rod as thick as my thumb and about a yard and a half long. Resting myself by walking, I followed a path parallel to his. His pasture was in a valley. He left the dog in charge of the little flock and climbed towards where I stood. I was afraid that he was about to rebuke me for my indiscretion,[5] but it was not that at all: this was the way he was going, and he invited me to go along if I had nothing better to do. He climbed to the top of the ridge, about a hundred yards away.

There he began thrusting his iron rod into the earth, making a hole in which he planted an acorn; then he refilled the hole. He was planting oak trees. I asked him if the land belonged to him. He answered no. Did he know whose it was? He did not. He supposed it was community property, or perhaps belonged to people who cared nothing about it. He was not interested in finding out whose it was. He planted his hundred acorns with the greatest care.

After the midday meal he resumed his planting. I suppose I must have been fairly insistent in my questioning, for he answered me. For three years he had been planting trees in this wilderness. He had planted one hundred thousand. Of the hundred thousand, twenty thousand had sprouted. Of the twenty thousand he still expected to lose about half, to rodents or to the unpredictable designs of Providence. There remained ten thousand oak trees to grow where nothing had grown before.

---

[5]**indiscretion**   rudeness

That was when I began to wonder about the age of this man. He was obviously over fifty. Fifty-five, he told me. His name was Elzéard Bouffier. He had once had a farm in the lowlands. There he had had his life. He had lost his only son, then his wife. He had withdrawn into this solitude where his pleasure was to live leisurely with his lambs and his dog. It was his opinion that this land was dying for want of trees. He added that, having no very pressing business of his own, he had resolved to remedy this state of affairs.

Since I was at that time, in spite of my youth, leading a solitary life, I understood how to deal gently with solitary spirits. But my very youth forced me to consider the future in relation to myself and to a certain quest for happiness. I told him that in thirty years his ten thousand oaks would be magnificent. He answered quite simply that if God granted him life, in thirty years he would have planted so many more that these ten thousand would be like a drop of water in the ocean.

Besides, he was now studying the reproduction of beech trees and had a nursery of seedlings grown from beechnuts near his cottage. The seedlings, which he had protected from his sheep with a wire fence, were very beautiful. He was also considering birches for the valleys where, he told me, there was a certain amount of moisture a few yards below the surface of the soil.

The next day, we parted.

Further reading

If you enjoyed this extract, it's well worth reading the whole book *The Man Who Planted Trees* by Jean Giono (Chelsea Green Publishing Company, 1985). Also, you might like to try *The Cone Gathers* by Robin Jenkins, published by Canongate Books, 2007.

A Christmas Carol

by Charles Dickens

Set in Victorian times, this is the opening of Charles Dickens's famous tale of Christmas, *A Christmas Carol*, in which Scrooge confronts Christmases past, present and future. 'Scrooge' has now passed into the English language as a person who is very mean with money, and many of Dickens's descriptions of Christmas live on today in our traditional thinking about this festive season.

Marley was dead: to begin with. There is no doubt whatever about that. The register of his burial was signed by the clergyman, the clerk, the undertaker, and the chief mourner. Scrooge signed it: and Scrooge's name was good upon 'Change, for anything he chose to put his hand to. Old Marley was as dead as a door-nail.

Mind! I don't mean to say that I know, of my own knowledge, what there is particularly dead about a door-nail. I might have been inclined, myself, to regard a coffin-nail as the deadest piece of ironmongery in the trade. But the wisdom of our ancestors is in the simile; and my unhallowed hands shall not disturb it, or the Country's done for. You will therefore permit me to repeat, emphatically, that Marley was as dead as a door-nail.

Scrooge knew he was dead? Of course he did. How could it be otherwise? Scrooge and he were partners for I don't know how many years. Scrooge was his sole executor,[1] his sole administrator, his sole assign,[2] his sole residuary legatee,[3] his sole friend and sole mourner. And even Scrooge was not so dreadfully cut up by the sad event, but that he was an excellent man of business on the very day of the funeral, and solemnised it with an undoubted bargain.

---

[1] **executor**   person who carries out the requests in someone's will
[2] **assign**   person to whom property is legally transferred
[3] **residuary legatee**   remaining inheritor

The mention of Marley's funeral brings me back to the point I started from. There is no doubt that Marley was dead. This must be distinctly understood, or nothing wonderful can come of the story I am going to relate. If we were not perfectly convinced that Hamlet's Father[4] died before the play began, there would be nothing more remarkable in his taking a stroll at night, in an easterly wind, upon his own ramparts, than there would be in any other middle-aged gentleman rashly turning out after dark in a breezy spot – say Saint Paul's Churchyard for instance – literally to astonish his son's weak mind.

Scrooge never painted out Old Marley's name. There it stood, years afterwards, above the warehouse door: Scrooge and Marley. The firm was known as Scrooge and Marley.

Sometimes people new to the business called Scrooge Scrooge, and sometimes Marley, but he answered to both names: it was all the same to him.

---

[4]**Hamlet's Father**   in Shakespeare's play *Hamlet*, Hamlet's father has been killed and appears as a ghost

Oh! But he was a tight-fisted hand at the grindstone, Scrooge! a squeezing, wrenching, grasping, scraping, clutching, covetous[5] old sinner! Hard and sharp as flint, from which no steel had ever struck out a generous fire; secret, and self-contained, and solitary as an oyster. The cold within him froze his old features, nipped his pointed nose, shrivelled his cheek, stiffened his gait;[6] made his eyes red, his thin lips blue; and spoke out shrewdly in his grating voice. A frosty rime[7] was on his head, and on his eyebrows, and his wiry chin. He carried his own low temperature always about with him; he iced his office in the dog-days; and didn't thaw it one degree at Christmas.

External heat and cold had little influence on Scrooge. No warmth could warm, nor wintry weather chill him. No wind that blew was bitterer than he, no falling snow was more intent upon its purpose, no pelting rain less open to entreaty. Foul weather didn't know where to have him. The heaviest rain, and snow, and hail, and sleet, could boast of the advantage over him in only one respect. They often 'came down' handsomely, and Scrooge never did.

Nobody ever stopped him in the street to say, with gladsome looks, 'My dear Scrooge, how are you? When will you come to see me?' No beggars implored him to bestow a trifle, no children asked him what it was o'clock, no man or woman ever once in all his life inquired the way to such and such a place, of Scrooge. Even the blindmen's dogs appeared to know him; and when they saw him coming on, would tug their owners into doorways and up courts; and then would wag their tails as though they said, 'No eye at all is better than an evil eye, dark master!'

But what did Scrooge care? It was the very thing he liked. To edge his way along the crowded paths of life, warning all human sympathy to keep its distance, was what the knowing ones call 'nuts' to Scrooge.

---

[5]**covetous**   grasping
[6]**gait**   way of walking
[7]**rime**   dew

Once upon a time – of all the good days in the year, on Christmas Eve – old Scrooge sat busy in his counting-house. It was cold, bleak, biting weather: foggy withal: and he could hear the people in the court outside go wheezing up and down, beating their hands upon their breasts, and stamping their feet upon the pavement-stones to warm them. The city clocks had only just gone three, but it was quite dark already: it had not been light all day: and candles were flaring in the windows of the neighbouring offices, like ruddy smears upon the palpable brown air. The fog came pouring in at every chink and keyhole, and was so dense without, that although the court was of the narrowest, the houses opposite were mere phantoms. To see the dingy cloud come drooping down, obscuring everything, one might have thought that Nature lived hard by, and was brewing on a large scale.

The door of Scrooge's counting-house was open that he might keep his eye upon his clerk, who in a dismal little cell beyond, a sort of tank, was copying letters. Scrooge had a very small fire, but the clerk's fire was so very much smaller that it looked like one coal. But he couldn't replenish it, for Scrooge kept the coalbox in his own room; and so surely as the clerk came in with the shovel, the master predicted that it would be necessary for them to part. Wherefore the clerk put on his white comforter,[8] and tried to warm himself at the candle; in which effort, not being a man of a strong imagination, he failed.

'A merry Christmas, uncle! God save you!' cried a cheerful voice. It was the voice of Scrooge's nephew, who came upon him so quickly that this was the first intimation[9] he had of his approach.

'Bah!' said Scrooge, 'Humbug!'

He had so heated himself with rapid walking in the fog and frost, this nephew of Scrooge's, that he was all in a glow; his face was ruddy and handsome; his eyes sparkled, and his breath smoked again.

---

[8]**comforter**   scarf
[9]**intimation**   indication

'Christmas a humbug, uncle!' said Scrooge's nephew. 'You don't mean that, I am sure.'

'I do,' said Scrooge. 'Merry Christmas! What right have you to be merry? What reason have you to be merry? You're poor enough.'

'Come, then,' returned the nephew gaily. 'What right have you to be dismal? What reason have you to be morose? You're rich enough.'

Scrooge having no better answer ready on the spur of the moment, said, 'Bah!' again; and followed it up with 'Humbug.'

'Don't be cross, uncle,' said the nephew.

'What else can I be,' returned the uncle, 'when I live in such a world of fools as this? Merry Christmas! Out upon Merry Christmas! What's Christmas time to you but a time for paying bills without money; a time for finding yourself a year older, and not an hour richer; a time for balancing your books and having every item in 'em through a round dozen of months presented dead against you? If I could work my will,' said Scrooge, indignantly, 'every idiot who goes about with "Merry Christmas" on his lips, should be boiled with his own pudding, and buried with a stake of holly through his heart. He should!'

'Uncle!' pleaded the nephew.

'Nephew!' returned the uncle, sternly, 'keep Christmas in your own way, and let me keep it in mine.'

'Keep it!' repeated Scrooge's nephew. 'But you don't keep it.'

'Let me leave it alone, then,' said Scrooge. 'Much good may it do you! Much good it has ever done you!'

'There are many things from which I might have derived good, by which I have not profited, I dare say,' returned the nephew: 'Christmas among the rest. But I am sure I have always thought of Christmas time, when it has come round – apart from the veneration[10] due to its sacred name and origin, if anything belonging to it can be apart from that – as a good time: a kind, forgiving, charitable, pleasant time: the only time I know

---

[10]**veneration**   respect

of, in the long calendar of the year, when men and women seem by one consent to open their shut-up hearts freely, and to think of people below them as if they really were fellow-passengers to the grave, and not another race of creatures bound on other journeys. And therefore, uncle, though it has never put a scrap of gold or silver in my pocket, I believe that it *has* done me good, and *will* do me good; and I say, God bless it!'

The clerk in the tank involuntarily applauded: becoming immediately sensible of the impropriety,[11] he poked the fire, and extinguished the last frail spark for ever.

'Let me hear another sound from *you*,' said Scrooge, 'and you'll keep your Christmas by losing your situation. You're quite a powerful speaker, sir,' he added, turning to his nephew. 'I wonder you don't go into Parliament.'

'Don't be angry, uncle. Come! Dine with us tomorrow.'

Scrooge said that he would see him – yes, indeed he did. He went the whole length of the expression, and said that he would see him in that extremity first.

'But why?' cried Scrooge's nephew. 'Why?'

'Why did you get married?' said Scrooge.

'Because I fell in love.'

'Because you fell in love!' growled Scrooge, as if that were the only one thing in the world more ridiculous than a merry Christmas. 'Good afternoon!'

'Nay, uncle, but you never came to see me before that happened. Why give it as a reason for not coming now?'

'Good afternoon,' said Scrooge.

'I want nothing from you; I ask nothing of you; why cannot we be friends?'

'Good afternoon,' said Scrooge.

'I am sorry with all my heart, to find you so resolute. We have never had any quarrel, to which I have been a party. But I have made the trial in homage to Christmas, and I'll keep my Christmas humour to the last. So A Merry Christmas, uncle!'

---

[11]**impropriety**   error

'Good afternoon!' said Scrooge.

'And A Happy New Year!'

'Good afternoon!' said Scrooge.

His nephew left the room without an angry word, notwith-standing. He stopped at the outer door to bestow the greetings of the season on the clerk, who, cold as he was, was warmer than Scrooge; for he returned them cordially.

'There's another fellow,' muttered Scrooge, who overheard him: 'my clerk, with fifteen shillings a-week, and a wife and family, talking about a merry Christmas. I'll retire to Bedlam.'[12]

This lunatic, in letting Scrooge's nephew out, had let two other people in. They were portly gentlemen, pleasant to behold, and now stood, with their hats off, in Scrooge's office. They had books and papers in their hands, and bowed to him.

'Scrooge and Marley's, I believe,' said one of the gentlemen, referring to his list. 'Have I the pleasure of addressing Mr Scrooge, or Mr Marley?'

'Mr Marley has been dead these seven years,' Scrooge replied. 'He died seven years ago, this very night.'

'We have no doubt his liberality[13] is well represented by his surviving partner,' said the gentleman, presenting his credentials.[14]

It certainly was; for they had been two kindred spirits. At the ominous word 'liberality', Scrooge frowned, and shook his head, and handed the credentials back.

'At this festive season of the year, Mr Scrooge,' said the gentleman, taking up a pen, 'it is more than usually desirable that we should make some slight provision for the poor and destitute, who suffer greatly at the present time. Many thousands are in want of common necessaries; hundreds of thousands are in want of common comforts, sir.'

'Are there no prisons?' asked Scrooge.

---

[12]**Bedlam**   an asylum
[13]**liberality**   generosity
[14]**credentials**   letter of introduction

'Plenty of prisons,' said the gentleman, laying down the pen again.

'And the Union workhouses?'[15] demanded Scrooge. 'Are they still in operation?'

'They are. Still,' returned the gentleman, 'I wish I could say they were not.'

'The Treadmill and the Poor Law are in full vigour, then?' said Scrooge.

'Both very busy, sir.'

'Oh! I was afraid, from what you said at first, that something had occurred to stop them in their useful course,' said Scrooge. 'I'm very glad to hear it.'

'Under the impression that they scarcely furnish Christian cheer of mind or body to the multitude,' returned the gentleman, 'a few of us are endeavouring to raise a fund to buy the Poor some meat and drink, and means of warmth. We choose this time, because it is a time, of all others, when Want is keenly felt, and Abundance rejoices. What shall I put you down for?'

'Nothing!' Scrooge replied.

'You wish to be anonymous?'

'I wish to be left alone,' said Scrooge. 'Since you ask me what I wish, gentlemen, that is my answer. I don't make merry myself at Christmas, and I can't afford to make idle people merry. I help to support the establishments I have mentioned: they cost enough: and those who are badly off must go there.'

'Many can't go there; and many would rather die.'

'If they would rather die,' said Scrooge, 'they had better do it, and decrease the surplus population. Besides – excuse me – I don't know that.'

'But you might know it,' observed the gentleman.

'It's not my business,' Scrooge returned. 'It's enough for a man to understand his own business, and not to interfere with other people's. Mine occupies me constantly. Good afternoon, gentlemen!'

---

[15]**workhouse**   Victorian institution for people with no money

Seeing clearly that it would be useless to pursue their point, the gentlemen withdrew. Scrooge resumed his labours with an improved opinion of himself, and in a more facetious[16] temper than was usual with him.

Further reading

Did you enjoy this extract? If so, try some more Dickens – *Oliver Twist* and *Great Expectations* are particularly good reads.

---

[16]**facetious**   joking

Silas Marner
by George Eliot

Silas Marner is set in the village of Raveloe in the 19th century. Molly is addicted to the drug opium and is returning to claim her rightful place as Godfrey Cass's wife. Silas Marner has recently experienced the theft of his treasured gold. Both Molly and Silas could be said to be 'outsiders'.

While Godfrey Cass was taking draughts of forgetfulness from the sweet presence of Nancy, willingly losing all sense of that hidden bond which at other moments galled[1] and fretted him so as to mingle irritation with the very sunshine, Godfrey's wife was walking with slow uncertain steps through the snow-covered Raveloe lanes, carrying her child in her arms.

This journey on New Year's Eve was a premeditated act of vengeance which she had kept in her heart ever since Godfrey, in a fit of passion, had told her he would sooner die than acknowledge her as his wife. There would be a great party at the Red House on New Year's Eve, she knew: her husband would be smiling and smiled upon, hiding *her* existence in the darkest corner of his heart. But she would mar his pleasure: she would go in her dingy rags, with her faded face, once as handsome as the best, with her little child that had its father's hair and eyes, and disclose herself to the Squire as his eldest son's wife. It is seldom that the miserable can help regarding their misery as a wrong inflicted by those who are less miserable. Molly knew that the cause of her dingy rags was not her husband's neglect, but the demon Opium to whom she was enslaved, body and soul, except in the lingering mother's tenderness that refused to give him her hungry child. She knew this well; and yet, in the moments of wretched unbenumbed[2] consciousness, the sense

---

[1]**galled**   irritated
[2]**unbenumbed**   not numbed or made dopey

of her want and degradation transformed itself continually into bitterness towards Godfrey. *He* was well off; and if she had her rights she would be well off too. The belief that he repented his marriage, and suffered from it, only aggravated her vindictiveness. Just and self-reproving thoughts do not come to us too thickly, even in the purest air, and with the best lessons of heaven and earth; how should those white-winged delicate messengers make their way to Molly's poisoned chamber, inhabited by no higher memories than those of a bar-maid's paradise of pink ribbons and gentlemen's jokes?

She had set out at an early hour, but had lingered on the road, inclined by her indolence³ to believe that if she waited under a warm shed the snow would cease to fall. She had waited longer than she knew, and now that she found herself belated in the snow-hidden ruggedness of the long lanes, even the animation of a vindictive purpose could not keep her spirit from failing. It was seven o'clock, and by this time she was not very far from Raveloe, but she was not familiar enough with those monotonous lanes to know how near she was to her journey's end. She needed comfort, and she knew but one comforter – the familiar demon in her bosom; but she hesitated a moment, after drawing out the black remnant, before she raised it to her lips. In that moment the mother's love pleaded for painful consciousness rather than oblivion – pleaded to be left in aching weariness, rather than to have the encircling arms benumbed so that they could not feel the dear burden. In another moment Molly had flung something away, but it was not the black remnant – it was an empty phial.⁴ And she walked on again under the breaking cloud, from which there came now and then the light of a quickly-veiled star, for a freezing wind had sprung up since the snowing had ceased. But she walked always more and more drowsily, and clutched more and more automatically the sleeping child at her bosom.

---

³**indolence**   lack of energy
⁴**phial**   small glass bottle

Slowly the demon was working his will, and cold and weariness were his helpers. Soon she felt nothing but a supreme immediate longing that curtained off all futurity[5] – the longing to lie down and sleep. She had arrived at a spot where her footsteps were no longer checked by a hedgerow, and she had wandered vaguely, unable to distinguish any objects, notwithstanding the wide whiteness around her, and the growing starlight. She sank down against a straggling furze[6] bush, an easy pillow enough; and the bed of snow, too, was soft. She did not feel that the bed was cold, and did not heed whether the child would wake and cry for her. But her arms did not yet relax their instinctive clutch; and the little one slumbered on as gently as if it had been rocked in a lace-trimmed cradle.

But the complete torpor came at last: the fingers lost their tension, the arms unbent; then the little head fell away from the bosom, and the blue eyes opened wide on the cold starlight. At first there was a little peevish cry of 'mammy', and an effort to regain the pillowing arm and bosom; but mammy's ear was deaf, and the pillow seemed to be slipping away backward. Suddenly, as the child rolled downward on its mother's knees, all wet with snow, its eyes were caught by a bright glancing light on the white ground, and, with the ready transition of infancy, it was immediately absorbed in watching the bright living thing running towards it, yet never arriving. That bright living thing must be caught; and in an instant the child had slipped on all fours, and held out one little hand to catch the gleam. But the gleam would not be caught in that way, and now the head was held up to see where the cunning gleam came from. It came from a very bright place; and the little one, rising on its legs, toddled through the snow, the old grimy shawl in which it was wrapped trailing behind it, and the queer little bonnet dangling at its back – toddled on to the open door of Silas Marner's cottage, and right up to the warm hearth, where there was a bright fire

---

[5]**futurity**   time to come
[6]**furze**   gorse

of logs and sticks, which had thoroughly warmed the old sack (Silas's greatcoat) spread out on the bricks to dry. The little one, accustomed to be left to itself for long hours without notice from its mother, squatted down on the sack, and spread its tiny hands towards the blaze, in perfect contentment, gurgling and making inarticulate communications to the cheerful fire, like a new-hatched gosling beginning to find itself comfortable. But presently the warmth had a lulling effect, and the little golden head sank down on the old sack, and the blue eyes were veiled by their delicate half-transparent lids.

But where was Silas Marner while this stranger-visitor had come to his hearth? He was in the cottage, but he did not see the child. During the last few weeks, since he had lost his money, he had contracted the habit of opening his door, and looking out from time to time, as if he thought that his money might be somehow coming back to him, or that some trace, some news of it, might be mysteriously on the road, and be caught by the listening ear or the straining eye. It was chiefly at night, when he was not occupied in his loom, that he fell into this repetition of an act for which he could have assigned no definite purpose, and which can hardly be understood except by those who have undergone a bewildering separation from a supremely loved object. In the evening twilight, and later when-ever the night was not dark, Silas looked out on that narrow prospect round the Stone-pits, listening and gazing, not with hope, but with mere yearning and unrest.

This morning he had been told by some of his neighbours that it was New Year's Eve, and that he must sit up and hear the old year rung out and the new rung in, because that was good luck, and might bring his money back again. This was only a friendly Raveloe-way of jesting with the half-crazy oddities of a miser, but it had perhaps helped to throw Silas into a more than usually excited state. Since the on-coming of twilight he had opened his door again and again, though only to shut it immediately at seeing all distance veiled by the falling snow. But the last time he opened it the snow had ceased, and the clouds were parting here and there. He stood and listened, and gazed for a long while – there was really something on the road coming towards him then, but he caught no sign of it; and the stillness and the wide trackless snow seemed to narrow his solitude, and touched his yearning with the chill of despair. He went in again, and put his right hand on the latch of the door to close it – but he did not close it: he was arrested, as he had been already since his loss, by the invisible wand of catalepsy,[7] and stood like a graven image, with wide but sightless eyes, holding open his door, powerless to resist either the good or evil that might enter there.

When Marner's sensibility returned, he continued the action which had been arrested, and closed his door, unaware of the chasm in his consciousness, unaware of any intermediate change, except that the light had grown dim, and that he was chilled and faint. He thought he had been too long standing at the door and looking out. Turning towards the hearth, where the two logs had fallen apart, and sent forth only a red uncertain glimmer, he seated himself on his fireside chair, and was stooping to push his logs together, when, to his blurred vision, it seemed as if there were gold on the floor in front of the hearth. Gold! – his own gold – brought back to him as mysteriously as it had been taken away! He felt his heart begin to beat violently, and for a few moments he was unable to stretch out his hand and grasp the restored treasure. The heap of gold seemed to glow and get larger beneath his agitated gaze. He leaned forward at last, and stretched forth his hand; but instead of the hard coin with the familiar resisting outline, his fingers encountered soft warm curls. In utter amazement, Silas fell on his knees and bent his head low to examine the marvel: it was a sleeping child – a round, fair thing, with soft yellow rings all over its head. Could this be his little sister come back to him in a dream – his little sister whom he had carried about in his arms for a year before she died, when he was a small boy without

---

[7]**catalepsy**   hypnotic trance

shoes or stockings? That was the first thought that darted across Silas's blank wonderment. *Was* it a dream? He rose to his feet again, pushed his logs together, and, throwing on some dried leaves and sticks, raised a flame; but the flame did not disperse the vision – it only lit up more distinctly the little round form of the child and its shabby clothing. It was very much like his little sister. Silas sank into his chair powerless, under the double presence of an inexplicable surprise and a hurrying influx of memories. How and when had the child come in without his knowledge? He had never been beyond the door. But along with that question, and almost thrusting it away, there was a vision of the old home and the old streets leading to Lantern Yard – and within that vision another, of the thoughts which had been present with him in those far-off scenes. The thoughts were strange to him now, like old friendships impossible to revive; and yet he had a dreamy feeling that this child was somehow a message come to him from that far-off life: it stirred fibres that had never been moved in Raveloe – old quiverings of tenderness – old impressions of awe at the presentiment[8] of some Power presiding over his life; for his imagination had not yet extricated[9] itself from the sense of mystery in the child's sudden presence, and had formed no conjectures of ordinary natural means by which the event could have been brought about.

But there was a cry on the hearth: the child had awaked, and Marner stooped to lift it on his knee. It clung round his neck, and burst louder and louder into that mingling of inarticulate cries with 'mammy' by which little children express the bewilderment of waking. Silas pressed it to him, and almost unconsciously uttered sounds of hushing tenderness, while he bethought himself that some of his porridge, which had got cool by the dying fire, would do to feed the child with if it were only warmed up a little.

---

[8]**presentiment**   foreboding
[9]**extricated**   removed

He had plenty to do through the next hour. The porridge, sweetened with some dry brown sugar from an old store which he had refrained from using for himself, stopped the cries of the little one, and made her lift her blue eyes with a wide gaze at Silas, as he put the spoon into her mouth. Presently she slipped from his knee and began to toddle about, but with a pretty stagger that made Silas jump up and follow her lest she should fall against anything that would hurt her. But she only fell in a sitting posture on the ground, and began to pull at her boots, looking up at him with a crying face as if the boots hurt her. He took her on his knee again, but it was some time before it occurred to Silas's dull bachelor mind that the wet boots were the grievance, pressing on her warm ankles. He got them off with difficulty, and baby was at once happily occupied with the primary mystery of her own toes, inviting Silas, with much chuckling, to consider the mystery too. But the wet boots had at last suggested to Silas that the child had been walking on the snow, and this roused him from his entire oblivion of any ordinary means by which it could have entered or been brought into his house. Under the prompting of this new idea, and without waiting to form conjectures, he raised the child in his arms, and went to the door. As soon as he had opened it, there was the cry of 'mammy' again, which Silas had not heard since the child's first hungry waking. Bending forward, he could just discern the marks made by the little feet on the virgin snow, and he followed their track to the furze bushes. 'Mammy!' the little one cried again and again, stretching itself forward so as almost to escape from Silas's arms, before he himself was aware that there was something more than the bush before him – that there was a human body, with the head sunk low in the furze, and half-covered with the shaken snow.

Further reading

If you liked reading this it might be worth trying the whole book – *Silas Marner* is a challenging and rewarding read. Another George Eliot novel that is recommended is *Adam Bede*.

Activities

Why the Whales Came

Before you read

1   Have you visited any small islands? Did you come across any inter-
    esting stories or legends surrounding them? What stories have you
    read with distinctive island settings? Talk about this in pairs and
    then present each other's experiences to the class.

What's it about?

2   In the first few pages, which words and phrases does the writer use
    to highlight the desperation of the whales? How does the author
    make us feel as though we too are on the beach? Discuss this in
    groups.

3   The whales are seen differently by the various people on the beach.
    Make a list of everyone on the scene. Who is sympathetic to the
    whales? Who is not? In what ways does Mother have such an
    impact on events?

4   From looking at the map of the Scilly Isles (page 2), plot out what
    happens where, as told in this extract.

Thinking about the text

5   We see everything though Gracie's eyes. Rewrite any of the scenes
    from
    a   Tim Pender's point of view and
    b   the Birdman's point of view.

6   How does the author build up the tension as to whether the whale
    will survive or not? Look carefully at the language he uses.

7   The chapter ends with the letters 'Z.W.'; these stand for Zachariah
    Woodcock, the Birdman's real name. Why do you think Michael
    Morpurgo finishes on these letters?

8   'The curse of Samson is redeemed, finished.' Use this as a starting
    point for your own short story. You could use some of the infor-
    mation from this extract, and then add your own details and ideas.

The Highwayman

Before you read

1   What kind of poetry do you most enjoy? Is it a poem that tells a story, or describes a particular scene, or one that focuses on people?

What's it about?

2   Talk in pairs about who might be described as the 'outsider' in this poem. Is there more than one outsider?

Thinking about the text

3   Why are the last two verses of the poem written in italics?

4   Alfred Noyes uses a wide range of poetic techniques in this narrative poem. Find examples of the following: metaphor; half-rhyme; alliteration; assonance; onomatopoeia; simile. Check your understanding of these words in your groups, using a glossary of technical terms if necessary.

5   The poem is alive with sounds and colours. Pick out words and phrases that you think are particularly successful in making the reader hear and see what is going on.

6   Prepare a dramatised reading of the poem for a small group of readers. Try to convey the various voices and people which feature.

7   Rewrite the poem as a short story, using your own words and phrases, to build upon those of the poet. You might like to illustrate a few scenes in the narrative.

The Pied Piper of Hamelin

Before you read

1 Talk in groups about stories you know in which someone is taught a very serious lesson because of what they have done.

What's it about?

2 A number of the words in the poem have been explained in the glossary, but there are many interesting words throughout the verses. Use a dictionary, thesaurus or Internet search engine to check your understanding of any unusual vocabulary.

3 Talk in pairs about the state of Hanover Town, as described in the opening three verses. How are the people feeling and thinking?

4 Draw your own picture of the Pied Piper, based on Browning's colourful description.

Thinking about the text

5 Re-read the first six verses and make a list of words, phrases and rhymes that you feel bring the scenes described vividly alive. Look for the way the poet uses end-rhymes. What effects does he create by doing this?

6 Write the word 'rats' at the centre of a page. Create a spider diagram to list around it all the adjectives that are used to describe the rats.

7 What do you think of the Mayor's and the Pied Piper's reactions in verses nine to eleven? Might you have been tempted to do the same as the Mayor? In your view, is the Pied Piper justified in his actions as he leads the children away? Draw up arguments for and against.

8 The final verse contains the moral of the tale. Should we always keep our promises? Discuss this question in small groups.

9 Write a short piece of literary criticism on the poem, giving your views about its content, its style, its moral and its overall effect on you.

The Third Man

Before you read

1 Who are your favourite spy characters and heroes, in book or film?

What's it about?

2 Write short character descriptions of Martins, Bates and the narrator, Calloway. What can you learn about them from the text? Look carefully.

3 There is a lot of movement in this extract. Draw a map that shows where each of the events described takes place. Include the café where the extract begins, the entrances to the sewer system and the sewer system itself. Mark on it the movements of Harry Lime, Martins, Bates, Calloway and the other policemen.

Thinking about the text

4 Discuss how the author builds up a sense of tension in the opening paragraphs. Look, for example, at the way he uses short sentences.

5 The chase takes place in the underground sewer system. Discuss in pairs how Graham Greene brings this setting alive for the reader. Make a list of the words and phrases that capture your imagination.

6 The narrator asks: 'What makes a man, without hope, cling to a few more minutes of existence? Is it a good quality or a bad one?' What are your thoughts on this? Debate your ideas.

7 Why is Harry's death described to us by Martins? What does this add to the impact and drama of Harry's death?

8 Harry Lime is a memorable 'fictional outsider'. Write a short character description of Harry, his appearance and personality as you imagine them. You might dip into a copy of the original novel to help you with this.

9 Recast as a short story the final hour of Harry's life, with Harry as the first-person narrator. Try to capture his increasing desperation as he finds there is no escape. Re-read carefully the final account by Martins on pages 34–35.

To Kill a Mockingbird

Before you read

1 Discuss with a partner: do children learn more from their parents, or do parents learn more from their children?

What's it about?

2 Make a list of all the characters (except Atticus Finch) who appear in this extract. Write short notes, including interesting quotations, about each one of them.

3 Using a spider diagram with the name of Atticus Finch at the centre, list a number of quotations that indicate he is an 'outsider' in his own community.

4 What picture do you have of Jem and Scout and their everyday lives? Look for clues in the text.

Thinking about the text

5 Look at the way this extract is told from the point of view of Scout. Discuss in pairs what you think are the advantages and disadvantages of the first-person narrator being a child. What can the author do, and not do?

6 In groups, discuss why it is that Scout and Jem are successful in seeing off the men who have come in search of Tom Robinson. Re-read carefully the conversations that take place between the children and the men.

7 What evidence can you find in this extract that indicates that the novel is set in the southern states of America in the 1930s? Get together with a partner and create an 'evidence list'.

8 Imagine you were directing this scene for television. Devise a short screenplay, including dialogue, direction to actors, and scene settings. You might also think about any mood music you could add.

9 Put yourself in Mr Underwood's shoes. Write a front-page article for the *Maycomb Tribune* which retells the events of that evening. You might want to inject a little bit of extra drama, given you are writing for the front page.

The Man Who Planted Trees

Before you read

1   Talk in your groups about the following serious but interesting question: imagine you die at the age of 90 – what would you most like to be remembered for?

What's it about?

2   Look carefully at the way the author describes the Provence landscape. How does he make it come alive for the reader? Pick out key words and phrases that you find do this for you as a reader.

3   In pairs, talk about the picture you have of the people who occupy this landscape. In what ways is the shepherd very different? Which phrases tell you this?

Thinking about the text

4   Re-read the first paragraph. Discuss in your group whether you agree with what it says about 'truly exceptional qualities'. Does Elzéard Bouffier show these qualities?

5   Read again the paragraph on pages 47–48 about the villagers always fighting and arguing. Improvise a scene that brings out the 'rivalry in everything'.

6   Imagine you are a local reporter and you have come to interview Elzéard Bouffier. Write up the feature article and interview for a magazine.

7   Hot-seat Jean Giono. He was an author who loved the country and its values. Plan a series of questions to ask him about how he came to write *The Man Who Planted Trees*.

8   The next part of this short book tells how the narrator returns to the same area many years later – and it has changed for the better. Imagine you are the narrator and write your own account of how the landscape and people have changed. How has the shepherd changed?

9   Is this a religious story in any way? As a class, debate arguments for and against.

A Christmas Carol

Before you read

1   Brainstorm in small groups: which characters from the novels of Charles Dickens have you heard of, either through reading or from television and film?

What's it about?

2   The scene is set in 19th-century Victorian London. Note down words and phrases that give you a strong sense of place and time.

Thinking about the text

3   What do you notice about Dickens's style of writing? Choose three or four paragraphs and read them with a partner. Ask yourselves:
    a   Is the language old-fashioned?
    b   How does Dickens create humour?
    c   How does he use dialogue?
    d   What do you notice about the punctuation?

4   With 'Scrooge' at the centre of a spider diagram, write down as many adjectives as you can find which Dickens uses to describe his central character. Use these notes as the basis for a short character description of Scrooge.

5   Turn this extract into a drama script which you and others in your class can act out. Use stage directions and notes to actors, alongside the dialogue itself. Think about some background music to include.

6   Imagine you meet Scrooge at the end of this scene. Ask him to explain his thoughts and actions to you. This could be improvised in pairs.

7   Charles Dickens always wrote to entertain – and educate at the same time. What ideas or themes does he want us to think about carefully in his creation of Scrooge? Research briefly into other themes that Dickens explored in two or three of his novels, for example *Oliver Twist* or *Hard Times*. Present these in a short talk to your group.

Silas Marner

Before you read

1   Which is more important – love or money? Hold a class debate.

What's it about?

2   What is Molly's sequence of thoughts during the text? Write them
in two or three paragraphs as a detailed journal entry that she
might have written for that day to describe her plans, what she did
and the consequences.

3   Draw a timeline for the period described in the text. Mark on it
what Molly, Silas Marner and Molly's child were doing.

Thinking about the text

4   Study the particular features of George Eliot's language and style.
Re-read a couple of her long paragraphs. Use a dictionary or
thesaurus to check out any vocabulary you are not sure of. Look at
how she constructs her sentences, with their many phrases and
clauses. Rewrite one of the paragraphs in a more direct, contem-
porary style. What is gained and lost, in comparison with the original?

5   What do you think has caused Molly to become a drug addict?
Write a series of her diary entries covering the weeks running up to
the events told here.

6   Imagine you are Silas Marner a few days later, thinking about what
happened on New Year's Eve. Write your own version of events as
you remember them.

7   Continue the story from where the extract ends, focusing on Molly,
the child and Silas.

8   Discuss in groups how Molly and Silas are presented as 'outsiders'.
Do you think the author tries to make the reader feel sympathetic
or not towards the two characters? Look for clues in the text.

Compare and contrast

1 Compare the two poems *The Highwayman* and *The Pied Piper of Hamelin*. What makes them successful narrative poems? Think about: descriptions of place; use of dialogue; characters; vocabulary; rhythm and rhyme; the tales they tell. Which do you prefer and why? Discuss in groups, then write up your findings. Add a few suitable illustrations.

2 Write a short study of the way in which Harper Lee, Jean Giono and Graham Greene present their 'outsiders'. Do you feel sympathy towards them? Do you like them as characters? In what way are they different from those around them?

3 Look again at a few paragraphs from the writings of Dickens and Eliot, both authors writing in the 19th century. Compare the way they use language to describe people and places. Which aspects of their style and language techniques do you enjoy?   Contrast the characters of Silas Marner and Scrooge. Write up your conclusions in a short study.

4 'A first reading makes you want to know what will happen; a second makes you understand why it happens; a third makes you think.' Discuss in groups how true you think this is of any of the extracts in this section.

2 Heroes and heroines

This section features a number of high-achieving individuals. In reading their stories you will see how they might be described as 'outsiders'. On the one hand is Lance Armstrong's incredible battle against cancer to become the greatest cyclist of his generation. On the other are the experiences of the handful of men who have glimpsed the dark side of the moon.

Activities

1 What for you defines success and failure? Talk about this in pairs and groups.

2 Make a list of your heroes and heroines. Why do you admire them? What have been their particular achievements? Have they battled against all odds to succeed? Do you think of them as 'outsiders'?

3 Debate in small groups whether you think that, in sport, 'It is only winning that matters'.

4 Draw up a list of books you have read or films you have seen that feature a sporting legend or feats of great physical endurance. What makes the books interesting and the films very watchable?

5 If you can, try to watch video clips from the Tour de France, the Isle of Man TT Races and *Touching the Void* alongside reading the extracts in this section.

Heroic Failures

by Stephen Pile

In one way or another, each of the people featured here stands apart from their fellow human beings. Enjoy the humour!

The Worst Bank Robbers

In August 1975 three men were on their way in to rob the Royal Bank of Scotland at Rothesay, when they got stuck in the revolving doors. They had to be helped free by the staff and, after thanking everyone, sheepishly left the building.

A few minutes later they returned and announced their intention of robbing the bank, but none of the staff believed them. When, at first, they demanded £5,000, the head cashier laughed at them, convinced that it was a practical joke.

Considerably disheartened by this, the gang leader reduced his demand first to £500, then to £50 and ultimately to 50 pence. By this stage the cashier could barely control herself for laughter.

Then one of the men jumped over the counter and fell awkwardly on the floor, clutching at his ankle. The other two made their getaway, but got trapped in the revolving doors for a second time, desperately pushing the wrong way.

The Worst Boxer

Ralph Walton was knocked out in 10½ seconds in a bout at Lewiston, Maine, USA, on 29 September 1946. It happened when Al Couture struck him as he was still adjusting his gum shield in his corner. The 10½ seconds includes 10 seconds while he was counted out.

The Worst Soccer Match

In 1973 Oxbarn Social Club football team arranged a friendly match in Germany. It was an opportunity for the lads, who play in the Wolverhampton Sunday League, to get a holiday abroad and also to meet some new opposition. Only when they entered their opponents' luxury stadium did they realize that they had mistakenly arranged a friendly with a top German first division side. For their part, SVW Mainz were expecting to play Wolverhampton Wanderers, then one of the strongest teams in Britain.

The Oxbarn Club secretary said, 'I thought it looked posh, and when I heard the other side were on an £80 bonus to win, I said to myself, "Something is wrong".'

After the fifteenth goal whistled into Oxbarn's net, their goalkeeper was seen to fall on to his knees. He seemed to be praying for the final whistle. It was around this time that the sixteenth and seventeenth were scored.

Naturally, the Mainz crowd were delighted to watch a team like Oxbarn instead of the mighty Wolverhampton Wanderers. 'They behaved very well,' said the Oxbarn secretary. 'Whenever we got the ball they gave a prolonged cheer.'

Oxbarn Social Club lost 21–0.

The Worst Save

This honour falls to Senhor Isadore Irandir of the Brazilian team Rio Preto who let in a goal after three seconds.

From the kick-off in the soccer match between Corinthians and Rio Preto at Bahia Stadium, the ball was passed to Roberto Rivelino who scored instantly with a left-foot drive from the halfway line. The ball went past the ear of Senhor Irandir, while he was on his knees finishing pre-match prayers in the goalmouth.

Further reading

There is a *Second Book of Heroic Failures* (Penguin Books, 1989) for those who enjoyed the first.

Blind Spanish Woman Makes Television History

by Julian Coman

▌ The headline speaks for itself.

When Nuria del Saz takes her seat to read the television news, she is fulfilling a childhood ambition.

The 25-year-old Spaniard has good reason to be proud of her achievement. Other newsreaders get help from the studio autocue, but she cannot see it. She is completely blind.

Ms del Saz, who presents the lunchtime bulletin for Spain's state-owned Canal 2 Andalucia, is thought to be the world's only blind newscaster. Her determined fight against disability to realise her childhood ambition has made her a star in her native Seville and a heroine for the country's blind people.

She had always wanted to be a broadcaster. While other girls played with dolls, she spent hours writing pretend scripts and read them to her parents. Then, aged 11, her sight worsened as a result of a progressive retinal disorder. By 13, she was totally blind.

She refused to be defeated by her handicap. Impressed by her dedication, the Spanish blind association ONCE paid for specially adapted equipment to help her through journalism school. She was noticed by a broadcast director while working for a student radio service, and was then chosen above non-disabled candidates for television training.

With the help of ONCE, she began to devise a way in which she could present the news as quickly and naturally as a sighted journalist.

'The problem was speed,' she said. 'I would write my script in braille, but it takes much longer to read than ordinary text because each letter is touched. So I began almost to memorise the whole broadcast, reading and re-reading before I went on air. Now I read the first part of a sentence and deliver the rest from memory while I move onto the next lines with my hands.'

She receives instructions from her producer via an earpiece. 'He always tells me when to begin, although I've done it so many times now that I don't need to be told. If something goes wrong with the images of a story, he tells me what's going on and I have to improvise.'

Memories from her sighted childhood help her to vary facial expression during broadcasts. An uninformed viewer would have no idea that she cannot see.

Her success has provided a welcome publicity coup for ONCE, which until recently ran its own radio station in an attempt to encourage the blind to take up journalism.

'It is a lesson and an encouragement for the whole blind community,' said a spokesman. 'If a blind person can read the news on prime-time television, it proves that almost anything is possible.'

Ms del Saz said: 'I have learnt to forget the negative parts of my life. My ambition is to live as normally as possible. I hope that what has happened to me will give other handicapped people some hope.'

Many people have written to tell her how her achievement has inspired others.

'One old man sent me a poem about the need to be strong in life,' she said. 'A grandmother rang me up in tears to tell me about her two-year-old grandson who is blind. She said it gave her hope for his future. As you can imagine, that made me feel pretty good.'

Further reading

The Bus People by Rachel Anderson, published by Oxford University Press (1989), recounts the stories of young people fighting against disabilities. One of the stories from this anthology is included later in this volume, in section 4, p. 244.

Marla Runyan

by Peter Sheridan

This is the amazing story of a girl who cannot see the running track but is a very successful athlete.

Marla Runyan triumphantly thrust her arms in the air as she crossed the 1,500-metre finishing line at the US Olympic athletics trials in Sacramento.

The crowd of 23,000 roared their approval and even her rivals stopped to applaud. Some had tears welling up in their eyes. Maria had come third – and just won herself a place as one of only three women to represent her country in the 1,500 metres at the Sydney Olympics.

The stadium buzzed with emotion. The crowd knew they were not just celebrating a personal victory but witnessing one of sporting history's greatest milestones. Because Marla Runyan is blind. In just over six weeks she will take her place alongside the best athletes in the world, to become the first ever blind Olympian to compete in the able-bodied games. By anyone's standards an Olympic place is a remarkable achievement, but for the 31-year-old athlete who needs a guide dog to walk down the street, and who cannot see the finishing tape at the end of the track, it is simply astonishing. She cannot see the Stars and Stripes that unfurls whenever she takes the winner's podium. She can only vaguely make out the track lanes beneath her feet and the blurred shapes of competitors around her. Yet she has carved out a running career that is not only astounding fellow athletes, but is inspiring blind and disabled people around the world.

Marla was born with an incurable, genetic, degenerative condition of the retina called Stargardt's disease. Although she has some peripheral sight, the damage to both retinas has left her with a hole at the centre of her vision, making her effectively blind.

Until she was nine, she lived an idyllic life with her family in Camarillo, a wealthy suburb of Los Angeles, California. Her father Gary was a banker and her mother Valerie was a music teacher. Marla spent her childhood playing with her brother Grady, two years her senior, riding ponies and fishing for bass in local rivers.

But one day at school, she found she couldn't pick out symbols on the blackboard and her parents took her to an optician. A year later, she was diagnosed with Stargardt's and doctors warned that she would never succeed at school, go to college, drive a car, have a regular job or compete in sport.

But Marla has proved them wrong. She went on to become an A-grade student at school, gained a masters degree in education at the prestigious San Diego State University, began a teaching job and will now become the first blind athlete to compete at an Olympic Games. The movie rights to her story were recently bought by Hollywood and Marla is also writing her autobiography.

She tries to make light of her disability, but to meet her is to see just how challenging her everyday life is. When running she has to keep looking straight ahead, but when talking she turns her head away from you, trying to see you out of the corner of her eye.

'I run towards an abyss of nothingness,' she said. 'It could be terrifying but I have spent my whole life facing my fears. I refuse to be defeated.

'What I represent is just achieving what you want to do in life. I think it's a matter of your attitude. Some people have a negative attitude, and that is their disability. I never wanted to be the first blind Olympian. I just wanted to make the Olympic team. I don't even think about being blind until somebody asks me about it. I would never say that if I could see, I could run three seconds faster. I can't make out anyone's facial features, I just see the colours of their kit. But there are no lanes in my event, so I don't have to worry about staying in a lane.'

Marla admits that she does run slightly wide for fear of bumping into other athletes. She can see 15 feet ahead, which translates to 1.5 seconds at her speed. Mostly, all she sees is the grey blur of the ground.

She said: 'If the field strings out, it's like running alone. I don't know who is in front or behind me, or how far. That can exhaust a lot of mental energy.

'And running in a new place is really hard. When I travelled to Seville in Spain for the world championships last year, I was really scared. I run, and I can't see what's ahead or behind me. I spend all my energy worrying about where I am.'

Marla – who now lives and trains in Eugene, Oregon – wants to be judged only on her athletic achievements. Last year she ranked second in America in the 1,500m and took second place at the US versus Britain games in Glasgow.

All this despite an injury to her left knee in 1996 and left foot in 1997 which stopped her from running for two depressing years.

And on a training run last month, Marla failed to see a little girl cycling by until she was almost on her. Twisting clear, she injured a muscle which stopped her training for a month, until only days before the Olympic qualifier.

'There are times I just sit down and cry,' she admitted. 'Just in the last few weeks, when it looked as if I wouldn't be fit for the Olympic trials, I was so upset. But that's all frustration at my fitness level, not at my blindness.'

Her boyfriend of two years – 26-year-old sports therapist and marathon runner Matt Lonergan – reads Marla the newspaper reports on her races, drives her to tournaments in unfamiliar towns and trains with her on new tracks. He said: 'Marla uses her disability as her motivation. Tell her she can't do something and she'll go out and do it.'

Her father Gary believes she is an Olympian perhaps because of, not despite, the disability. She transformed herself from being a rather ordinary athlete at school into an exceptional one in adulthood as a result of the blindness. 'She has put herself through a lot of pain not to fail,' he said. 'I think a lot of it is driven by a lack of eyesight, and wanting to succeed in spite of it.'

Marla said: 'My parents were amazingly supportive. They always told me there are no limitations, but it took me a long time to learn that. I didn't have many friends at school. Because

I could hardly see, people always thought I was being rude when I passed them in the corridor and never said hello.

'Looking back, I suppose I liked sport because of the sense of independence it brought. It was a place I could succeed on my own.'

She was transferred to a school for the visually impaired but said: 'It was as if everyone had lowered their standards, with no expectations of success. I couldn't take that. I'd get angry and frustrated, seeing people who didn't expect more of themselves. I was always persevering.

'But as far as the sport goes I wasn't a teenage phenomenon. I loved football but I had to give it up at 14 because I'd reached the point where I couldn't follow the ball around the field. That's when I took up running.'

Her athletic career soared at college, mastering the seven events of the heptathalon. She painstakingly measured out each long jump and high jump, and counted the paces between hurdles. In 1996 she entered the Paralympics in Barcelona, and won four gold medals. She still holds the disabled world record in ten events.

'But that was just like lowering my expectations again,' she explained. 'I needed to compete against able-bodied athletes to prove my worth.'

She has certainly proved that but by doing so the pressures on her have intensified. In her qualifying race she almost fell on the third lap when a slight collision forced her to reach out and touch the back of another runner to keep her balance. And as the first blind athlete to compete at an Olympic Games she is painfully aware that there must be no mistakes – as a direct result of her disability – that might affect other people's future chances.

So far, it has not proved a problem. 'I've never had any complaints,' she said. 'Everyone is very aware of positioning during a race. I have been involved in a couple of tumbles, but not of my causing.'

But the spectre of Mary Decker's fall when she was tripped by Zola Budd in the 1984 Los Angeles Olympics is terrifying.

And she now also has the pressure that comes with being a role model for others. She said: 'I can't tell you the number of letters I've had from parents and teenagers with the same or similar condition. It makes me feel good to affect people in such a positive way. It was never my motivation to be a role model. But I realise the influence I can have, and I don't want to let anyone down.

'I'm not running to escape my blindness', she insists. 'I'm running to take my blindness where everyone told me it could never go – to the Olympics. And whether I come home with a medal or not, I'm a winner already.'

Further reading

If you'd like to read more about athletics and running, take a look at Roger Bannister's *The Four Minute Mile* (Lyons Press, 1994), or try *The Perfect Mile* (Marimer Books, 2005) by Neal Bascomb.

Touching the Void
by Conn and Hal Iggulden

This extract is adapted from Joe Simpson's original book *Touching the Void* and tells an extraordinary tale of individual survival.

In May 1985, two young English climbers set off to conquer the unclimbed west face of Siula Grande – a 21,000-foot (6,400 m) peak in the Andes. There are no mountain rescue services in such a remote region, but Joe Simpson (25) and Simon Yates (21) were experienced, confident and very fit. Their story is an extraordinary one. Apart from being made into a book and a film, it has inspired intense debate among that small group of expert climbers with experience enough to judge what happened.

The two men tackled the face in one fast push, roped together and taking everything they needed with them. They

carried ice axes and wore boots with spikes (crampons), using ice screws and ropes for the ascent.

They climbed solidly that first day until darkness fell and they dug a snow cave and slept. All the second day, they climbed sheet ice, reaching 20,000 feet when high winds and a blizzard hit them on an exposed vertical slope. At that point, they were climbing flutes of powder snow, the most treacherous of surfaces and incredibly dangerous. It took five to six hours to climb just 200 feet in the dark before they found a safe place for a second snow cave.

The third morning began with a clear blue sky. By 2 p.m., they reached the north ridge at last – the first men ever to climb that face of Siula Grande. Both men felt exhausted after some of the hardest climbing of their lives, but they decided to follow the ridge towards the peak.

They reached it, but with the weather uncertain, they couldn't stay for long. Only half an hour into the descent, clouds came in and they were lost in a whiteout on the ridge, completely blind. On one side was a drop of thousands of feet and the ridge itself was made of overhanging cornices of snow that could break off under their weight. Yates saw the ridge through a break in the clouds and climbed back up to it. The cornice broke under his weight and he fell, saved by the rope attached to Simpson. He shouted up that he had found the ridge. In such conditions, progress was very slow. By the time darkness came, they were still at 20,000 feet.

The fourth day began with good weather once more. The two men came to a cut in the ridge and Simpson started to climb down a face of sheer ice. He hammered in one of his ice axes and didn't like the sound it made. As he pulled one out to get a better contact, the other gave way without warning and he fell.

He hit hard, his shinbone going through his knee and into the upper leg. As Yates climbed down, he tried to stand on it, appalled at the pain and grating of the bones. The two men looked at each other in desperation. Simpson expected his friend to leave him. There was no other choice – a broken leg so far from civilisation meant that he was dead. Instead, Yates stayed and they discussed a plan to lower Simpson on two ropes, knotted together. Yates would dig himself a seat in the snow and lower Simpson the first 150 feet. The knot wouldn't pass through the lowering device, so Simpson would dig in until Yates had retied it and could lower away once more.

The laborious process began, with Simpson face down. His broken leg jarred constantly, but it had to be fast as neither their endurance nor the light would last for long. Yates's snow seats crumbled quickly in the time it took to lower his friend. As the hours passed, a full storm hit the mountain with wind chill of −80 degrees. Darkness came upon them and both men were exhausted. They had no gas to make tea or get warm. They continued on in the dark, one rope at a time.

Simpson felt the powder snow change to hard ice and called out to stop. His voice wasn't heard and he slipped over the edge of an overhang, dangling below it. He couldn't reach a surface and, crucially, was unable to take his weight off the rope. Above him in the dark, Yates waited alone and freezing, with the wind roaring around him.

At first, Simpson attempted to climb back up the rope using a 'prussic loop', a knot that locks solid once pressure is applied. He needed two and managed to fix the first with frozen hands. The second one escaped his numb fingers and he watched it fall with his last hopes. He waited then to drag Yates to his death.

Yates waited and waited as his seat began to crumble under the unrelenting[1] weight. All he could do was hang on until he began to slide down. He remembered he had a penknife and made a decision in an instant, using it to cut the rope. The rope snaked away and below the overhang Simpson fell into darkness, losing consciousness. Yates dug himself a snow cave out of the storm and waited for daylight.

---

[1]**unrelenting**   constant

Simpson awoke in pitch blackness on a narrow slope, sliding. He had fallen more than a hundred feet into a crevasse, ending up on an ice ledge next to another drop into infinite darkness. He screwed in an ice screw anchor very quickly.

His helmet torch revealed the rope going up to a small hole eighty feet above. He thought Yates was on the end of it, dead. Simpson thought the rope would come tight on Yates's body. He pulled it to him and it fell. When he saw the end, he knew it had been cut and guessed what had happened. He was pleased Yates was alive, but realised his own chances of survival had dropped to almost nothing.

In the dark, he turned off the torch to save the batteries. Alone, he despaired.

Yates continued to climb down the next day, feeling desperately guilty about cutting the rope. He lowered himself past the over-hang and the crevasse, convinced that Simpson was dead. He went on numbly, following tracks back to the base camp that he had made with Simpson only days before.

When no one answered his shouts, Simpson tried to climb out of his crevasse, but eighty feet of sheer ice was impossible with only one working leg. He didn't believe anyone would ever find him. His only course seemed to be to sit and wait to die – or to lower himself into the crevasse to see if there was another way out in the darkness below. He took this terrifying decision, but didn't put a knot on the end of the rope. He decided that if he reached the end and there was nothing beneath him, he would rather fall than be stuck and slowly freeze.

Joe lowered himself eighty feet and found he was in an hourglass-shaped crevasse. He reached the pinch point and found a crust of snow there that had a chance of taking his weight. He heard cracking and movement beneath him, but there was light nearby, at the top of a slope he thought he could climb, bad leg or not. This was the way out.

Though every jarring step brought him close to fainting, he made it onto the mountainside to see a blue sky and bright sunshine. He lay there and laughed with relief at his deliverance.

After the initial exhilaration,[2] he looked further down and realised that he still had miles of glacier to cross as well as a treacherous maze of crevasses. He thought at first that he couldn't do it, but there was no point in simply sitting and waiting. He could see Yates's tracks and knew that they would lead him through the crevasse field.

He made progress sitting down, with his legs flat on the snow and pushing himself along backwards. Snow and high winds came again, and he kept going as darkness fell, terrified at losing sight of Simon's tracks.

The tracks had gone by the morning of the sixth day, but Simpson struggled on, reaching at last the jumbled boulders that meant the end of the glacier. He wrapped his sleeping mat around the broken leg, using his ice axes to try and support himself over the broken ground. He fell at almost every step and each fall was like breaking the leg again. Somehow, he kept going. He ate snow for water, but there was never enough to quench a brutal thirst. He could hear streams running under the rocks, but maddeningly he could not find them. He pushed himself on and on until he collapsed and lay looking at the sky as it grew dark once more.

As Day 7 dawned, he could barely move at first. He believed he was going to die, but kept crawling. He found a trickle of water and drank litres of it, feeling it make him stronger. Despite this, he was becoming delirious.

Simpson reached the lake by the camp by four in the afternoon of the seventh day. He knew the camp was in a valley at the far end, but he had no idea if Yates would be there. He tried to make faster progress, plagued by the thought that he would get there too late.

2exhilaration   excitement

Clouds came down as the day progressed and, by the time he looked into the valley, it was white with mist. He lay there for a long time, delirious and hallucinating. Eventually, he moved on as night fell and it began to snow once more.

He dragged himself through the latrine area of the camp and the sharp smell acted like smelling salts, bringing him back. He began to call for Yates and when no one came at first he believed he had been left behind.

Yet Simon Yates had stayed and he woke as he heard his name called. When he heard his name again, he went out and began to search. He found his friend a couple of hundred yards from the camp and dragged him back to the tent. Yates could not believe it. He had cut the rope and seen the drop and the crevasse. He *knew* Simpson could not have survived.

As Joe Simpson became conscious, he sought to ease his friend's guilt. His first words were,

'Don't worry, I would have done the same.'

Adapted from *Touching the Void* by Joe Simpson, published by Jonathan Cape

Further reading

Have a look at the website www.noordinaryjoe.co.uk if you are interested in Joe Simpson's experiences. The original book *Touching the Void* is available in most bookshops published by HarperCollins in 2006 and a film was also made in 2003 which had very good reviews.

On Being John McEnroe

by Tim Adams

Great sporting heroes need each other, and nowhere was this truer than in the tremendous rivalry between tennis players John McEnroe and Björn Borg, two of the very best of their generation. This is an account of their famous Wimbledon final in 1980, in a chapter entitled *Sudden Death*.

Every tennis fan remembers where they were on Sunday 5 July 1980. Nelson Mandela had managed to persuade his guards on Robben Island to provide a radio so he could listen to the World Service commentary. Andy Warhol had got up early in his mother's old house on East 66th Street, Manhattan, to catch the game on the networks. Sachin Tendulkar, in Bombay, destined to be the world's greatest cricketer, was dressed, aged 7, in a tennis kit and scarlet headband in homage to his hero, McEnroe. And I was struggling with the aerial on an old portable TV in a caravan, in a field overlooking the grey sea on the coast of west Wales, where the same rain – and hail – that had interrupted that year's tournament had also served to dampen an already angsty teenage family holiday. For me, the tension of the match was heightened by the fact that I had hardly been outside for a week, except in a cagoule. And also because, on crucial points, the television picture had a tendency to begin revolving at a furious rate, causing McEnroe, crouched interminably to serve, to begin frantically chasing several versions of his crouched self up and down the screen.

He started, I remember, too easily. Though it was McEnroe who had had the tougher semi-final, against Connors the day before, it was Borg who looked stiff and even a little slow. The Swede was chopping short arm returns into the net, jabbing at forehands, unable to find any feel for the ball. McEnroe was dominating with serve, punching and feathering volleys by turns. Many tennis matches (including almost all the ones I ever played in) simply carry on this way. One player (invariably this was me) is unable to summon any semblance of rhythm or grace, and simply throws the match away in a series of unforced errors.

In the first set, at least, that looked like it might just be the case for Borg in 1980. As a result, walking back to his chair having established his lead, McEnroe seemed particularly ill at ease: just as he hated to lose, so he apparently took no pleasure at all in winning too comfortably. He scratched his head, picked at his socks, bit his lip. 'I get a feeling from time to time,' he would say, speaking for many of us, 'when it feels like things are going too well, that something bad has to happen.' Something, on this occasion, was very horribly wrong: he was 6–1 up against the four-time champion.

Up in the stands, Borg was being watched by Mariana Simionescu, who was keeping notes on her feelings during the match, in preparation for a book that was to be her wedding present to him. The previous night, at the Holiday Inn, she'd had a dream: 'I am in Greece and Björn is far out to sea, and he comes back with a lot of fish. We cook the fish on the beach. Our little house is far above and you have to climb exactly 134 steps to get to it, and we eat there, on the sand, with wooden spoons, and Björn has never been a tennis player.' She is not quite sure what to make of this dream, but somehow it does not seem like a good omen. Her star sign has told her: 'If possible, don't leave your house today.'

When the players came out for the second set Borg still looked awkward, but seemed untroubled by the way he was playing. He made no effort to shake life into his arms, or to stretch his legs. He played, that is, as he always played, looking for the next shot and the next point. The crowd, which sounded equally split between the two players, was muted though, as if wondering if this was it: the King of Wimbledon was going to give up his crown with hardly a whisper. McEnroe had been saying before the match that he thought that the 'Wimbledon crowd just wants Borg to win for ever', but that this time, 'McEnroe was in his way.'

It seemed odd for him to talk about himself in the third person, as if he were not sure he had a real say in the matter.

Apart from a few diehard partisans the allegiance of a tennis crowd, and in particular a British tennis crowd, tends to shift depending on the state of the match. If it is a close struggle, or a final, then it will support the player who is just behind, in order that the game is prolonged into something memorable (and the spectators get their money's worth). This is not how the crowds feel in football, say, when there is a finite length to the match, whatever the score. But a one-sided tennis match is hardly a match at all. For this reason, having been rooting for McEnroe, I recall now willing Borg to come back, to make something more of it.

Replaying the match again, it looks as if McEnroe wants to feel his way through the second set, to get it over with quietly. Recognising that Borg is not on top of his game, he also starts to play just a little within himself, not hitting the lines but just inside. But still he is well on top. Borg gets nowhere near his serve and clings on desperately to hold his own. Then, at five games all, Borg locates his timing for just a couple of points. Once he starts hitting the ball he starts moving better, and suddenly he has served a love game and has broken McEnroe for the first time, to take the set.

McEnroe looks, at this point, like he has been ambushed and humiliated. He squats down on his haunches, juts out his lower lip; tears seem a possibility. A man in the crowd with a pink silk open-necked shirt and a cigar clamped between his teeth stands up to cheer the Swede. Mariana Simionescu in the stands is angry at herself for having ever doubted that her betrothed, King Borg, would let her down.

At one set all, now it is McEnroe's turn to look stiff and out of sorts. The American player Gene Meyer remarked how, the first time he played McEnroe, on any given point his opponent 'never seemed quite ready, whether serving or receiving'. And he does not seem ready now, twitching a little, taking an age to wind up his serve. He overhits a couple of volleys, sets up Borg at the net twice. And he is 3–0 down in the third set, having dominated the whole match. At changeover he takes off both his shoes and peers inside, as if looking for what has gone wrong. He then bites furious lengths of sticking plaster off a roll and makes little loops of them which he lines up along his thigh, before attending angrily to his shoelaces. A couple of weeks earlier, at Queens,[1] his opponent, Sandy Meyer, Gene's brother, had offered to tie the laces up for him, believing he was using it as a tactic to disrupt his serve. McEnroe had replied as Woody Allen might have done: 'I'm just a very fidgety person . . . I don't know why . . . I always like my laces to be very tight, especially for crucial points.' Before he goes out to serve he leaves a little pile of sticking plaster loops beside his chair.

Borg does not worry about anything, apart from his rackets, the strings of which he taps to listen for a reassuring tone. Other than this, he occasionally blows lightly on his fingers. At changeovers he looks up without expression at Simionescu and Bergelin. He and his wife-to-be have a code during matches. Sometimes he feels he wants her to leave, believes she is getting in the way of things, and he indicates this by making a curt slicing motion with his hand, down by the pocket of his shorts – the kind of behaviour which perhaps, in retrospect, did not augur[2] particularly well for their marriage. On this occasion, she is pleased to see, he is happy for her to stay, and she makes mental notes as he wins the third set. 'The crowd now seems to breathe in a special way,' she senses, 'as if everyone is adjusting to his pulse.'

The most memorable tennis matches are those which invent their own rhythm. In the early sets you begin to notice little patterns within points, themes and metres, which are then returned to and tested under the greatest pressure at or near the death. We remember the 1980 final primarily for the

---

[1]**Queens**   a tennis tournament
[2]**augur**   promise

tiebreak. But there were epic moments before that drama which seemed to enable it to be possible. There were the three break points Borg saved at 4–4 in the second set, the loss of any of which would almost certainly have put him down two sets to love. And then there was the twenty-point game he served at 4–2 in the third set, with McEnroe always an inch or two away from breaking him back and restoring parity. On both occasions it was Borg who had held his nerve and prevailed, as he always prevailed. These exchanges were stored in the memory of both the players and the audience, and as the tension developed, both we and they subconsciously perhaps, expected them to be repeated.

In the fourth set both players play at a pace and with a confidence that had not previously been apparent. McEnroe goes through his full repertoire of shots – stop volleys and drop volleys, angled passes and lobs – but Borg is chasing nearly everything down now and passing McEnroe at the net on both sides. On other occasions, in other matches, McEnroe could become overwhelmed by the sense that, 'I'm out there on the line, by myself, fighting to the death in front of people who are eating cheese sandwiches, checking their watches, chatting about the stock market.' Now, though, no one is eating their sandwiches, and he has what he has always required: the crowd's fullest attention.

Even so, just an hour after he appeared to have the match and the title within sight, he is now facing defeat. Matches involving Borg often seemed to work out like that. Vitas Gerulaitis, Borg's closest friend, who had never beaten him in sixteen attempts, once said: 'Every time I play Borg I come out with some thirty new ideas which should get me victory. And each time Björn breaks each one of the thirty to pieces, like a clay pigeon shooter.' The Swede looks in that mood now, his eyes apparently getting closer together, zeroing in, and eventually, at 40–15 and 5–4 down, McEnroe faces two match points.

Before he settled himself to receive the first of these serves you could see – even, I remember, on my intermittently revolving

TV screen – McEnroe searching his armoury at this moment, wondering what he might throw at Borg. It looks a bit like the wonderful frame or two in the film *When We Were Kings* when the camera lingers on the face of Muhammad Ali,[3] who, having exhausted what he thought was everything against George Foreman, quietly determines simply to let himself be hit for a few rounds to tire Foreman out. In something like this spirit McEnroe looks down at the ground and swipes at a piece of loose dirt at the service line, wonders what manner of man he is playing. And then he conducts two entirely thoughtful rallies, different from what has gone before, pushing the ball around the court, letting Borg feel the pressure, and ending with nerveless passing shots. He finishes off the game with two extraordinary backhands, not so much struck as guided over the net. And having been dead, he is now alive.

The very greatest competitors are, it seems, always motivated not by the glory of success but by the abject fear of the pain that attends defeat. Boris Becker[4] once described this sensation very clearly. 'When you are a young man, you are looking for your own identity, and winning is a way of expressing yourself. When I lost, I wanted to die. And because I thought in victory I became somebody, in defeat, it followed, I was nobody.' In the showers at Wimbledon, after he had successfully retained his title at the age of 18, Becker bleakly shouted through to his coach that he did not feel as strongly about having won the championship as he had a couple of years before when an ankle ligament injury had forced him to withdraw. 'Winning,' noted his coach, 'never lifts him as high as losing drags him down.' It was the same with McEnroe, too, who talked about being 'diminished' in defeat; of not being the man he hoped he was.

In a tiebreak, as in a penalty shoot-out in football, the burden of this kind of little death is only ever a shot or two away.

---

[3]**Muhammad Ali**   a world champion boxer
[4]**Boris Becker**   another Wimbledon champion

This fact is reflected in the emotion of the crowd: its empathy is not at all with the person who will win the match but entirely with the person who will lose it.

The tiebreak had been introduced in 1971 and McEnroe had grown up with it. His father once told a story about a tiebreak he had watched his son play at the Pepsi Junior tournament in Forest Hills, when he was 16. 'He had six or eight match points, some were net cord balls, and luck was against him. When it was over he was on court with his face in his hands and a towel over his head. I don't normally do it, but I went over to him on court, and said: "Don't worry about it son, it's not so bad." He didn't want to talk to me, though – he was too upset. I was upset, too. I mean, it was a *horrible thing* to witness.'

Günther Bosch, Becker's coach, suggested that 'in a tiebreak there are no benevolent[5] spirits you can pray to, it's not a poker game or voodoo. A player must be peaceful and calm inside. He must open the door and go quietly into the room.' But the Wimbledon final did not allow that kind of calm, at least not to McEnroe. If the match was Borg's to win, it was his to lose. 'Somehow,' he later remembered feeling, 'maybe because I'd saved those match points earlier, I could sense that people who didn't want me to win the match, wanted me to win the tiebreaker. They just didn't want this match to end. And the match itself did not seem to want to end.'

The idea of a tiebreak is a simple one: kill or be killed. On this occasion, though, I remember thinking how the two players seemed to be anxious to explore a third option: that of a death indefinitely postponed. As the points stacked up, the commentators' talk turned from 'the long walk' and 'staring down the barrel' to desperate hopes of closure. 'Well, *surely* now . . . ', 'And *finally* the champion serves for the match, for the *sixth time* . . . '

At 11–11, we were told, there was 'nothing left now to happen'. But there was plenty more to happen. Once they are into the teens the points seem to go faster, and the possibility of

---

[5]**benevolent**   kind

ending seems oddly further off. There is a net call on match point; a service called out is overruled before McEnroe has a chance to explode; and then he misses two easy volleys. Watching the close-up of him now, at 14–14, he seems to be wondering if he should give up the game for good.

Simionescu, meanwhile, smoking with her cigarette cupped in her hand below the ledge in front of her, so that Borg won't notice, starts producing metaphors at the rate of one a point. Having thought initially that the tiebreak was 'like the drum beating that heralds the tumbril carrying the convicts sentenced to death . . . like a dawn in the Middle Ages when all the balconies are booked because no one wants to miss the moment of the beheading', she now believes 'that the stadium is a boat at the mercy of a giant wave, bobbing on the crest only to be sucked into the abyss the next moment'. At 15–15, 'The audience is still, even the heads have stopped turning from right to left, from left to right. These fortunate few are watching, in fact, two men walking on a tightrope between two tall buildings, who go steadily ahead to meet at the middle, where one will have to fall.' At 16–16 she feels she is witnessing a moon landing; at 17–16 they are all in an aquarium. And then, 18–16, she watches Borg fall from his tightrope at the twentieth floor; the scoreboard wipes everything away, and comes back up with two simple numbers, 2–2, and the players return to their seats.

After the tiebreak, having lost seven match points, Borg quietly checks his rackets again. McEnroe begins violently chewing something; he sends a ball boy on an errand that the ball boy clearly does not understand, but which he is far too scared to question. Their brief exchange ends with McEnroe telling him to just 'go, go now'.

And then there follows a moment which must rank among the greatest in sport. It is the moment when Borg walks out to serve once more, two sets all, one set to play, as if nothing had happened. 'I thought Borg would be physically deflated after losing the tiebreaker,' McEnroe said. 'But whatever he had inside him was beyond anything I could imagine.'

McEnroe had forgotten his fatigue during the tiebreaker, but now he was beginning to remember it. 'At one point I started getting cramp in my foot. Then my knee hurt. But I pushed myself anyway. I felt I did my best. It was, like . . . like I was playing from within.'

Borg, though, had got to that place first. He won the final set 8–6, winning all of his last five service games to love. Afterwards, when he was sitting in his chair, zipping his rackets up, the camera caught him for the first time in what looked like reflection. He tried an odd half-smile, and muttered something to himself, a single word, in Swedish. The word was 'unbelievable'.

He had not been dethroned, but for the first time Borg admitted in the post-match interview to something in his head that he had not allowed the public or his opponents to see before at Wimbledon: doubt. When asked if he was unsure of the eventual winner at certain stages during the match, he said, 'Yes, of course.' It felt like a moment to reach for the book of quotations. Richard Evans, writing in *Tennis Week*, observed: 'Thank god for McEnroe for otherwise Borg would indeed "bestride this narrow world and hold the palm alone".'

Immediately after the interview Borg phoned his parents in Sweden. They were asleep at nine o'clock. He apologised for having woken them up. He then did not speak for a couple of hours, not to Bergelin, not to his fiancée Simionescu. Later he went to a reception at the Clermont Hotel where Petula Clark and Shirley Bassey sang to him 'Happy Wimbledon to you'. Someone produced a cake. Two weeks after that, he and Simionescu were married.

Further reading

If this was of interest to you, it's well worth reading the whole book, *On Being John McEnroe* by Tim Adams, published by the Yellow Jersey Press.

The Madness of Man

by Andrew Alderson

> Every year on the Isle of Man the celebrated motor-cycling TT races
> take place. This is an account of one year's death-defying races.

The Isle of Man TT is the last truly eccentric mass sporting
event left in Britain – and the most dangerous, with seven people killed in the past fortnight alone. Andrew Alderson discovers its addictive allure.

It is only in the pit lane minutes before race time that you begin
to understand the obsession. As the sound of 80 revved engines
grows from a gentle hum to a fierce roar, the air is filled with an
intoxicating cocktail of motor oil, hot rubber and worn
leathers: one lungful can hook a person for life.

This is the Isle of Man TT 2000, where only a combination
of adrenaline, testosterone and back-slapping camaraderie prepares competitors for the most challenging and dangerous race
in the world.

As they tear off at 10-second intervals on to the 37.73 mile
circuit, riders know that they will reach speeds of up to 195 mph
on roads that range from snaking mountain passes to what are
usually busy town highways.

It is not necessary to be clinically insane to participate in one of the ten races, but with riders regularly thundering down a tree-lined hill with a one-in-seven gradient on two wheels at 150 mph inches away from the bike in front in a thunder storm, it helps.

This year the Isle of Man TT fortnight has claimed seven lives on the island where the local population of 75,000 is boosted by 30,000 motorbike enthusiasts. To put the level of danger into perspective, during the past decade just two men have died participating in Formula 1 racing – hardly a sport for the faint-hearted but one in which the cars are now so sturdily built that they offer a level of protection that no motorcycle rider will ever enjoy.

Since the TT races began in 1907, between 170 and 200 riders have died either in qualifying or racing the course. It may not be entirely coincidental that Douglas's vast cemetery is opposite the main TT grandstand.

It is not only human error that causes a TT rider not to require his (or her, for there are a handful of women riders) return ticket home. Over the years everything from a wet manhole cover to a burst tyre, a stray farm animal and discharged diesel on the road, have claimed lives.

Many racers seem happy, well-balanced family men when you begin talking to them but as the conversation turns to motorbikes their eyes light up and their passion for a sport that has claimed the lives of many of their friends and relatives is unmistakable.

Bill Smith, a cheerful, stocky, father of three from Chester, is entitled to draw his state pension. Last week, the 65-year-old was competing in his 81st TT race, having won four previously and gained 51 TT replicas – earned for finishing close to the winning time, and a total topped only by another race veteran, Joey Dunlop.

Smith, who competed in his first TT race in 1957, considers himself 'lucky' to have had only one bad crash while racing, in the 1983 TT. Yet, when he starts to describe his injuries, it soon becomes apparent that it is the sort of 'luck' that most of us would happily do without.

'It was my own fault. I was talking to the BBC the night before and saying how safe I had been for 27 years and the next day I was fighting for my life in intensive care,' he says, with a chuckle. 'It will teach me not to shoot my mouth off in future.

'The gear box locked up and I hit Ballaugh Bridge when I was doing about 110mph. I broke just about every bone in my body: both my legs, both my arms and my back. I was a mess: seven breaks in the right leg, and four in the left.

'My elbows were completely smashed up. Afterwards I had plastic elbows and they had to lock my arms in just one position. I just got them to set them in a position that I could still ride a bike rather do the washing up.

'My kidneys had stopped working so I had to be on a dialysis machine pretty quickly. Thanks to a helicopter ambulance, it was 7 minutes 20 seconds from the time I hit the wall to the time I was on the operating table. If it had been just a few more minutes without my kidneys working, I would have been a goner.'

He spent the next three months in hospital and was unable to race again for four years. He defied the advice of both friends and his wife, Ann, and began competing again in 1987. Yet even as he lay in his hospital bed, he was plotting his return to racing. 'The thing was that it wasn't my own fault. If it had been my mistake I would have accepted that the time had come to pack it in, but it was a mechanical fault so I couldn't blame myself or the circuit.

'I just had the urge to race again. It's the course: there is no other circuit like it in the world. It has mountains, it has bad weather. It's the ultimate challenge.'

Smith, whose son Mark, 21, also races motorbikes, has long given up trying to convert his wife to the merits of the sport. 'I suppose having a husband and a son racing plays on her emotions,' he says with masterly understatement.

Smith, who chaired the sport's ruling body, the Auto Cycle Union, for six years until 1997, has no plans to retire. 'I will pack it in when I don't feel physically fit. But I am still racing okay at the moment. On the course, you are the master of your own destiny and every year your knowledge and mastery of the track increases.'

Even those who lose loved ones tend to be forgiving towards the sport. Last week Stan Beck, a company director from Preston, Lancashire, was on the Isle of Man to support two young race riders even though his son, Simon, a leading competitor, died in last year's TT.

'It's been sad in some ways coming back and I have had one or two quiet moments by myself, but Simon died doing what he loved,' said Mr Beck, who was in the grandstand with his daughter, Jayne, when his son was killed during qualifying.

'The circuit wasn't to blame and if Simon came down from the heavens now he would say: "Dad, I made a mistake." He was going just a bit too quick.'

Isle of Man TT fortnight is more than just watching 350 riders from 22 countries compete for £750,000 of prize money on bikes ranging from 125 to 1,000 ccs.

Thirteen thousand of the 30,000 visitors to the island bring their own motorbikes. This is the island where – for a fortnight in June and a fortnight in late summer for the Manx Grand Prix – everyone from doctors to dustmen who share a passion for the sport spend their days either competing or watching the races and their evenings either trying the race circuit out for themselves or watching a rerun of the races from every possible camera angle on a giant screen on Douglas seafront.

Death and serious injury are accepted as part of the sport and – as if the sport is in denial – often receive little or no media coverage. *Motor Cycle News*, the riders' weekly 'Bible', last week devoted 13 pages to TT coverage, but only a lengthy paragraph on page 51 to the death of five riders (two more died after its publication).

Three racers, Steve Wood, 40, Chris Ascott, 36, and Raymond Hanna, 49, died in successive TT practice sessions. Three others, including two in a head-on collision, died when riders were on the course while the roads were open to the public, and a seventh man, Douglas Hook, 39, died in an accident during sand racing on Douglas beach.

On the course, bouquets of flowers and the occasional wooden and brass plaque mark the spots where riders have perished over the years. Many roadside memorials have fresh bunches placed every year by friends and family returning for their annual pilgrimage to the TT.

Peter Kneale, the chief press officer for the event and who has seen every race on the course since 1946, said everything was done to make the event as safe as possible and only competitors with an international race licence could take part. 'Three competitors dying is three too many. High-speed sports are dangerous and there is no disguising it. But the TT course is to top riders what Mount Everest is to mountaineers and they want to tackle it.'

On the Isle of Man, where the TT races cost £1.5 million to stage but bring in millions in tourism, there is barely a dissenting voice despite the heavy death toll.

'Sos' Whelan, one of 1,000 volunteer marshals and who has witnessed three fatal crashes at Greeba Bridge, said: 'The throttle works two ways and nobody says that the riders have to take part and no one is telling them how fast they have to go.'

The island's 220-strong police force closes the roads on the 226-square-mile island half an hour before each race and puts up road signs in German urging Continental riders, who have caused countless deaths over the years, to ride on the left when the roads are open to the public.

Acting Chief Inspector Gary Roberts, who is in charge of uniformed policing on the island, supports the race even though he concedes that the motorbikers' invasion brings dangers to competitors and islanders alike. 'From a policing point of views, it is a challenge for us, too,' he said. 'And, in the end, you just have to admire the sheer, mad courage of them.'

Further reading

If motorcycles and racing are your thing, have a look at www.ttwebsite.com and also www.motorcycle.com for more information, and have a browse in your local bookshop in the sports section.

It's Not about the Bike

by Lance Armstrong

Lance Armstrong has known greater sporting success than most sportsmen of his generation. He has also known the appalling realities of living with and fighting against a severe form of cancer. In this extract he draws very interesting parallels between the sport and the illness.

That afternoon, I walked into yet another non-descript brown brick medical building for my first chemotherapy[1] treatment. I was taken aback by how informal it was: a simple waiting room with some recliners and La-Z-Boys[2] and assorted chairs, a coffee table, and a TV. It looked like somebody's living room full of guests. It might have been a party, except for the giveaway – everybody was attached to his or her very own IV drip.[3]

Dr Youman explained that the standard treatment protocol[4] for testicular cancer was called BEP, a cocktail of three different drugs, and they were so toxic that the nurses wore radioactive protection when handling them. The most important ingredient of the three was cisplatin, which is actually platinum, and its use against testicular cancer had been pioneered by a man named Dr Lawrence Einhorn, who practiced at the Indiana University medical center in Indianapolis. Prior to Einhorn's discovery, testicular cancer was almost always fatal – 25 years earlier it had killed a Chicago Bears football star named Brian Piccolo, among many others. But the first man who Einhorn had treated with platinum, an Indianapolis schoolteacher, was still alive.

Had I lived 20 years ago, I would have been dead in six months, Youman explained. Most people think Piccolo died of

---

[1]**chemotherapy**   cancer treatment
[2]**La-Z-Boys**   reclining chairs
[3]**IV drip**   medical equipment for giving medicines directly into a vein
[4]**protocol**   procedure for a course of treatment

lung cancer, but it started as testicular cancer, and they couldn't save him. He died in 1970 at the age of 26. Since then, cisplatin has become the magic bullet for testicular cancer, and Einhorn's first patient, the Indianapolis teacher, has been cancer-free for over two decades – on his anniversaries they have a big party at his house, and Dr Einhorn and all his former nurses come to visit him.

I thought, *Bring it on, give me platinum*. But Youman warned that the treatment could make me feel very sick. The three different anti-cancer toxins would be leaked into my system for five hours at a time, over five straight days. They would have a cumulative effect. Anti-emetics would be given to me along with the toxins, to prevent me from suffering severe nausea, but they couldn't curb it entirely.

Chemo is so potent that you can't take it every day. Instead it's administered in three-week cycles; I would take the treatment for one week, and then have two weeks off to allow my body to recover and produce new red blood cells.

Dr Youman explained everything carefully, preparing us for what we were about to face. When he finished, I had just one question. It was a question I would ask repeatedly over the next several weeks. 'What's the cure rate for this?' I asked. 'What are my chances?'

Dr Youman said, 'Sixty to sixty-five percent.'

My first chemo treatment was strangely undramatic. For one thing, I didn't feel sick. I walked in and chose a chair in the corner, the last one along a wall in a row of six or seven people. My mother kissed me and went off to do some errands, and left me with my fellow patients. I took my place among them.

She had prepared me to be disturbed by my first encounter with other cancer patients, but I wasn't. Instead, I felt a sense of belonging. I was relieved to be able to talk to other people who shared the illness, and compare experiences. By the time my mother got back, I was chatting cheerfully with the guy next to me. He was about my grandfather's age, but we hit it off, and we were jabbering away when my mother walked in. 'Hey, Mom,' I said brightly. 'This is Paul, and he's got prostate cancer.'

I had to keep moving, I told myself. Every morning during that first week of chemo I rose early, put on a pair of sweats and my headphones, and walked. I would stride up the road for an hour or more, breathing and working up a sweat. Every evening, I rode my bike.

Bart Knaggs returned from Orlando with a Mickey Mouse hat he had picked up at Disney World. He handed it to me and told me he knew I would need something to wear when I lost my hair.

We would go riding together, and Kevin Livingston often joined us. Bart made huge maps for us, as large as six feet in diameter. He would get maps of counties from the Department of Highways and cut and paste them together, and we would stand over them choosing new routes for ourselves, long winding rides out in the middle of nowhere. The deal was to always find a new road, someplace we hadn't been before, instead of the same old out-and-back. I couldn't stand to ride the same road twice. The training can be so monotonous that you need newness, even if half the time you end up on a bad piece of road, or get lost. It's okay to get lost sometimes.

Why did I ride when I had cancer? Cycling is so hard, the suffering is so intense, that it's absolutely cleansing. You can go out there with the weight of the world on your shoulders, and after a six-hour ride at a high pain threshold, you feel at peace. The pain is so deep and strong that a curtain descends over your brain. At least for a while you have a kind of hall pass, and don't have to brood on your problems; you can shut everything else out, because the effort and subsequent fatigue are absolute.

There is an unthinking simplicity in something so hard, which is why there's probably some truth to the idea that all world-class athletes are actually running away from something. Once, someone asked me what pleasure I took in riding for so long. 'Pleasure?' I said. 'I don't understand the question.' I didn't do it for pleasure. I did it for pain.

Before the cancer, I had never examined the psychology of jumping on a bicycle and riding for six hours. The reasons weren't especially tangible to me; a lot of what we do doesn't make sense to us while we're doing it. I didn't want to dissect it, because that might let the genie out of the bottle.

But now I knew exactly why I was riding: if I could continue to pedal a bike, somehow I wouldn't be so sick.

The physical pain of cancer didn't bother me so much, because I was used to it. In fact, if I didn't suffer, I'd feel cheated. The more I thought about it, the more cancer began to seem like a race to me. Only the destination had changed. They shared gruelling physical aspects, as well as a dependence on time, and progress reports every interval, with checkpoints and a slavish reliance on numbers and blood tests. The only difference was that I had to focus better and harder than I ever did on the bike. With this illness, I couldn't afford impatience or a lapse in concentration; I had to think about living, just making it through, every single moment. The idea was oddly restorative: winning my life back would be the biggest victory.

I was so focused on getting better that during that first round of chemotherapy I didn't feel anything. Nothing. I even said to Dr Youman, 'Maybe you need to give me more.' I didn't realize that I was extremely lucky in how my body tolerated the chemo. Before it was over I would meet other patients who had uncontrollable vomiting after the first cycle, and by the end of my own treatments I would experience a nausea that no drug could get a grip on.

The only thing that suffered at first was my appetite. When you undergo chemotherapy, things taste different because of the chemicals in your body. My mother would fix me a plate of food, and she'd say, 'Son, if you're not hungry and you don't want to eat this, it won't hurt my feelings.' But I tried to eat. When I woke up from a nap, she would put a plate of sliced fruit and a large bottle of water in front of me. I needed to eat so I could keep moving.

Move, I told myself. I would get up, throw on my warmup clothes, put my Walkman on, and walk. I don't even know how far. I'd walk up the steep hill and out of the front gates, and trudge on up the road.

As long as I could move, I was healthy.

A couple of days after I started chemo, we opened a notification letter from the hospital: *Our records show that you have no health insurance.*

I stared at the letter, uncomprehending. That wasn't possible. I had a health plan with Motorola, and I should have been fully covered. Irritated, I picked up the phone and called Bill Stapleton to read him the letter. Bill calmed me down, and told me he would check into it.

A few hours later, Bill called back. It was a lousy piece of timing, he said. I was in the midst of changing employers, and although my contract with Cofidis had taken effect, the cancer was a pre-existing medical condition, for which I was not covered by the Cofidis group plan. My insurance with Motorola had expired. I would have to pay for hospitalizations and the treatments myself, unless Bill could figure something out.

I had cancer, and I had no health insurance.

A lot of terrible realizations hit me one after another in those first few days, and this was only a material matter. Still, it was potentially ruinous. I looked around my house, and started thinking about what to sell. I was wiped out financially, I assumed. I had just gone from making $2 million a year, to nothing. I had some disability insurance, but that was about it. I would have no income, because the companies that sponsored me or paid me would cut me off, surely, since I couldn't race. The Porsche that I so treasured now seemed like an item of pure decadent self-indulgence. I would need every penny to pay the medical bills. I started planning the fire sale. I'd get rid of the Porsche, and some art, and a few other toys.

Within days, the Porsche was gone. I did it for two reasons, first and foremost because I thought I might need every dime for my treatment, and I'd have to live on what was left for the rest of my life. But I think, too, that I was beginning to need to simplify things.

I became a student of cancer. I went to the biggest bookstore in Austin and bought everything there on the subject. I came home with ten different volumes: diet books, books on coping emotionally, meditation guides. I was willing to consider any option, no matter how goofy. I read about flaxseed oil, which was supposed to be 'a true aid' against arthritis, heart infarction, cancer, and other diseases. I read about soy powder, a 'proven anti-cancer fighter'. I read *Yoga Journal*, and became deeply if only momentarily interested in something called The Raj, 'an invitation to perfect health'. I tore out pages of *Discover* magazine, and collected newspaper stories on far-off clinics and far-fetched cures. I perused a pamphlet about the Clinic of the Americas in the Dominican Republic, describing 'an absolutely certain cure for cancer'.

I devoured what Bart had given me, and every time he called, I said, 'What else you got?' I had never been a devoted reader, but now I became voracious. Bart went to Amazon.com and cleaned them out on the subject. 'Look, do you want me to feed you what I find?' he asked.

'Yeah, I want everything. Everything, everything.'

Here I was, a high-school graduate who'd received an eclectic[5] education in Europe, and now I was reading medical journals. I had always liked to study financial magazines and architectural-design magazines, but I didn't care much for books; I had an impossibly short attention span and I couldn't sit still for that long. Now all of a sudden I had to tackle blood counts and basic oncology.[6] It was a second education, and there were days that I thought, *Well, I might as well go back to school and try to become a doctor, because I'm becoming so well-versed in this.*

---

[5] **eclectic**   broad
[6] **oncology**   the study of tumours

I sat on the sofa flipping through books, talking on the phone, reading off numbers. I wanted to know exactly what my odds were, so I could figure out how to beat them. The more research I did, the better I felt my chances were – even though what I was reading suggested that they weren't very good. But knowledge was more reassuring than ignorance: at least I knew what I was dealing with, or thought I did anyway.

There was an odd commonality in the language of cancer and the language of cycling. They were both about blood. In cycling, one way of cheating is to take a drug that boosts your red bloodcell count. In fighting cancer, if my hemoglobin fell below a certain level, the doctors would give me the very same drug, Epogen. There was a baseline of numbers I had to meet in my blood tests, and the doctors measured my blood for the very same thing they measured in cycling: my threshhold for physiological stress.

I began to receive mountains of mail, get-well cards, best wishes, and off-the-wall suggestions for cures, and I read them all. Reading the mail was a way to keep from brooding, so in the evenings Lisa and my mother and I would sort through the letters, and answer as many as possible.

One evening, I opened a letter with an embossed letterhead from Vanderbilt University's medical center. The writer was a man named Dr Steven Wolff, the head of the bone-marrow transplant department. In the letter, Dr Wolff explained that he was a professor of medicine and an oncologist, as well as an ardent cycling fan, and he wanted to help in any way he could. He urged me to explore all the various treatment options, and offered to be available for any advice or support. Two things about the letter drew my attention; the first was Wolff's obvious cycling knowledge, and the other was a paragraph that urged me in strong terms to get a second opinion from Dr Larry Einhorn himself at Indiana University because he was the foremost expert on the disease. Wolff added, 'You should note that there are equally effective chemotherapy treatments that could minimize possible side effects to not compromise your racing capabilities.'

I picked up the phone and dialed Wolff. 'Hi, this is Lance Armstrong,' I said. Wolff was taken aback, but he recovered quickly, and after we exchanged a few pleasantries, he began a hesitant inquiry about my treatment. Wolff explained that he was reluctant to encroach on the authority of my doctors in Austin, but he wanted to help. I told him that I was on the standard treatment protocol for testicular cancer with lung metastasis, BEP.

'My prognosis[7] isn't good,' I said.

Further reading

It's Not about the Bike and *Every Second Counts* by Lance Armstrong, both published by Yellow Jersey Press, provide vivid accounts of the author's battle with cancer and his cycling triumphs.

---

[7]**prognosis**   forecast of the probable course of an illness

Moondust

by Andrew Smith

Of the astronauts who walked on the moon, only nine are alive today. Andrew Smith set out to find and interview the moon-walkers who have experienced what no other human being has. He finds that their lives were changed for ever. Astronaut Gene Cernan features in this extract.

'Well, you know, I flew when I was thirty-two, thirty-five, thirty-eight, and I had no idea where I was gonna go or what I was gonna do. I looked at the space-shuttle programme, but by that time I was forty-three, I'd had twenty years in the Navy and the shuttle was still five or six years out there into the future. And even at the age of forty to forty-two, five years is a long time. I'd like to have flown the shuttle, cos it's a great flying machine, but I'd been there and done that, and it doesn't go anywhere. And let me tell you, when you've seen the Earth from the Moon, staying home isn't good enough. So I had to decide whether to stick around or go out and find something new, and that's what I chose.'

Which must have been hard.

'Yeah. Just cos you go to the Moon doesn't mean you're an expert at everything, obviously. And it's harder to find something when you're on the hot seat all the time, training for crews and backup crews. You almost take those things for granted, and then all of a sudden you get off and you look for the next mountain to climb. And you don't find one with the challenge, with the risk, with the adventure and the reward. So you keep searching until . . . you know, I guess I'm the kind of personality that can't just sit back and put up a sign saying, "I've been to the Moon – you all owe me somethin''. I had to go and find something else. And I guess until I grew up and hit grandkids and one thing or another . . . I'm satisfied now, although I'm still probably this type whatever-it-is personality . . . '

And I find myself thinking, 'But you never did find anything else,' and wondering what the difference was between those who were expanded by the journey and those left with ennui[1] and frustration; between the trips that were good and the trips that were bad. I wonder what I would have found and whether it's perhaps better not to know . . . whether quiet, Earthly contentment beats shooting for the Moon in the end, the way a pair of threes beats an ace in poker. It draws on me that this question lies behind nearly all of the others I've been asking in regard to both the astronauts and the Apollo programme itself, and that it has a special resonance for me, because amused friends have begun to point out that when I'm finished with the Moon men, I'm going to be in a similar, if much less spectacular, position to the one they faced at the end of 1972. Where am I going to find something to absorb me the way they have? In this moment I feel a heightened empathy for Cernan, even if he maintains that he's as passionate about space as he ever was.

You still feel passionate about it? I ask.

---

[1] **ennui**   boredom

'Oh yeah, that's one reason why I'm tending to respond to requests like this. I'm finally seeing something come together that I've been trying to say for a long time. And that's that we haven't had an agenda. We've got a series of space events that we can't define, that we can't justify. And they're going nowhere. We need something out there to entice our kids. Claire, how long have I been saying that?'

'Twenty years.'

He continues as if he hasn't heard.

'Twenty-five years. And finally we've got a president who's saying the same thing I'm saying. So that's what I'm passionate about, that's what I'm excited about.'

After NASA,[2] Cernan worked in oil, energy, marketing, and ran a small airline for a while. You don't need to be a rocket scientist to appreciate that none of those could rival the thrill of leading a species to its apparent destiny in space and in time they all palled. Like Buzz Aldrin,[3] he wound up returning to the Moon in the sense that it's his life again; it's what he does and takes his identity from. It's where he sees himself.

'Yeah, going to the Moon in front of the whole world is a tough one to top,' he confirms, leaving me to wonder whether he thinks his Moonwalker colleagues experienced the same sense of let-down that he did, reacting as he would have expected them to, or whether they surprised him.

'Some of them surprised me and some haven't. Some have gone on and decided that they've done it, don't want to be bothered, and live a cloistered life. Others are very ambitious and want to go out and do something and make something happen in business. And then others sort of, ah . . . I've gotta be careful with my words here . . . sort of prostituted[4] to some degree their celebrity status. And I think there's somewhere in-between where you can make use of it.'

---

[2]**NASA**   National Aeronautics and Space Administration (the US space agency)
[3]**Buzz Aldrin**   another moonwalker
[4]**prostituted**   abused for their own benefit

There's little doubt in my mind as to who he's talking about here, although it seems to me that if anyone fits that third category, he does.

'You've got a lot of opportunities, but a lot of responsibilities go with it. Twelve of us travelled to the Moon. I don't have to keep telling people about it, but some guys feel they do. So there's that three categories of people.'

Does he get fed up with the obvious questions – what did it feel like to walk on the Moon etc.? He smiles.

'What's it feel like? What's it look like? Did you feel closer to God? Were you scared? How do you go to the bathroom in space? What's one-sixth gravity like? I mean, you just can't get it from looking at a picture. What's it like? I can't tell you what it's like in a few words. What's it like to look back at the Earth surrounded by the infinity of space and concepts we can't even understand, like *time*. I can't tell you it's unbelievable, or it's awesome, because that doesn't answer your question. We gotta sit here and talk about it. That's what enticed me to write a book . . . So do you get tired of hearing that question? Yes and no. You get tired of the fact that you can't give that person the ten-second voice-bite that he wants in order to feel good about what you've said. You've gotta spend time, like I'm trying to do with you now, talking about being there at that moment in space and time and history. You feel inadequate that you can't give people the answer they want.'

Suddenly I feel bad about my earlier impatience. When I told him what I was searching for, I never meant to suggest that I was expecting Kierkegaard[5] in response, the grand answers from him alone, but that's obviously what he heard. No wonder there was a look of panic in his eyes as he tried to figure where to start.

We talk about celebrity for a while and Cernan complains at the way its modern form fails to distinguish between 'someone who's cut somebody's throat or drowned their pregnant

---

[5]**Kierkegaard**   a philosopher

wife', or 'a ballplayer who made sixty home runs, then got kicked outta the game because he's a druggy', or Britney Spears, who's just got hitched for a day in Vegas ('she's just a bad influence on my grandkids, as far as I'm concerned'), or him.

'But we didn't put ourselves in front of the public, which is what celebrities tend to do. We just got thrust there.'

He talks about his 'love affair' with the Saturn V.

'Standing up at night and the lights are on it and all this oxygen and hydrogen are boiling over the sides, it's *alive*, it's moving cos the wind makes it sway, and that's going to take you a quarter of a million miles to another planet . . . and when you get in it, you've got control of it.'

Only later do I recall Buzz's insistence that, as an astronaut, one thing you *didn't* have was control over the rocket.

We move on to the Carpenter family's allegation of a *coup*[6] in the Astronaut Office and Cernan holds the official line that Scott 'screwed up'. He's complimentary about Carpenter's best pal John Glenn, though, who flew into space once more aboard the shuttle in 1998, at the age of seventy-seven. I ask whether he'd like to go for an encore and he says that he'd be happy to take the shuttle up for a quick spin, but not to spend two weeks sliding around in low Earth orbit on the space station.

'Would I like to go back to the Moon, though? Sure I would. Because I would like to go back to a place that I once lived, to see what it's like, like going back to the old farmhouse that you grew up in when you were a kid, that you haven't seen in thirty years. You know, *What is it like today?*'

He'll repeat this thought for TV cameras tomorrow and Jay Leno[7] will be making fun of him on the *Tonight Show* in the evening, pointing out that unless some alien civilisation has snuck up there and shifted stuff around like a frat house prank it's going to look the same. But when Cernan adds that 'the place we lived was frozen in time before we got there and it's

---

[6]**coup**   sudden action to take over power
[7]**Jay Leno**   American TV chat show host

been frozen in time since we left, with the flag and my space-craft and the rover and my daughter's initials in the dust, and our footsteps just eternally blazed in time', I can see what he means. If it was a surreal adventure in the first place, how much more surreal it would be to go back and survey the scene again. That sensation has the potential to be felt by only nine people, but unless Bush the Younger[8] has something very spectacular up his sleeve, it will never be felt by anyone.

'Yeah, I'd like to go back. As you get older, you get more his-torically-minded. You go places where important things have happened and know that the only thing which separates this place from what happened then is something we know nothing about – time. How could you turn it down?'

We talk a bit about Mars and his inconvenient but valid contention that the chemical propulsion systems used today are inadequate to take us there, because 'six or seven months' travel time is unacceptable', but six to eight weeks would be OK. Right now, astronauts would have to stay there for eight-een months until the planets were correctly aligned for a return flight. In my mind, Mars moves further away as he says this.

'But you've got more technology under the dashboard of that rental car you're driving than I had going to the Moon, which tells you what's happened in those thirty or forty years. And there's gonna need to be that same kind of technological evolution, that's gonna be moved forward through necessity. Technology evolves through necessity, not by accident. Now we're going to see another explosion of technology if the presi-dent's policy goes through. I mean, when I was a kid, Dick Tracy[9] used to talk through his watch and it was, like, 'Gimme a break!' Now we can talk through 'em and take pictures and find out where the nearest coffee shop is. I mean, this is *wild* technology we have today. Anything you can imagine, you can

---

[8] **Bush the Younger**   George W. Bush, American President
[9] **Dick Tracy**   police detective in a popular American cartoon strip

make happen. But we do need to advance our technology in several key areas even to get to the Moon.'

Yet the question remains: Why is any of this important?

'I don't know, maybe just because it's there,' he muses, echoing Sir Edmund Hillary's[10] possibly apocryphal[11] response to the question of why people climb mountains. Taken at face value, this is obviously the most nonsensical reason a person could have for doing anything more complex than tying a shoelace, and I assume Hillary to have meant that mountains and Moons excite the imagination for reasons we don't understand, which are irrational yet in some way quintessentially[12] human.

Further reading

Have a look at the website www.nasa.gov for more information about space travel. If you really enjoyed the extract, you might like to read the whole book *Moondust* by Andrew Smith, published by Bloomsbury.

---

[10]**Sir Edmund Hillary**   Everest mountaineer
[11]**apocryphal**   untrue
[12]**quintessentially**   very particularly

Activities

Heroic Failures

Before you read

1   What kind of humour really makes you laugh? Are there certain subjects which comedians should not tell jokes about?

What's it about?

2   These heroic failures are all true stories. Which did you find
    a   the funniest?
    b   the most absurd?
    c   the hardest to believe?

3   Choose two of the (safer) tales and recreate them as short drama scripts or improvisations for group performance.

Thinking about the text

4   Why do we laugh at these incidents? Are they all failures? What makes the people heroic? Debate these questions in small groups.

5   Talk in groups about how you might consider the people involved in these tales to be 'outsiders'. What makes them different? What do you think motivated them to act in the way that they did?

Blind Spanish Woman Makes Television History

Before you read

1   If you had a choice of a television department you could work in, what area would you choose? Would it be behind the scenes as a producer? Or presenting sport? Might it be working on nature documentaries? Or reality shows? Would you like to be a newsreader?

What's it about?

2   Discuss what particular problems Nuria del Saz has had to overcome to realise her ambition to become a newsreader.

3   Do you think she considers herself to be an 'outsider'? Debate this question in your group.

Thinking about the text

4   You are a journalist sent to interview Nuria for a magazine. Write a feature article about her life and achievements which will serve to inspire others.

5   Write 'A Day in the Life of Broadcaster Nuria del Saz' from her point of view. This could be done as a series of diary entries.

6   Using the websites below and related websites, research into Braille script, its origins and current usage. Present your findings to others in the group.

www.wikipedia.org
www.nbp.org
www.rnib.org

Marla Runyan

Before you read

1   This text is about a blind runner. To get a brief impression of what it would be like to be unable to see, try some of the following wearing a blindfold:

- Arrange in front of you – and in the correct order – the books and equipment you need for each lesson today.
- Follow instructions from a partner to move to specific places in the room.
- Find your way around an obstacle course laid out in the room.
- Write your name and address.

Discuss how you felt at the end of each activity.

What's it about?

2   This is very well-crafted piece of journalism. What techniques of content, style and language does Peter Sheridan use to keep the reader's interest? Make notes under the following headings:

- human interest items
- organisation of ideas
- use of paragraphs
- use of quotations
- biographical detail
- wider references to the Olympics.

3   Marla talks about the people around her who have supported her efforts. What particular contributions have been made by her family and friends? What has their role been in her achievements? Discuss your ideas in pairs.

Thinking about the text

4   Marla Runyan says, 'Some people have a negative attitude, and that is their disability.' Use this as starting point for a group discussion.

5   There are a number of striking images created in this feature article. Imagine you are a photographer sent to cover the story. Draw up some notes to yourself about five key photos you'd like to take to accompany the article.

6   Present a short illustrated talk (perhaps with Powerpoint slides) about the Olympics and the Paralympics.
See www.london2012.org for some ideas.

Touching the Void

Before you read

1   Women and men attempt amazing feats around the world, climbing mountains, sailing across oceans, walking across deserts. Which do you think are the most impressive or inspiring? Is there a particular physical challenge that you would like to tackle in years to come?

What's it about?

2   Re-read the first two sections. How successful is the writer in creating a vivid picture of the conditions the men were climbing in? In pairs, make a list of words and phrases that appeal to the five senses.

3   What technical vocabulary about climbing do you learn from this passage? Compile a list of the technical vocabulary and use a dictionary to write clear definitions. Is this vocabulary key to understanding what the author is writing about?

4   'He remembered he had a penknife and made a decision in an instant, using it to cut the rope.'

Simon Yates has been much criticised by climbers everywhere about this decision. He was made to feel a real outsider within the climbing community. Why did he choose to cut the rope? Should he have done so? What were his alternatives? Debate these key questions in small groups.

Thinking about the text

5   Writing as Yates back at base camp, draft a series of diary entries covering the time up to and including Simpson's miraculous return.

6   What techniques of language and style does the writer use to emphasise how desperate Simpson is during his crawl back to base camp? Look carefully at the vocabulary used.

7   Discuss in pairs your reaction to the final sentence of the passage.

8   Select any point in the passage where the action takes a turn in direction and rewrite the rest of the account in a different way from that of the original.

Being John McEnroe

Before you read

1 Discuss with a partner: what do you expect from your sporting heroes and heroines? Should they be good role models to young people?

What's it about?

2 Write the name John McEnroe at the centre of a spider diagram. Note down ten words and phrases that describe him. Look out in particular for aspects of his competitive character.

3 Now draw a similar spider diagram for Björn Borg. Again, search for clues as to his extraordinary reactions under pressure.

4 The writer tries to pick out a few of the two players' relative weak spots as humans and competitors. Make a list of these.

Thinking about the text

5 What stylistic techniques does Tim Adams use to capture the sheer excitement and tension of their great Wimbledon final? Write these up as a short critique.

6 'The very greatest competitors are, it seems, always motivated not by the glory of success but by the abject fear of the pain that attends defeat.' Debate this statement in groups, thinking about other great competitors you have seen in action.

7 Note down the names of the other sportsmen mentioned in this chapter. Research their sporting achievements.

8 Imagine you had the opportunity as a radio reporter to interview both Borg and McEnroe several months after their epic final. Draw up a series of questions you would want to ask each of them. With a partner, role-play the two interviews.

The Madness of Man

Before you read

1 From your reading and your watching of film and television, what is the most dangerous sport you have come across? Why is it particularly dangerous? Are you tempted to try it?

What's it about?

2 'It is only in the pit lane minutes before race time that you begin to understand the obsession.' Make a note of all the 'obsessive' aspects of TT racing that Andrew Alderson covers in this article.

3 On your own, pick out a few of the descriptions that you feel bring the racing scenes on the Isle of Man vividly alive. In small groups, explain your selection. Are there one or two scenes that everyone has found particularly striking? Discuss the reasons for this.

4 You have been commissioned to produce a fact file on the TT races for a website. Include in your fact file all the facts and figures included in the article. Try to present them in an interesting format for the TT website. Have a look at www.ttwebsite.com

Thinking about the text

5 What do you think of Stan Beck's attitude to the TT races? Can you understand how he feels?

6 Write a short argument essay on how these riders, as extreme sportsmen and sportswomen, can be viewed as 'outsiders'. Try to explain their passion and their motivation.

7 Put yourself in the place of one of the racers who returns year after year. From his viewpoint, keep a diary covering a typical fortnight. Try to capture all the drama of what happens before, during and after the races.

8 Exploring the theme of 'being an outsider', choose one of the following as a starting point either for a short story or for a newspaper article:
   - *You are the master of your own destiny.*
   - *The gear box locked up and I hit Ballaugh Bridge when I was doing about 110mph.*
   - *Dad, I made a mistake.*
   - *High-speed sports are dangerous and there is no disguising it.*
   - *You just have to admire the sheer, mad courage of them.*

It's Not About the Bike

Before you read

1 Do you know or have you heard about people who have managed to overcome terrible illness or disability to achieve something special to them? In small groups, discuss what you know of these people. Make suggestions as to what might have helped them.

What's it about?

2 'I didn't do it for pleasure. I did it for pain.' Use this as the starting point for a character description of Lance Armstrong. Use other clues in the extract to help you build this picture.

3 What parallels does Armstrong draw between cycling and cancer? What is your reaction to his analysis?

4 Do you think Armstrong's attitude to his illness and his career helps explain (a) his great sporting achievement and (b) how he overcame such severe cancer?

5 In this extract, what does Armstrong say were the worst aspects of living with cancer? Discuss these points in small groups.

Thinking about the text

6 'I felt a sense of belonging. I was relieved to be able to talk to other people who shared the illness, and compare experiences.' Why do you think Armstrong feels this way towards other cancer patients?

7 Lance Armstrong now works for his own cancer charity (www.livestrong.org) and presents talks to inspire others to fight cancer. Using ideas from this extract, draft out a short talk that he might give to a group of cancer patients. Try to make it both hard-hitting about the realities of cancer and inspiring!

Moondust

Before you read

1   It is predicted that within 20 years you will be able to take a flight into space as a regular passenger. Talk with a partner about whether you would go or not.

2   Carry out a brief bit of research (library or web-based) to find out the names of all the astronauts who have walked on the moon. Who was the first, and what were his famous words when first stepping onto the moon's surface?

What's it about?

3   What does Andrew Smith learn from his interview with Gene Cernan about the personalities of many of the moonwalkers?

4   Which sentences and phrases in the text indicate that those who had walked on the moon then found life back on Earth very difficult?

5   Talk in your groups about what Cernan says about actually being on the moon. What are the sights, sounds and images? How does it make a human being feel?

Thinking about the text

6   Imagine yourself as a moonwalker. Using the first person 'I' narrator, tell your story of the landing, your walkabout and then your return to Earth.

7   'Anything you can imagine, you can make happen.' Use this as a starting point for writing a short story.

8   Cernan observes, 'Technology evolves through necessity, not by accident.' Stage a debate on this subject, with two speakers (a proposer and a seconder) arguing for this proposition and two arguing against it.

9   Re-read the final paragraph. Reflect on the following: 'mountains and Moons excite the imagination for reasons we don't understand, which are irrational yet in some way quintessentially human'. Write a short speech from Gene Cernan's viewpoint, in which he is talking to an audience about the special experience he had.

Compare and contrast

1 Think about the athletes and sportsmen and women in this section
   and consider:
   a what they have in common
   b how they are different
   c how they respond to adversity
   d how they view danger and even death.

2 Which of the extracts did you enjoy most? Write a review of your
   favourite extract from this section that will make other people want
   to read it.

3 Why does someone behave in the way they do? What causes them
   to take one line of action rather than another? What motivates the
   central figures in these extracts? Working in groups, choose one of
   the people you have read about. S/he is placed in the witness box
   and quizzed as to how s/he succeeded and why s/he acted in a particular way.

4 Nuria del Saz and Marla Runyan have interesting parallel experiences to share. Script a conversation between them in which they
   discuss how they overcame their disabilities to achieve success.

5 Based on the Lance Armstrong and Andrew Alderson extracts,
   present a short talk on what you think cyclists and motorcyclists
   have in common, in terms of their pursuit of their sport almost at
   any cost.

6 How do those around Lance Armstrong help him to fight his cancer? Compare this with how people around Nuria del Saz and
   Marla Runyan helped them overcome obstacles.

3 Moving places, moving lives

This section covers what is perhaps more familiar 'outsider' territory, with stories that allow us to step inside someone else's shoes. Floella Benjamin and Benjamin Zephaniah describe what it is like to arrive as a child in another culture, while Mirad's and Zlata's stories take us to the heart of children's desperate, lonely experiences in wartime.

Activities

1 Have you had any personal experience of moving places, and there-fore moving your life and home? Was the change very dramatic? Was it easy or difficult? Did some family members find it more dif-ficult than others? What do you particularly remember about the move? Talk about these questions in your groups.

2 Have you encountered incidents of deliberate racism, either towards you or towards family and friends? What happened? Can you explain *why* you think it happened? What was the outcome? How were you left feeling?

3 Which short stories, diaries, plays or novels have you read that focus on children and young people caught up in war? Discuss what happened to them and how they reacted. Were they caught up in particularly interesting tales of survival? Are there any films you have seen which you felt were successful in bringing home to you the *realities* of war, from a young person's perspective?

Coming to England

by Floella Benjamin

Floella was one of six children who, with her mother (Marmie) and father, moved from Trinidad to start a new life in England in the 1960s. This extract presents her first steps into a new school. Her brother Junior and sister Cynthia had come to England a little earlier.

It took us a few days to get over our disappointment and to adjust to living in the big city of London. During that time we got used to being with Junior and Cynthia again who had both changed quite a lot. They had made so many presents for us at nursery school and had also painted pictures of what they thought we would look like, which was most amusing. They had longed to be with us and asked so many questions about Trinidad and our adventurous voyage. They loved hearing the story of Ellington nearly falling into the ocean, which got more and more exaggerated depending on who was telling the tale. The room was our playground and the noise we made inside those four walls was unbelievable. We were forever being told to be quiet, that we were not in Trinidad now where we could run free and play in the yard. Our new home didn't have a garden and Marmie would never allow us to play in the streets because it was far too dangerous.

One of the few times we were allowed to go outside was to collect the bottles of silver- and gold-topped milk left on the doorstep. At first I thought someone had left them as a free gift for us until I realized Marmie had to pay for the milk at the end of the week. In Trinidad, we used to buy milk from a man who came round on a bicycle with a small tank full of cow's milk on the back.

Marmie had made arrangements for us to go to a local school and after just ten days of being in England, I was on my way to my first English school.

When I arrived at the school, many of the children rushed over and touched me then ran away giggling. I thought they were being nice to me. At that time I didn't realize it was because I was different, a novelty, something to be made a fool of and to be laughed at. The dingy Victorian building squatted in the large grey playground like a bulldog ready to attack. It was surrounded by high wire fencing, a hopscotch game was marked out on the ground and on one of the walls a bull's-eye pattern was painted.

Above the school's main door were some letters engraved in the stone; they were Latin words and I never did find out what they meant. Inside the school the walls of the long corridors were tiled halfway up, making the building feel cold. The tiles had been painted a mushy green, some of it flaking off where it had been scratched over the years by passing children. The ceilings and upper half of the walls were a dull beige colour and the floors were covered with worn and splintering wooden parquet. Off the corridors were separate, unwelcoming classrooms, each one with its own door, not partitions like the ones in Trinidad. But the desks and the blackboards were the same. I felt a little comforted when I saw them. At least they were something I'd seen before.

The structure of the day was also a familiar routine: lessons, playtime, more lessons, lunch and play, then ending the day with

more lessons. The work the teacher gave us was so easy and simple compared to the work I was used to. Yet the teacher treated me like an idiot because she couldn't understand my Trinidadian accent even though I could understand her. I felt like a fish out of water.

School took a great deal of getting used to, especially during the first few weeks. I found some things new and exciting – simple things like the taste of cold milk during the morning break. I would grip the small glass bottle tightly as I plunged the straw into the silver foil top and sucked out the creamy liquid. The only thing I wasn't so keen on was the thick, furry feeling it left in my mouth afterwards. There wasn't a stall selling treats in the playground but the children did play clapping and skipping games which made me feel at home. There was one game, however, which I didn't understand at first but in no time at all I began to hate. The first time I saw the children play it, I knew it was wrong and cruel. I was standing next to the wall with the painted bull's-eye when some boys came up and spat strange words at me, words that I had never heard before but from their faces I knew they were not nice. They were words which told me that I was different from them and that they felt my kind shouldn't be in their country. I looked at them, confused and baffled like a trapped, helpless creature. What was 'my kind' and why shouldn't I be in the country I was brought up to love? The land of hope and glory, mother of the free. I began to feel angry and violent as I stood and watched their ugly faces jeering at me. But they might as well have been talking in a foreign language because I didn't understand the words they were shouting. I didn't let them make me cry though; I had learnt how to be tough during the time Marmie had left us in Trinidad. When I got home and asked Marmie what the words meant, she looked sad and sat us all down and slowly explained that because of the colour of our skin some people were going to be cruel and nasty to us. But we must be strong, make something of ourselves and never let them get the better of us. That was the day I realized that in the eyes of some people in this world I was not a person but a colour.

I looked down at my hands and desperately tried to understand why my colour meant so much to some and disturbed them so deeply. In Trinidad there were people of different races, from all over the world, and they lived together in harmony. No one felt threatened or was made to feel bad because of his or her colour. So why all the fuss in England? I felt so confused. A picture flashed up in my mind of Sandra and me holding hands and laughing as we skipped along Marabella main street to our friendly wooden two-storey school. Tears welled up in my eyes and I wished I was back there, happy and innocent again. For that was the day I had lost a certain innocence, and I would never be the same again. I, too, would now see a person's colour first and wonder whether he or she was going to hate me.

The next time the boys shouted racist words at me *they* ended up against the wall. My battle for survival had begun. I was determined not to be the loser and I never was because Marmie told me over and over that no one was better than me and to be proud of who I was and of the colour of my skin. I liked myself and if anyone had a problem with my colour it was going to be their problem, not mine.

Further reading

If the issues in this extract interested you, you might like to try *The Lonely Londoners* by Samuel Selvon, published by Longman, 1989.

Refugee Boy

by Benjamin Zephaniah

> Alem Kelo's father is Ethiopian and his mother is Eritrean; their two countries are at war. Alem comes to London for safety to live with a foster family, Mr and Mrs Fitzgerald and their daughter, Ruth. But, as a refugee, he then gets caught up in the British justice system. His father has recently arrived in England to meet up with Alem. Mariam and Sheila from the Refugee Council have been working with the family.

After school on Monday, Alem ran home as fast as he could to cook his father's meal.

'Did you get the spaghetti?' he asked Mrs Fitzgerald as he hung up his jacket and went into the kitchen.

'Yes, I got it,' she replied.

'And is it Italian?'

'Yes.'

'Actually made in Italy?'

'Yes, yes, yes! It says "produce of Italy" on the packet and the shopkeeper said he knows the Italian family who export it.' She handed him the packet. 'You can't get more Italian than that. Now wash your hands.'

Mrs Fitzgerald guided him around the kitchen and helped him prepare the spaghetti and the sauce. Ruth came home as the cooking was ending and laid the table for them before going to her room to listen to some music. Not sure exactly what time Mr Kelo was coming, the household went into a state of limbo. Mr Fitzgerald was happily rearranging things in the garden shed, Mrs Fitzgerald began washing used pots and cleaning the kitchen, and Alem went upstairs and started to tidy his room.

Then the doorbell rang and everybody headed for the front door. Alem leaped down the stairs and beat everyone to it. He opened the door to find Mariam and Sheila standing there. He looked beyond them and to the left of them and to the right of them, hoping that there was a surprise or a trick in store, but he could see by the expressions on their faces that they were playing no games.

'Where's my father?' Alem asked.

Mrs Fitzgerald came up behind Alem. 'Let them come in, Alem.'

They all went into the living room without saying a word until Mariam spoke. She directed her words to Alem. 'I went with your father today to the Home Office to help him with his application and he was arrested and taken to Campsfield.'

No one spoke. Alem stared at her. He felt like crying, he felt like shouting, but instead he just whispered, 'What is Campsfield?'

'Campsfield is a detention centre where they detain asylum seekers.'

'You mean it's a prison?' Alem asked.

'Well, officially it's not a prison,' Mariam replied. 'However, I'm afraid that everyone I've known who's been there has said it's just like a prison.'

'What can we do?' said Ruth.

'There's not much we can do,' Mariam said. 'We'll be using Nicholas Morgan again, Alem's barrister. He'll get to work first thing tomorrow. Until then there really is very little that can be done.'

Sheila reminded Alem that she was there if he needed her. Alem thanked them both and went to his room. He felt as if his life was a roller-coaster going from one extreme to the other. He considered his age and asked himself if this was the way his life would continue. He sat silently. He heard Sheila and Mariam leave. He heard the Fitzgeralds talking; he had no intention of joining them.

When Mrs Fitzgerald stood outside his door urging him to eat something before the food went cold, he just said, 'I can't eat now, Mrs Fitzgerald.'

As the Fitzgeralds were eating, he went to the bathroom, but after that he never left his room for the rest of the night.

The next morning to everyone's surprise Alem was up early. He had breakfast as usual and went to school. Mrs Fitzgerald tried to get him to stay home but he insisted on going, saying that he had to learn as much as he could. But at school everyone could see that something was wrong with him. Robert knew it was serious but, instead of asking, he hoped that Alem would tell him what it was.

Alem walked home alone and when he arrived, Mrs Fitzgerald, who was in the middle of a phone conversation, opened the door. 'Alem has just come in now,' she said to the person on the phone. 'Would you like to speak to him? OK, here he is,' she said, handing him the phone.

'Hello. This is Nicholas Morgan here, Alem.'

'Hello,' Alem replied.

'Look,' Nicholas continued, 'I don't want you to get too worried. We're going to apply for bail.[1] He really doesn't have to

---

[1] **bail**   money paid or promised as a guarantee that a person will return to court

be in there and we think that we have a strong case. So don't worry too much, all right?'

'All right,' Alem said.

'I'll let you know what's happening as soon as I know anything. Now can you put Mrs Fitzgerald back on?'

'Yes,' said Alem. He handed the phone back to Mrs Fitzgerald.

'OK,' she said. 'OK – will do – no problem – thank you – goodbye,' and she put the phone down. 'Don't worry, son,' she said to Alem.

'I'm all right,' Alem replied. He went to his room, turned on his computer and changed his clothes.

He didn't say much but he ate with the family as normal that evening, retiring to his room early again. Soon after there was a knock on the door.

It was Ruth.

'Can I come in?' she said, opening the door ever so slightly.

'Of course.'

She entered the room and sat on the bed next to Alem. 'I really don't know what to say. If I were in your place, I would have cracked up by now. You've had to deal with so much.'

'I suppose it's my life so I have to deal with it.'

'I don't think it's as simple as that. You have to be tough.' She had a small package in her hand which she handed to Alem. 'I have a present for you. I took a chance – you may hate them but I thought I'd give it a try.'

Alem took the gifts from her. They were in a brown paper bag. He held it at one end and let the gifts fall into the other hand. It was two CDs, one of Eritrean traditional music and one of Ethiopian traditional music. The minute beginnings of a smile appeared on Alem's face.

'There is a problem,' he said mock seriously. 'You didn't get me any Tigrean music nor any Somalian music.'

'Gosh, Alem, I don't know the difference. I'll take them back if you don't like them,' Ruth said, holding her hand out.

'Only joking, silly,' Alem said, holding the CDs to his chest. 'They're great.'

Ruth rolled her eyes and smiled. 'I looked hard for those. I was trying to find an Ethiopian band but I couldn't find any.'

After Ruth left the room, Alem went to his computer and played the CDs. He had never been interested in music and he certainly was not the type to listen to traditional music, but this was different. The recording quality was basic, as if recorded in a field or by someone simply placing a microphone in front of the musicians. It didn't have the clean, polished sound of a studio recording but it had a profound effect on Alem. The stringed instruments, the drumming and most of all the chanting meant that he was hearing the sounds of home. These were the birth songs, the death songs, the wedding songs and the love songs that he had for so long taken for granted. He closed his eyes and drifted from the Ethiopian town of Harar to the Eritrean city of Asmara; then he drifted into sleep.

There was a knock on the door. Alem woke up. It was Mrs Fitzgerald. 'Alem, maybe you should get in bed now, it's almost midnight.'

Alem couldn't believe he had been asleep so long. 'Yes, Mrs Fitzgerald. I'm sorry, I fell asleep.'

The next time Alem woke up it was morning. The sound of pop music was blaring out from Ruth's room as she was busy getting ready for work. Before she left, Alem caught her on the landing and thanked her for the CDs again. 'I don't know what you were thinking but all I can say is that it was just what I needed.'

His mood that day at school was a bit better and he managed to explain to Robert and Buck what had happened, how his father came and how he went.

'We have to do something,' Robert said. 'It's not fair!'

'There's nothing we can do now,' Alem replied.

When Alem arrived home, Mrs Fitzgerald had a message for him. She told him to go and get changed and then to wait in the living room. Alem just didn't know what to expect but the seriousness of her tone made him very worried. She came into the living room and sat opposite Alem.

'Well, Nicholas Morgan has been on the phone to me again today and he sounded hopeful. Tomorrow morning your father will appear in court and Nicholas will be making an application for bail on his behalf. He thinks that there's a good chance that bail will be granted but he said he couldn't be one hundred per cent sure.'

Alem didn't know how to take the news, he wasn't sure whether it was good or bad.

'Do I have to go to court as well?' he asked.

'Nicholas said no. He said that we don't want to be seen taking you out of school for this and that he will have your file with him anyway because it may help your father's case.'

'So I just carry on as normal?'

'That's just what he said,' Mrs Fitzgerald replied. 'It's going to be difficult waiting for the results of the hearing but Nicholas does know his business.'

Alem looked her in the eye and said, 'I'm sorry for being such a problem.'

Mrs Fitzgerald rose to her feet. 'Nonsense!' she said. 'The only problem I have is you thinking you're a problem. Now stop saying sorry and stop saying problem, will you?' She looked down at him most seriously but then quickly winked at him.

Alem smiled. 'Yes, Mrs Fitzgerald.'

'And Alem?'

'Yes, Mrs Fitzgerald?'

'Remember, there's a lot of people who love you.'

'Yes, Mrs Fitzgerald.'

Further reading

If you'd like to read another book with a similar theme, try *Sumitra's Story* by Rukshana Smith (Coward McCann, 1983). For more information about the author and his work, have a look at the website www.benjaminzephaniah.com

What's Your Problem?

by Bali Rai

This story is about racism in England. Jaspal and his family have moved from Leicester to a village near Nottingham, where his father runs a shop. Jaspal has begun to meet some racist bullies.

The next day I got on the bus and found a seat next to Jemma and Katie. I looked towards the back where Steggsy and his crew always sat. He wasn't there but two of the other lads were, the skinny, rat-faced one called Chas, and the fat, blonde one, Cutler.

I stared at them, expecting some abuse, but they looked at anything but me. Down at the floor, out the window. Just not at me. *Typical,* I thought, as I sat down, *no balls when their leader wasn't around.*

Katie and Jemma started asking me about my black eye and the cuts on my face.

'It's nothing,' I told them, looking away.

'Nothing?' said Jemma, frowning, 'You look like you've run into a wall or something.'

'Who was it, Jas?' asked Katie.

'It wasn't anyone . . . just some trouble. Nothing I can't handle. I'll deal with it my way,' I told them.

Katie and Jemma looked at me with a mixture of pity and concern. I went red and looked out of the window, wishing that they would leave it alone.

I spent the morning of my second day at my new school unable to concentrate on a word the teachers were saying. My mind was on Steggsy and his mates and how I was going to deal with them the next time they came for me. It wasn't a question of *whether* they would come. More of *when*. I was thankful when the bell went for lunchtime.

After lunch I sat in a dream through biology and history. I wanted to get home to my bedroom where I could lock the door and put on my headphones and listen to my music.

Jemma picked up on my mood on the way home and kept asking me what was up. I was grateful for her interest but I didn't tell her about the attack.

But I could think of nothing else. I felt ashamed that I hadn't put up a better fight. That I had felt scared. That wasn't how I'd been brought up. That wasn't what I'd learned in Leicester, where an attack like that would have been dealt with the same night. Only in Leicester I'd have had back-up. Here in the perfect English village I had just me.

When I got in I put some hip-hop on and turned up the volume, getting lost in each track, but still not forgetting what was on my mind. I didn't even hear my mum knocking on my door until she just about broke it down. Taking off my headphones, I jumped off my bed and unlocked the door.

'Are you deaf, Jaspal?' she shouted, in Punjabi.

'Sorry, Mum, I was listening to some music,' I replied in English.

'Go downstairs and help your father.'

'Why?' I asked. I didn't think the shop was all that busy.

'He is doing some paperwork so he needs you to mind the counter,' replied my mum.

'Cool.'

I turned off my stereo and headed downstairs and out into the shop.

'You watching counter, *beteh*,' said my dad in English.

'OK.'

'I'll be in back doing papers . . . '

'No problem, Dad. I ain't got no homework anyway,' I replied.

He shuffled off into the back with a big red file full of his order sheets and stuff.

I settled down on the stool and waited for a customer, watching the small telly that my dad had under the counter.

Every two or three minutes people came in and bought the evening paper or fags. Most of them were polite but one or two made comments under their breath, mainly stuff I couldn't understand because they had mumbled it. I ignored it all and waited for my dad to finish what he was doing.

It was nearly an hour later when two men came in, sneering at me and then smiling to each other. I sensed trouble straight away. There was just something in the way that they were looking at me. And each other. The taller of the two was shaven-headed and wearing a Nottingham Forest shirt with combat trousers and boots. A spider's web tattoo crawled up the right side of his thick neck and he had a bulldog wrapped in the Union Jack on his left arm with the letters *BWF* underneath it.

The other man was shorter than me but twice as wide and had a five-inch-long scar running down the left side of his face. He was wearing a combat jacket, jeans and boots, and he too was close-shaven. He was the sort of racist thug that you meet in your nightmares. One of the 'NFs' my dad always told me about. National Front. Racist scum.

As if to confirm this, he pulled up his jacket sleeves. On one arm he had a tattoo of a Union Jack with *NF* in the middle of the red cross and *England's Pride* written above and below. On the other arm was a naked lady. A dagger dripped blood between her breasts. I caught myself staring and looked away quickly. The shorter man spoke first.

'Twenny B&H.' Just like that. No please. No mate.

I coughed. My dad must have realised that I was trying to catch his attention, because he walked in and looked at the two men. He told me to sit down, in Punjabi, and faced the shorter man.

'What you after, mate?' he asked, smiling.

'What's your problem – can't you speak?' said the shorter man, in a deep growl of a voice, looking at me and ignoring my dad.

'He busy – I serving. What you want?' my dad asked.

The taller man sneered and leaned into my dad's face.

'You know what we want,' he said. 'And don't call him "mate" – he ain't no mate of yours.'

The shorter man smiled and showed two gold teeth.

'Twenny B&H,' he spat out.

My dad turned and got the fags from the shelf and put them down on the counter. He waited for the money. The taller man looked around and then pulled a 20 pound note from his trousers, screwed it up and threw it into my dad's face. I got angry and stood up but the man just laughed at me and then his face got deadly serious.

'Sit down, Paki,' he whispered to me. 'I'm not here to hurt yer unless you make me.'

I stood my ground and stared into his pale blue eyes. They didn't blink once.

'Leicester's easy to go back to,' he told my dad.

'You can just jump in yer Paki wagon and 40 minutes from now you'll be back in Pakistan,' added the short one.

My dad told them the price of the fags and waited. I could tell that he was fuming, but he didn't show it.

'Just a friendly piece of advice,' said the taller man. He picked up the 20 from the counter where it had fallen and smoothed it before putting it back on the counter.

My dad picked it up and cashed up the fags, laying the change down on the counter. The shorter man picked up the money and pocketed it while the other one started to sniff the air.

'Smell that?' he whispered, to no-one in particular. 'Smells like petrol.'

He looked me in the eye and smiled.

'Just like petrol,' he repeated before both of them left the shop.

My dad went around to the front of the counter after the two men and locked the door behind them. He turned to me and tried to smile. Tried to pretend it was nothing.

'They just idiots, innit,' he said, not looking me in the eye.

'I think you should report them to the coppers,' I said, trying to stay calm.

'No point, *beteh*. They not doing anything. Just messing 'bout,' replied my dad, not looking at all sure about what he was saying.

'Dad – they weren't messing about. At least report them – that way . . . '

'No, Jaspal. I don't care about them mens. It's my country too.'

I shook my head and went back upstairs, wondering when the next warning would come.

Further reading

If you'd like to read more by the same author, try *Dream On* (Barrington Stoke Ltd., 2002) and *(Un)arranged Marriage* (Random House, 2001) by Bali Rai. You could also take a look at the website www.balirai.com

A Boy Called 'Grenade'

by Fergal Keane

BBC journalist Fergal Keane has reported on wars from around the world. He has been named Reporter of the Year in the Amnesty International Press Awards. This article is set in Rwanda, the scene of a bloody civil war.

Kigali, Rwanda, April 1997

Today's correspondents meet many people who've suffered loss or been traumatized by war and violence. Sometimes it can prove an educational experience. This was the case when the author interviewed a young survivor of the Rwanda massacres which cost the lives of hundreds of thousands of people. He ended up questioning the very way he and other news-gatherers work.

Like nearly every other survivor of the genocide[1] I have met, Placide always looked away when answering questions about what had happened to him. He did not look into my face, but rather into some unreachable distance, in whose limitless spaces he seemed lost. Yes, he could tell me his story and he could remember names, dates, places and incidents. But he would not meet my eyes and so that most fundamental of human contacts evaded me through the long hour I spent with him. Later, I would find out why. But only after I had made a very foolish and hurtful mistake.

We were sitting in the church where he had seen his parents murdered, where he had seen children's heads smashed and pregnant women disembowelled, where he had seen what no child should ever see. And as I have done before in other zones of conflict, in other ruined countries, I listened, asked questions and recorded. He was patient with me. Most survivors are incredibly patient. But it was at the end of a day of stories, a day

---

[1]**genocide**   deliberate slaughter of a race of people

when the stories seemed to get worse and worse and by the end, sitting there in the church, I think I had started to lose my concentration. This is not by way of an advance apology for the mistake I made, but rather an explanation of how one can lose the sense of what one is doing.

You see, earlier in the day, somebody had told me that Placide's nickname was Grenade; this because he'd had a grenade thrown at him during the massacre and the shrapnel had badly marked his legs. I was given to understand that he liked the name, that he had laughed when someone mentioned it. It was background information, the kind of thing you store away and maybe or maybe not use when writing the script. But I decided to ask Placide about the nickname; it just might prove useful in building a picture of his life after the genocide.

'I understand you have a nickname,' I said. For the first time in the interview he looked directly at me. 'Is it true that your nickname is Grenade?' I asked. Placide's eyes began to fill with tears, in a few seconds he was crying uncontrollably. A soldier who had been helping us to interpret stood and took him by the hand and led him outside. I knew within an instant that my question had deeply hurt the child. Perhaps in front of his friends he had to pretend to like the nickname, but it was clear now that he felt ashamed, marked out and different because of his wounds. Grenade. The name singled him out and I, for the sake of one thoughtless question, had summoned up all of the pain it caused him.

I got up from my seat and walked out of the church, into a garden where, three years before, I had walked among the recently murdered bodies of Placide's family and hundreds of other local Tutsis.[2] The bodies had been buried and a gardener had planted some brilliant yellow flowers along the pathway. Late golden African light played across the valley beyond. I could hear only birdsong and the quiet sobbing of the little boy.

---

[2]**Tutsis**   one of the native groups of people in Rwanda; it is estimated that 77% of the Tutsi population were killed during the 1994 genocide

I began to think of the times I had faced other victims of violence and misery and asked them questions which had made them cry. It happens all the time in the world of news and current affairs. Reporters like me arrive in a place like Rwanda or Belfast or Dunblane and we come into people's homes to hear and record their stories and many of them do weep and their testimony very often moves our audiences. But what happened with Placide has caused me to pause and question my questioning.

It has caused me to ask if the need to bear witness is worth the pain it can cause to others. For when we ask, 'How do you feel?' is it not a question calculated to probe and bring into the public domain the deepest emotions, and does the asking of such questions not impose upon us some responsibility for the emotional well-being of the person we are interviewing?

---

[3]**disinter**   dig up

It is not the first time that I have asked this question, but never before has it been so acutely defined for me as in that Rwandan church. For I move on as other reporters elsewhere move on. But the people whose grief we disinter[3] are left to their lives and memories. In my case, the reporting of genocide and man's inhumanity to man has brought me professional praise and awards and many letters of thanks from listeners and viewers. But you must forgive me if I say that in the Rwandan church I felt ashamed of myself and the hurt which my question had caused. Of course, the world in which I work is full of difficult questions, questions which often demand an answer. But let me say only that Placide has reminded me to think carefully before opening my mouth; he has reminded me that humanity must come before everything else.

Further reading

If this writing had a strong impact on you and you'd be interested to read more, try *Letters Home* (Penguin, 1999) and *Season of Blood* (Penguin, 1996), also by Fergal Keane.

Mirad, a Boy from Bosnia
by Ad de Bont

This extract comes from a play about Mirad and his family, who have been caught up in the 1980s civil war in the former Yugoslavia: Bosnia, Croatia and Serbia. The bitter conflicts were mostly between the Serbs on one side and the Bosnians, Croats or Albanians on the other. Thousands of refugees, like Mirad, ended up fleeing their shattered homelands to seek a new life in other parts of Europe. (Mirad eventually goes to Holland.)

Fazila and Djuka, who live in Sarajevo, the capital of Bosnia, are Mirad's aunt and uncle. They tell his story in this drama.

Scene 10

FAZILA:

After the defeat of Foca,
three months after the start of the war,
and after the death of his father,
Mirad fled to us,
to Sarajevo.[1]

DJUKA:

That was the beginning of July 1992.
Sarajevo was under siege.
Every day we were shot at and everywhere snipers[2] were hiding,
but Mirad didn't know where else to go.

FAZILA:

He could not go to his grandparents, the Balics.
They were in jail,
in the old town hall of Foca.

DJUKA:

He didn't dare to go to his grandmother and
grandfather Kovac,

---

[1]**Sarajevo**   Bosnia's capital
[2]**snipers**   people who shoot from a hiding place

for they lived in Bistrica,
in Serbia.

FAZILA:

Aunt Vineta and Uncle Stipo
had fled to Sweden in May.

DJUKA:

Aunt Marika and Uncle Bozo had been
chased out of the city
with seven thousand other Muslims.

FAZILA:

And Aunt Liljana and Uncle Milos
were out of the question
because Uncle Milos,
the brother of his mother,
was an officer in the Serbian army.

DJUKA:

So to Sarajevo.

FAZILA:

Foca to Sarajevo is ninety kilometres.

DJUKA:

And it took Mirad four days.
Or rather four nights because he
slept during the day
and walked through the night.

FAZILA:

Along the road
hundreds of houses were burnt out,
everywhere bodies,
crippled, half wasted, swollen bodies.

DJUKA:

One night,
just when he wanted to start walking again,
Mirad saw how two soldiers drove their bayonets into
some swollen bodies.

FAZILA:

He almost vomited.

DJUKA:

> But later, in Sarajevo,
> when he saw all the bodies in the streets,
> he understood the soldiers did it
> because the bodies could explode
> and spread all kinds of diseases.

FAZILA:

> How he passed all those Serbian control posts,
> alone without identity papers,
> I have no idea.
> But one night
> just before curfew,
> he arrived at our door.

DJUKA:

> He looked like a ghost.
> More than skinny,
> dead pale,
> totally filthy,
> and his whole body trembling.

FAZILA:

> We were shocked.
> We hadn't seen him since January
> and at the time he was a healthy boy.

DJUKA:

> He was shocked to see us.
> We looked like idiots after two months in the cellars.

FAZILA:

> Then he told us everything.
> We were speechless.

DJUKA:

> First we tried to smarten him up,
> as far as possible of course,
> for without water, without food and without
> medicine you cannot do much.

FAZILA:

> Don't forget all those shells and mortars
> day and night,
> it was enough to drive you crazy.
> So one thing was clear:
> Mirad had to get out of Sarajevo
> as soon as possible.

DJUKA:

> So did we but we thought
> we can't just up and leave everything
> just like that.

FAZILA:

> We shouldn't have been that stupid,
> maybe we could have got away in time.

DJUKA:

> If we had fled earlier
> Mirad would have arrived at an empty house.

FAZILA:

> No, the three of us,
> we should've all tried to get out of
> this damned city, all three.

DJUKA:

> Then they would have caught all three of us.
> That way, at least you would have escaped.

FAZILA:

> Well, whatever,
> we agreed Mirad had to leave the city,
> but where to?

DJUKA:

> Suddenly I thought of Serbian friends in Krupac,
> just outside Sarajevo in the mountains.
> Very nice people with a son about Mirad's age.
> They would take him in.

FAZILA:

> Djuka would go with him,
> we thought it irresponsible to let

him go on his own
with all those snipers in a strange city.

DJUKA:

And I knew how you could get out of the city.
At least I thought I knew.

FAZILA:

It was the evening of the 25th of July.
I remember quite well,
it had been so hot that day,
but rather quiet.
No shooting I mean.
I had been with a friend
that afternoon,
Evica,
a Serbian woman,
very nice.
We drank Turkish coffee.
When I told her our plans
she said, 'Wait'
and she put her cup upside down
on the saucer.
The coffee grounds dribbled down
and she stared at them.
I said, 'Come on, Evica,
you don't believe in that?'
'It's war,' she said,
'and my grandmother always told me:
"If this can help you, why not?"'
After that she concentrated on the cup
and after she'd shaken it again
she said,
'Don't let them go.
Not tonight.
Maybe tomorrow or the day after,
but not tonight.'

DJUKA:

We should have listened to her.

FAZILA:

That's what I said

but you had to leave.

DJUKA:

I couldn't keep beating my head against

a brick wall.

FAZILA:

Why are you always so stubborn?

DJUKA:

Yes, why?

Who knows?

FAZILA:

So they left.

In the evening around eleven o'clock.

DJUKA:

It went very well,

I knew the way we had to go

and it was all just as I expected

until we got to one of the last control posts.

'It should be behind the water tower,'

they said,

but it had been moved in front.

Suddenly we stood in plain view

of some Serbian soldiers,

fully armed

and we couldn't get away.

If we ran they would shoot us.

So I said to Mirad:

'Quiet.

Stay quiet,

maybe we have a chance.'

And we strolled to the post

as if we were going to the zoo.

I don't think
there are many people
who have walked so quietly into a trap
as we did.
And then it started,
that bloody circus of questions,
threats, sufferings and tortures.
The first camp,
Keraterm,
was the worst,
so I was very glad that Mirad was let out after
two weeks
because he would never have come
through it alive.
That he would be allowed to go to Holland
directly after leaving that camp
I didn't know then.
Of course.
That was a chance you could only dream about.

Scene 11

FAZILA:
Nunspeet, 29th September 1992.
Dear Sir,
I am Mirad Balic from Foca.
You asked me to write down what happened
to my father.
That's what I am going to do for you now.
Please excuse my handwriting
because I tremble a bit sometimes.
That is because of the war.
In school in Foca I didn't tremble at all.
The last time I saw my father
was on the 6th July.
After that nobody saw him
because he didn't exist any more.

That day we were taken out of the prison
that we had been put in some days before.
When the Serbs took Foca,
we didn't get anything to eat,
only some water
and we were beaten up many times.
I knew one of the guards,
he used to be our neighbour.
The second night
some of the men were taken outside
and beaten terribly with sticks,
gunbutts and chains.
My father was one of them
and he told me
that our neighbour had beaten him with an iron
stick on the soles of his feet.
The man used to be friendly and polite.
My father couldn't understand,
nor could I.

DJUKA:

That day about fifty men and boys
were taken for a 'technical expedition',
they said.
We walked out of the city
and reached a field full of clover.
We had to stand next to each other
and join hands.
Then the Serbs told us to walk slowly
into the clover-field.
Suddenly one of the prisoners,
Mister Poljac,
the father of my friend Ante,
cried out: 'Don't do it, don't go,
the field is heavily mined.'
As he cried out he was shot.
Nobody was allowed to pick him up.

Not even Ante.
Then we walked into the mined field.
Never before had I been so afraid,
not all my life,
because every step could be your last.
But I was most afraid for my father,
that he would step on a mine.
My father didn't walk beside me,
that was forbidden,
he was at a distance at the end of the line.
The line was a bit curved
so that I could see him.
I was glad about that.
And then it happened.
I looked at the ground
for I saw something small sticking out
and I was afraid it was a mine.
Then I heard a loud explosion.
Somebody had stepped on a mine.
I looked to my father
but all I saw
was a cloud of mud and blood.
I shouted 'Daddy'
and I ran without thinking
right over the field
to the spot where my father had walked.
Then, one right after another
there were more explosions.
Everybody wanted to run away in panic
but the Serbs were still behind us
and started to shoot with machine guns.
All over the field were dead bodies and wounded people.
Some men were crying horribly
because their arms or legs had been blown off by a mine.
So the Serbs left the engine of their tank running,
very loudly,

so that nobody could hear the
shooting and crying any more.
They kept shooting until nobody walked
over the clover-field any more.
Then they left.
I was lying very still all the time,
as if I was shot at the first firing.
But also because I'd found the hand of my father,
the hand with the little finger
without a nail.
So I knew he was dead.
I felt dead too.
All the shooting and crying didn't bother me any more.
I don't know how long I lay in the clover-field
holding my father's hand in my hand.
When it grew dark I stood up.
I buried my father's hand
and started walking.
Away from Foca.
Later I thought I could go to Sarajevo,
to Uncle Djuka and Aunt Fazila.

Scene 12

FAZILA:

There's not much more to tell.
My husband was in three different camps.
What he went through there is impossible to describe.
He does not want to talk about it,
it is too painful for him.
I was in Sarajevo all the time
so I knew nothing.
Not where he was.
Not whether he was alive,
not even what happened.
Nothing. Horrible.
It was only when Mirad arrived in Holland

that I heard via the International Red Cross
that they were caught that night together.
I decided to wait for my husband in Sarajevo
so that he could find me
if he was set free.
Finally, after a terrible winter,
they let him out on 4th April 1993.
In exchange for Serbian prisoners of war.
They brought them on buses to a reception centre in
Croatia.
There was an official letter for him
saying that he was invited to come to Holland as a
selected refugee.
As his wife and Mirad's aunt, that was also valid for me.
So I travelled in a Red Cross convoy
from Sarajevo to Karlovac.

DJUKA:
There I saw Fazila for the first time in nine months.

Further reading

A good book to read if you are interested in the issues that come up in
this text is *Mischling, Second Degree* by Ilse Koehn, published by Puffin in
1981.

Zlata's Diary

by Zlata Filipovic

Zlata was an 11-year-old caught up in the civil war in Sarajevo in the early 1990s, like Mirad in the previous extract. Her diary takes us powerfully inside the experience of war.

Saturday, 2 May 1992

Dear Mimmy,

Today was truly, absolutely the worst day ever in Sarajevo. The shooting started around noon. Mummy and I moved into the hall. Daddy was in his office, under our flat, at the time. We told him on the interphone to run quickly to the downstairs lobby where we'd meet him. We brought Cicko [Zlata's canary] with us. The gunfire was getting worse, and we couldn't get over the wall to the Bobars, so we ran down to our own cellar.

The cellar is ugly, dark, smelly. Mummy, who's terrified of mice, had two fears to cope with. The three of us were in the same corner as the other day. We listened to the pounding shells, the shooting, the thundering noise overhead. We even heard planes. At one moment I realized that this awful cellar was the only place that could save our lives. Suddenly, it started to look almost warm and nice. It was the only way we could defend ourselves against all this terrible shooting. We heard glass shattering in our street. Horrible. I put my fingers in my ears to block out the terrible sounds. I was worried about Cicko. We had left him behind in the lobby. Would he catch cold there? Would something hit him? I was terribly hungry and thirsty. We had left our half-cooked lunch in the kitchen.

When the shooting died down a bit, Daddy ran over to our flat and brought us back some sandwiches. He said he could smell something burning and that the phones weren't working. He brought our TV set down to the cellar. That's when we learned that the main post office (near us) was on fire and that they had kidnapped our President. At around 20.00 we went back up to our flat. Almost every window in our street was broken. Ours were all right, thank God. I saw the post office in flames. A terrible sight. The fire-fighters battled with the raging fire. Daddy took a few photos of the post office being devoured by the flames. He said they wouldn't come out because I had been fiddling with something on the camera. I was sorry. The whole flat smelled of the burning fire. God, and I used to pass by there every day. It had just been done up. It was huge and beautiful, and now it was being swallowed up by the flames. It was disappearing. That's what this neighbourhood of mine looks like, dear Mimmy. I wonder what it's like in other parts of town? I heard on the radio that it was awful around the Eternal Flame. The place is knee-deep in glass. We're worried about Grandma and Grandad. They live there. Tomorrow, if we can go out, we'll see how they are. A terrible day. This has been the worst, most awful day in my eleven-year-old life. I hope it will be the only one.

Mummy and Daddy are very edgy. I have to go to bed.
Ciao!
Zlata

Sunday, 3 May 1992

Dear Mimmy,
Daddy managed to run across the bridge over to Miljacka and get to Grandma and Grandad. He came running back, all upset, sweating with fear and sadness. They're all right, thank God. Tigr Street looks awful. The heavy shelling has destroyed shop windows, cars, flats, the fronts and roofs of buildings. Luckily, not too many people were hurt because they managed to take shelter. Neda (Mummy's girlfriend) rushed over to see how we were and to tell us that they were OK and hadn't had any damage. But it was terrible.

We talked through the window with Auntie Boda and Bojana just now. They were in the street yesterday when that heavy shooting broke out. They managed to get to Stela's cellar.
Zlata

Tuesday, 5 May 1992

Dear Mimmy,

The shooting seems to be dying down. I guess they've caused enough misery, although I don't know why. It has something to do with politics. I just hope the 'kids' come to some agreement. Oh, if only they would, so we could live and breathe as human beings again. The things that have happened here these past few days are terrible. I want it to stop for ever. PEACE! PEACE!

I didn't tell you, Mimmy, that we've rearranged things in the flat. My room and Mummy's and Daddy's are too danger-ous to be in. They face the hills, which is where they're shooting from. If only you knew how scared I am to go near the windows and into those rooms. So, we turned a safe corner of the sitting room into a 'bedroom'. We sleep on mattresses on the floor. It's strange and awful. But, it's safer that way. We've turned every-thing around for safety. We put Cicko in the kitchen. He's safe there, although once the shooting starts there's nowhere safe except the cellar. I suppose all this will stop and we'll all go back to our usual places.

Ciao!

Zlata

Thursday, 7 May 1992

Dear Mimmy,

I was almost positive the war would stop, but today . . . Today a shell fell on the park in front of my house, the park where I used to play with my girlfriends. A lot of people were hurt. From what I hear Jaca, Jaca's mother, Selma, Nina, our neighbour Dado and who knows how many other people who happened to be there were wounded. Dado, Jaca and her mother have come home from hospital, Selma lost a kidney but I don't know how she is, because she's still in hospital. AND NINA IS DEAD. A piece of shrapnel lodged in her brain and she died. She was such a sweet, nice little girl. We went to kindergarten together, and we used to play together in the park. Is it possible I'll never see Nina again? Nina, an innocent eleven-year-old little girl – the victim of a stupid war. I feel sad. I cry and wonder 'why?' She didn't do

anything. A disgusting war has destroyed a young child's life. Nina, I'll always remember you as a wonderful little girl.
Love, Mimmy,
Zlata

Wednesday, 13 May 1992

Dear Mimmy,
Life goes on. The past is cruel, and that's exactly why we should forget it.

The present is cruel too and I can't forget it. There's no joking with war. My present reality is the cellar, fear, shells, fire.

Terrible shooting broke out the night before last. We were afraid that we might be hit by shrapnel or a bullet, so we ran over to the Bobars'. We spent all of that night, the next day and the next night in the cellar and in Nedo's flat. (Nedo is a refugee from Grbavica. He left his parents and came here to his sister's empty flat.) We saw terrible scenes on TV. The town in ruins, burning, people and children being killed. It's unbelievable.

The phones aren't working, we haven't been able to find out anything about Grandma and Grandad, Melica, how people in other parts of town are doing. On TV we saw the place where Mummy works, Vodoprivreda, all in flames. It's on the aggressor's side of town (Grbavica). Mummy cried. She's depressed. All her years of work and effort – up in flames. It's really horrible. All around Vodoprivreda there were cars burning, people dying, and nobody could help them. God, why is this happening?

I'M SO MAD I WANT TO SCREAM AND BREAK EVERY-THING!
Your Zlata

Thursday, 14 May 1992

Dear Mimmy,
The shelling here has stopped. Daddy managed to run over to Grandma's and Grandad's to see how they are, how they've been coping with the madness of the past few days. They're all right,

thank God. Melica and her family are all right, and Grandma heard from Vinko that Meda and Bojan (an aunt and her son) are also all right.

The situation at the Marshal Tito barracks and in the new parts of town is terrible. It's a madhouse around the electricity board building and the radio and television centre. I can't watch television any more. I can't bear to. The area around O seems to be the only place that is still quiet. Mummy's brother Braco and his family live there. They're so lucky, there's no shooting where they live.

Zlata

Sunday, 17 May 1992

Dear Mimmy,

It's now definite: there's no more school. The war has interrupted our lessons, closed down the schools, sent children to cellars instead of classrooms. They'll give us the grades we got at the end of last term. So I'll get a report card saying I've finished fifth grade.

Ciao!

Zlata

Wednesday, 20 May 1992

Dear Mimmy,

The shooting has died down. Today Mummy felt brave enough to cross the bridge. She saw Grandma and Grandad, ran into various people she knows and heard a lot of sad news. She came back all miserable. Her brother was wounded on 14 May, driving home from work. Her brother is hurt and she doesn't find out about it until today – that's terrible. He was wounded in the leg and is in hospital. How can she get to him? It's like being at the other end of the world now. They told her he's all right, but she doesn't believe them and keeps crying. If only the shooting would stop, she could go to the hospital. She says: 'I won't believe it until I see him with my own eyes.'

Zlata

Thursday, 21 May 1992

Dear Mimmy,

Mummy went to see Braco in the hospital today. He's alive. That's the most important thing. But he's badly wounded. It's his knee. Two hundred wounded were brought to the clinic that day. They were going to amputate his leg, but his friend Dr Adnan Dizdar (the surgeon) recognized him, cancelled the amputation and took him into the operating theatre. The operation lasted four-and-a-half hours and the doctors say it was a success. But he'll have to stay in bed for a long, long time. He has some rods, a cast, all sorts of things on his leg. Mummy is terribly worried and sad. So are Grandma and Grandad (that's what Mummy tells me, because I haven't seen them since 12 April; I haven't been out of the house). In the end he was lucky. I hope it will turn out all right. Hold on there, Braco!!!
Your Zlata

Saturday, 23 May 1992

Dear Mimmy,

I'm not writing to you about me any more. I'm writing to you about war, death, injuries, shells, sadness and sorrow. Almost all my friends have left. Even if they were here, who knows whether we'd be able to see each other. The phones aren't working, we couldn't even talk to each other. Vanja and Andrej have gone to join Srdjan in Dubrovnik. The war has stopped there. They're lucky. I was so unhappy because of that war in Dubrovnik. I never dreamed it would move to Sarajevo. Verica and Bojana have also left.

I now spend all my time with Bojana and Maja. They're my best friends now. Bojana is a year-and-a-half older than me, she's finished seventh grade and we have a lot in common. Maja is in her last year of school. She's much older than I am, but she's wonderful. I'm lucky to have them, otherwise I'd be all alone among the grown-ups.

On the news they reported the death of Silva Rizvanbegović, a doctor at the Emergency Clinic, who's Mummy's friend. She

was in an ambulance. They were driving a wounded man to get him help. Lots of people Mummy and Daddy know have been killed. Oh, God, what is happening here???
Love,
Zlata

Wednesday, 27 May 1992

Dear Mimmy,
SLAUGHTER! MASSACRE! HORROR! CRIME! BLOOD! SCREAMS! TEARS! DESPAIR!

That's what Vaso Miskin Street looks like today. Two shells exploded in the street and one in the market. Mummy was nearby at the time. She ran to Grandma's and Grandad's. Daddy and I were beside ourselves because she hadn't come home. I saw some of it on TV but I still can't believe what I actually saw. It's unbelievable. I've got a lump in my throat and a knot in my tummy. HORRIBLE. They're taking the wounded to the hospital. It's a madhouse. We kept going to the window hoping to see Mummy, but she wasn't back. They released a list of the dead and wounded. Daddy and I were tearing our hair out. We didn't know what had happened to her. Was she alive? At 16.00, Daddy decided to go and check the hospital. He got dressed, and I got ready to go to the Bobars', so as not to stay at home alone. I looked out the window one more time and ... I SAW MUMMY RUNNING ACROSS THE BRIDGE. As she came into the house she started shaking and crying. Through her tears she told us how she had seen dismembered bodies. All the neighbours came because they had been afraid for her. Thank God, Mummy is with us. Thank God.

A HORRIBLE DAY. UNFORGETTABLE.

HORRIBLE! HORRIBLE!
Your Zlata

Further reading

Another war diary by a young person worth trying is the well-known *Diary of Anne Frank* which you should be able to find easily in a local library.

Shooting an Elephant

by George Orwell

As a young man in the 1920s, George Orwell served as a police officer in Burma. Here he tells a gripping story of how one day he was expected to shoot an elephant. He is very much the European 'outsider', with the Burmans having particular expectations of him.

In Moulmein, in Lower Burma, I was hated by large numbers of people – the only time in my life that I have been important enough for this to happen to me. I was subdivisional police officer of the town, and in an aimless, petty kind of way anti-European feeling was very bitter. No one had the guts to raise a riot, but if a European woman went through the bazaars alone somebody would probably spit betel juice over her dress. As a police officer I was an obvious target and was baited whenever it seemed safe to do so. When a nimble Burman tripped me up on the football field and the referee (another Burman) looked the other way, the crowd yelled with hideous laughter. This happened more than once. In the end the sneering yellow faces of young men that met me everywhere, the insults hooted after me when I was at a safe distance, got badly on my nerves. The young Buddhist priests were the worst of all. There were several thousands of them in the town and none of them seemed to have anything to do except stand on street corners and jeer at Europeans.

All this was perplexing and upsetting. For at that time I had already made up my mind that imperialism[1] was an evil thing and the sooner I chucked up my job and got out of it the better. Theoretically – and secretly, of course – I was all for the Burmese and all against their oppressors, the British. As for the job I was doing, I hated it more bitterly than I can perhaps make clear. In a job like that you see the dirty work of Empire at close

---

[1] **imperialism**   where a country controls other countries through colonisation

quarters. The wretched prisoners huddling in the stinking cages of the lock-ups, the grey, cowed faces of the long-term convicts, the scarred buttocks of the men who had been flogged with bamboos – all these oppressed me with an intolerable sense of guilt. But I could get nothing into perspective. I was young and ill-educated and I had had to think out my problems in the utter silence that is imposed on every Englishman in the East. I did not even know that the British Empire is dying, still less did I know that it is a great deal better than the younger empires that are going to supplant it. All I knew was that I was stuck between my hatred of the empire I served and my rage against the evil-spirited little beasts who tried to make my job impossible. With one part of my mind I thought of the British Raj as an unbreakable tyranny, as something clamped down, *in saecula saeculorum*,[2] upon the will of prostrate peoples; with another part I thought that the greatest joy in the world would be to drive a bayonet into a Buddhist priest's guts. Feelings like these are the normal by-products of imperialism; ask any Anglo-Indian official, if you can catch him off duty.

One day something happened which in a roundabout way was enlightening. It was a tiny incident in itself, but it gave me a better glimpse than I had had before of real nature of imperialism – the real motives for which despotic[3] governments act. Early one morning the sub-inspector at a police station the other end of the town rang me up on the phone and said that an elephant was ravaging the bazaar. Would I please come and do something about it? I did not know what I could do, but I wanted to see what was happening and I got on to a pony and started out. I took my rifle, an old .44 Winchester and much too small to kill an elephant, but I thought the noise might be useful *in terrorem*[4]. Various Burmans stopped me on the way and told me about the elephant's doings. It was not, course, a wild

---

[2] *in saecula saeculorum*   down through the ages, for ever
[3] **despotic**   very powerful, especially in a cruel way
[4] *in terrorem*   as a warning

elephant, but a tame one which had gone 'must'. It had been chained up, as tame elephants always are when their attack of 'must' is due, but on the previous night it had broken its chain and escaped. Its mahout, the only person who could manage it when it was in that state, had set out in pursuit, but had taken the wrong direction and was now twelve hours' journey away, and in the morning the elephant had suddenly reappeared in the town. The Burmese population had no weapons and were quite helpless against it. It had already destroyed somebody's bamboo hut, killed a cow and raided some fruit-stalls and devoured the stock; also it had met the municipal rubbish van, and, when the driver jumped out and took to his heels, had turned the van over and inflicted violences upon it.

The Burmese sub-inspector and some Indian constables were waiting for me in the quarter where the elephant has been seen. It was a very poor quarter, a labyrinth of squalid huts, thatched with palm-leaf, winding all over a steep hillside. I remember that it was a cloudy, stuffy morning at the beginning of the rains. We began questioning the people as to where the elephant had gone and, as usual, failed to get any definite information. That is invariably the case in the East; a story always sounds clear enough at a distance, but the nearer you get to the

scene of events, the vaguer it becomes. Some of the people said that the elephant had gone in one direction, some said that he had gone in another, some professed not even to have heard of any elephant. I had almost made up my mind that the whole story was a pack of lies, when we heard yells a little distance away. There was a loud, scandalized cry of 'Go away, child! Go away this instant!' and an old woman with a switch in her hand come round the corner of a hut, violently shooing away a crowd of naked children. Some more women followed, clicking their tongues and exclaiming; evidently there was something that the children ought not to have seen. I rounded the hut and saw a man's dead body sprawling in the mud. He was an Indian, a black Dravidian[5] coolie,[6] almost naked, and he could not have been dead many minutes. The people said that the elephant had come suddenly upon him round the corner of the hut, caught him with its trunk, put its foot on his back and ground him into the earth. This was the rainy season and the ground was soft, and his face had scored a trench a foot deep and a couple of yards long. He was lying on his belly with arms crucified and head sharply twisted to one side. His face was coated with mud, the eyes wide open, the teeth bared and grinning with an expression of unendurable agony. (Never tell me, by the way, that the dead look peaceful. Most of the corpses I have seen looked devilish.) The friction of the great beast's foot had stripped the skin from his back as neatly as one skins a rabbit. As soon as I saw the dead man I sent an orderly to a friend's house nearby to borrow an elephant rifle. I had already sent back the pony, not wanting it to go mad with fright and throw me if it smelt the elephant.

The orderly came back in a few minutes with a rifle and five cartridges, and meanwhile some Burmans had arrived and told us that the elephant was in the paddy fields below, only a few hundred yards away. As I started forward practically the whole

---

[5]**Dravidian**   from south India
[6]**coolie**   labourer

population of the quarter flocked out of the houses and followed me. They had seen the rifle and were all shouting excit-
edly that I was going to shoot the elephant. They had not
shown much interest in the elephant when he was merely ravaging their homes, but it was different now that he was going
to be shot. It was a bit of fun to them, as it would be to an
English crowd; besides, they wanted the meat. It made me
vaguely uneasy. I had no intention of shooting the elephant – I
had merely sent for the rifle to defend myself if necessary – and
it is always unnerving to have a crowd following you. I marched
down the hill, looking and feeling a fool, with the rifle over my
shoulder and an ever-growing army of people jostling at my
heels. At the bottom, when you got away from the huts, there
was a metalled road and beyond that a miry waste of paddy
fields a thousand yards across, not yet ploughed but soggy from
the first rains and dotted with coarse grass. The elephant was
standing eight yards from the road, his left side towards us. He
took not the slightest notice of the crowd's approach. He was
tearing up bunches of grass, beating them against his knees to
clean them and stuffing them into his mouth.

I had halted on the road. As soon as I saw the elephant I
knew with perfect certainty that I ought not to shoot him. It is
a serious matter to shoot a working elephant – it is comparable
to destroying a huge and costly piece of machinery – and obviously one ought not to do it if it can possibly be avoided. And
at that distance, peacefully eating, the elephant looked no more
dangerous than a cow. I thought then and I think now that his
attack of 'must' was already passing off; in which case he would
merely wander harmlessly about until the mahout came back
and caught him. Moreover, I did not in the least want to shoot
him. I decided that I would watch him for a little while to make
sure that he did not turn savage again, and then go home.

But at that moment I glanced round at the crowd that had
followed me. It was an immense crowd, two thousand at the
least and growing every minute. It blocked the road for a long
distance on either side. I looked at the sea of yellow faces above

the garish clothes – faces all happy and excited over this bit of fun, all certain that the elephant was going to be shot. They were watching me as they would watch a conjurer about to perform a trick. They did not like me, but with the magical rifle in my hands I was momentarily worth watching. And suddenly I realized that I should have to shoot the elephant after all. The people expected it of me and I had got to do it; I could feel their two thousand wills pressing me forward, irresistibly. And it was at this moment, as I stood there with the rifle in my hands, that I first grasped the hollowness, the futility of the white man's dominion in the East. Here was I, the white man with his gun, standing in front of the unarmed native crowd – seemingly the leading actor of the piece; but in reality I was only an absurd puppet pushed to and fro by the will of those yellow faces behind. I perceived in this moment that when the white man turns tyrant it is his own freedom that he destroys. He becomes a sort of hollow, posing dummy, the conventionalized figure of a sahib.[7] For it is the condition of his rule that he shall spend his life in trying to impress the 'natives', and so in every crisis he has got to do what the 'natives' expect of him. He wears a mask, and his face grows to fit it. I had got to shoot the elephant. I had committed myself to doing it when I sent for the rifle.

A sahib has got to act like a sahib; he has got to appear resolute, to know his own mind and do definite things. To come all that way, rifle in hand, with two thousand people marching at my heels, and then to trail feebly away, having done nothing at all – no, that was impossible. The crowd would laugh at me. And my whole life, every white man's life in the East, was one long struggle not to be laughed at.

But I did not want to shoot the elephant. I watched him beating his bunch of grass against his knees, with that preoccupied grandmotherly air that elephants have. It seemed to me that it would be murder to shoot him. At that age I was not

---

[7]**sahib**   gentleman

squeamish about killing animals, but I had never shot an elephant and never wanted to. (Somehow it always seems worse to kill a *large* animal.) Besides, there was the beast's owner to be considered. Alive, the elephant was worth at least a hundred pounds; dead, he would only be worth the value of his tusks, five pounds, possibly. But I had got to act quickly. I turned to some experienced-looking Burmans who had been there when we arrived, and asked them how the elephant had been behaving. They all said the same thing: he took no notice of you if you left him alone, but he might charge if you went too close to him.

It was perfectly clear to me what I ought to do. I ought to walk up to within, say, twenty-five yards of the elephant and test his behaviour. If he charged I could shoot, if he took no notice of me it would be safe to leave him until the mahout came back. But also I knew that I was going to do no such thing. I was a poor shot with a rifle and the ground was soft mud into which one would sink at every step. If the elephant charged and I missed him, I should have about as much chance as a toad under a steam-roller. But even then I was not thinking particularly of my own skin, only of the watchful yellow faces behind. For at that moment, with the crowd watching me, I was not afraid in the ordinary sense, as I would have been if I had been alone. A white man mustn't be frightened in front of 'natives'; and so, in general, he isn't frightened. The sole thought in my mind was that if anything went wrong those two thousand Burmans would see me pursued, caught, trampled on and reduced to a grinning corpse like that Indian up the hill. And if that happened it was quite probable that some of them would laugh. That would never do. There was only one alternative. I shoved the cartridges into the magazine and lay down on the road to get a better aim.

The crowd grew very still, and a deep, low, happy sigh, as of people who see the theatre curtain go up at last, breathed from innumerable throats. They were going to have their bit of fun after all. The rifle was a beautiful German thing with cross-hair sights. I did not then know that in shooting an elephant one should shoot to cut an imaginary bar running from ear-hole to ear-hole. I ought, therefore, as the elephant was sideways on, to have aimed straight at his ear-hole; actually I aimed several inches in front of this, thinking the brain would be further forward.

When I pulled the trigger I did not hear the bang or feel the kick – one never does when a shot goes home – but I heard the devilish roar of glee that went up from the crowd. In that instant, in too short a time, one would have thought, even for the bullet to get there, a mysterious, terrible change had come over the elephant. He neither stirred nor fell, but every line of his body had altered. He looked suddenly stricken, shrunken, immensely old, as though the frightful impact of the bullet had paralysed him without knocking him down. At last, after what seemed a long time – it might have been five seconds, I dare say – he sagged flabbily to his knees. His mouth slobbered. An enormous senility[8] seemed to have settled upon him. One could have imagined him thousands of years old. I fired again into the same spot. At the second shot he did not collapse but climbed with desperate slowness to his feet and stood weakly upright, with legs sagging and head drooping. I fired a third time. That was the shot that did for him. You could see the agony of it jolt his whole body and knock the last remnant of strength from his legs. But in falling he seemed for a moment to rise, for as his hind legs collapsed beneath him he seemed to tower upwards like a huge rock toppling, his trunk reaching skywards like a tree. His trumpeted, for the first and only time. And then down he came, his belly towards me, with a crash that seemed to shake the ground even where I lay.

I got up. The Burmans were already racing past me across the mud. It was obvious that the elephant would never rise again, but he was not dead. He was breathing very rhythmically with long rattling gasps, his great mound of a side painfully rising and falling. His mouth was wide open – I could see far down

---

[8]**senility**   old age

into caverns of pale pink throat. I waited a long time for him to die, but his breathing did not weaken. Finally I fired my two remaining shots into the spot where I thought his heart must be. The thick blood welled out of him like red velvet, but still he did not die. His body did not even jerk when the shots hit him, the tortured breathing continued without a pause. He was dying, very slowly and in great agony, but in some world remote from me where not even a bullet could damage him further. I felt that I had got to put an end to that dreadful noise. It seemed dreadful to see the great beast lying there, powerless to move and yet powerless to die, and not even to be able to finish him. I sent back for my small rifle and poured shot after shot into his heart and down his throat. They seemed to make no impression. The tortured gasps continued as steadily as the ticking of a clock.

In the end I could not stand it any longer and went away. I heard later that it took him half an hour to die. Burmans were bringing dahs[9] and baskets even before I left, and I was told they had stripped his body almost to the bones by the afternoon.

Afterwards, of course, there were endless discussions about the shooting of the elephant. The owner was furious, but he was only an Indian and could do nothing. Besides, legally I had done the right thing, for a mad elephant has to be killed, like a mad dog, if its owner fails to control it. Among the Europeans opinion was divided. The older men said I was right, the younger men said it was a damn shame to shoot an elephant for killing a coolie, because an elephant was worth more than any damn Coringhee coolie. And afterwards I was very glad that the coolie had been killed; it put me legally in the right and it gave me a sufficient pretext for shooting the elephant. I often wondered whether any of the others grasped that I had done it solely to avoid looking a fool.

Further reading

If you like Orwell's style, have a look for *Selected Essays* and *Animal Farm*, both by the same author, and give them a go.

---

[9]**dahs** knives

A Stranger's Eye

by Fergal Keane

In 1999 the journalist Fergal Keane travelled through Britain to uncover lives of poverty and exclusion, after years of travelling around the world to war zones. This extract records the stories of the tenant farmers in the Welsh hills whose way of life is vanishing. These farmers are 'outsiders' in their own country.

The house in which they lived dated back to 1560. They knew this because a group of local historians had turned up one day to look around the farm. People had been farming on the mountain for at least four centuries, they said.

It was a cold house that had never known central heating. Gwylithin lit big wood fires in the sitting room, but the cold lay in perpetual ambush beyond the narrow radius of the fire. There were three small bedrooms, a living room and a kitchen. Part of the upstairs ceilings and walls were mottled with damp. Most of the time Gwylithin and her children congregated in the kitchen around an old range they'd bought from a neighbour. At school she'd won lots of prizes for her cooking, and the kitchen invariably smelled of baking. Whenever there was a party or an *eisteddfod*[1] at the chapel down in the valley, Gwylithin would be called into action.

The farmhouse and land were rented from an English land-lord. They never said much about the landlord; they were dependent on his goodwill and understandably reluctant to talk about the relationship publicly. They saw him rarely, only when he came up during the season to shoot grouse. On the first day I met her, Gwylithin had just finished doing the accounts. It was a weekly ritual, the taking down of the big ledger and the realization that yet again they had failed to make ends meet. The family owed £30,000 to the bank, all of it borrowed

---

[1] *eisteddfod*   music and poetry competition

to pay for livestock and machinery. Now the livestock was virtually worthless. Across Wales farmers were dumping sheep in public places in symbolic protests; there was an oversupply of sheep and the large supermarkets were essentially able to pay what they liked. And so the ewe that Arwen sold at 56 pence a kilo ended up costing the consumer £12.60 a kilo. It was a mark-up of over 2,000 per cent. The supermarkets could argue all they liked about hygiene, marketing, transport and labour costs, but they would never convince the likes of Arwen Jones that he wasn't being made a fool of. It was the law of supply and demand all right, and the big chains held all the power.

Ten years ago when Arwen and Gwylithin had come to the farm, prices were relatively stable. They knew they would have to work hard, but there was a fair chance of a living wage. Now Arwen earned less than £80 a week. This was his return for a winter working day that began at seven in the morning and ended at nine in the evening; in summer he didn't get back to the farmhouse until half past midnight. It was his life seven days a week, fifty-two weeks a year. The couple were now receiving family credit of £104 a week. Arwen was ashamed of that, said Gwylithin. It made him feel like a failure. There were tens of thousands of tenant farmers in the same position across Britain, but that was scant consolation to Gwylithin as she waited for her husband night after night. 'He's like a robot. He's a workaholic. It's not fair what life is doing to him. He just works, works, works, and you can't do that. He's OK now 'cos he's young, but give him ten, fifteen years I don't think he'll manage.'

Arwen wanted Gwylithin to get a job. But she wanted to be at home for the children. 'What would they do on their own up here in the school holidays? Who would meet them off the bus, at the end of the school day? It's not fair on them. They want to see their mum when they get home from school. It's hard to say this in the modern age, you know. But I feel I need to be here for them. I get their meals and do their homework with them. And I work here at home on the farm. If he is working on another farm or away at his other fields, I need to watch for the cow that is calving, and do all the other jobs around the farm.' Still, she'd signed up for a computer course just in case.

The children saw little of their father. 'They adore him, but they don't see him. I'm the one they try things on with, I have to discipline them. The good days are when he is home and I can help him outside. Sometimes you want an adult to talk to, but he's never around.' This was not said in an angry or bitter voice. Gwylithin was twenty-seven years old and lonely; by the time I met her in the last months of 1999, she was also starting to get very scared. If the bank decided that Arwen was wasting his time and the money wouldn't ever be repaid, they might decide to foreclose.[2] And if that happened, the family owned nothing. The house belonged to someone else, the remaining livestock and machinery would be sold off by the bank. There was no collateral[3] to allow them to start up again when the rural economy improved. And where would they go? To a council house in the village if they were lucky, with Arwen labouring on another man's farm, though with farmers going to the wall[4] everywhere the work was by no means guaranteed.

Gwylithin divided her days into those she called 'good', 'bad' and 'very bad'. On the very bad days she cried all the time. The day before I called at the farm the doctor had prescribed anti-depressants. She tried to talk to Arwen about the problems on the farm, but he didn't want to face them. He just kept working hard, hoping things would change. 'He's proud,' she said. 'You know up here, you're not talking about nineties man. You're talking about 1890s man. They keep their troubles to themselves. I know it must be affecting him, but he doesn't want to face reality.'

I tried to talk to Arwen about the farm difficulties. He could give you the figures, but he avoided drawing any conclusions. He spoke in short sentences and then lapsed into long silences.

---

[2]**foreclose**   stop allowing someone to borrow money
[3]**collateral**   financial security
[4]**going to the wall**   going out of business

Our conversations were painfully awkward. It was intimidating at first, and then you got used to his shyness and the deep worry that must have been filling every hour of his day. Instead I talked to him about rugby. He was a big man, six feet tall and broad, and he still occasionally played for the village team. He joked about how terrible the Irish team was and I agreed with him. One day he took me to the market and I saw that he was as quiet with his friends as he was with strangers. Mind you, there were very few talkative men at that market; there was an air of exhaustion – that is the only word that will do – about the whole place.

But at home with the children Arwen was transformed; he would gather them up in his arms when he walked through the door, smiling and asking questions about their day. He looked – how can I describe it? – almost carefree; and in those moments you could glimpse the young man who'd charmed Gwylithin on her seventeenth birthday at a barn dance for the Penyfed Sheepdog Association. 'Oh, the sparks flew, I can tell you. He had this lovely smile. I thought he must have been going with someone. But he asked me if I wanted a lift home and that was the beginning of it all.' They started going out, and Gwylithin became pregnant with Alau, their first daughter. The couple married in October 1993 and moved into a village house. But Arwen wanted to find a farm of his own. He was the son of an agricultural contractor who travelled around the farms with his JCB,[5] digging ditches and repairing drains. Arwen had gone to agricultural college and then out to work as a farm labourer. He had been given two fields by his parents, and these he'd sold to get money for livestock. Now all he needed was a farm to rent.

One Friday evening Gwylithin's mother telephoned to say a farm had become vacant on the mountain. They phoned the land agent and he told them they could view Pentry-Mawr Farm the following Monday. Gwylithin knew the place well. Every curve of the mountain path on Pentry-Mawr was woven into her memory. Each summer of her childhood had been spent at the

---

[5]JCB   digger

farm next door, where Gwylithin's grandmother lived with her son Ivor. She remembered summer lunchtimes and her grandmother's kitchen filled with hungry neighbours who'd come to help with the lambing; on Sunday mornings before chapel she would lie in her grandmother's bed, listening to fairy stories. Gwylithin's gran made her feel special. At home there were three other sisters competing for her mother's attention; on the farm she was her gran's pet. Eventually her uncle Ivor found a farm with better drainage further along the valley and they moved on; there were no more summer holidays at Pentry-Mawr.

She went back there with Arwen on a summer's day. There hadn't been rain for weeks and the mountain was dry, the grass brittle and shaded brown. The feeling as they walked around the land was 'something like magic', she said, like coming home at the end of a long, long journey. They moved in soon after. 'The day we were due to come, it was 14 October, and I was up at six in the morning, I was so excited. All the colours were turning on the hills. The furze[6] was going from yellow to brown. Oh, it was magical.'

One afternoon I walked with Gwylithin to the top of the mountain. In a few days she and Arwen would come up to drive the ewes down to the sheds before taking them to market. She often came up here. The stony path took her away from her worries for an hour.

'Just stand quiet and listen,' she said.

I heard only the sound of the wind funnelling through the valley and, below that, faintly discernible, the noise of water rushing through the farm stream.

'You hear that? It's magic. I can stand here and believe I'm the only person in the world.'

Gwylithin began to name the farms dotted along the valley. They were the places where four generations of her family had reared their families. 'Over that way is uncle Hwyel, over there is uncle Wynne's place. That is where my grandmother grew up, and that was my uncle Ivor's farm.'

---

[6]**furze**   gorse

Gwylithin was reminding me how bound in she was to this land.

'What a place for children to grow up! They know the names of trees, birds and different breeds of animals. You don't get that in town. Up here you don't worry about what might happen to your kids the way people have to in the town. I love the life, that's the thing that conquers it.'

Weeks later I was reading an anthology of local writings when I came across a poem that Gerard Manley Hopkins had written while sitting at a waterfall not far from where Gwylithin and Arwen were farming. They were some of the most plaintive lines I'd read about the claims of landscape on being.

> *The sun on falling waters writes the text*
> *Which yet is in the eye or in the thought.*
> *It was a hard thing to undo this knot.*

For Gwylithin and Arwen the knot was being pulled asunder[7] before their eyes. Without money to pay the bills, the land and all it symbolized – childhood memory, the future of their children – was slipping away from them. It was happening bit by bit, the incremental[8] departure of dreams.

Back in the kitchen, I asked Gwylithin if she thought they'd survive.

'I want to stay here more than anything. But when the bills are coming in, you've got to be realistic. I don't see a future, not as it is.'

There were 320 acres. Arwen had followed the general advice of the time: you had to be big to have a reasonable chance of survival in modern agriculture. And for a while they seemed to be making a go of things – until the unholy trinity of BSE,[9] falling prices and rising costs came creeping up the

---

[7]**asunder**   apart
[8]**incremental**   increasing
[9]**BSE**   a brain disease affecting cows; it led to huge losses in the British beef industry in the 1990s

road and started to strangle the life out of the farm. Arwen rented more land – another 152 acres – to try to make the economies of scale work in his favour. But they didn't. He and Gwylithin were never a big spending couple, not in the sense of buying clothes and going out for meals or taking holidays. So when it came to economizing, there was very little fat to be trimmed from their lives. They went out exactly three times a year: on the night of Arwen's birthday, on the night of the Cerrigydrudion show, and on the Saturday before Christmas for a meal with the other farmers in the valley. As a rule they didn't go on holidays. The previous year they had taken two days off to take the girls to the seaside. They went to Caernarvon and walked around the castle. The girls wanted to go inside but the admission fee was more than their parents could afford. There was a choice of having their tea in a café or going inside the castle. The children didn't complain; according to Gwylithin, they rarely complain. They pick out clothes and toys in the catalogues Gwylithin keeps by the television, and hope that by some chance their father will bring home a windfall. 'I'd like to go to the cinema once or twice, but the cash isn't there for it,' she said. 'You think it would be easy to say we're going to set aside £10 for it every couple of weeks, but the money just isn't there for that. I'd much rather spend it on shoes for the children. Wouldn't you?'

I was in the house on the morning of Alau's birthday. Gwylithin had bought her a mirror and a bottle of sparkling nail varnish. The presents had cost £4.50 in the village store. Alau had wanted a compact disc by the pop group Steps, but she smiled and looked happy for her mother when she unwrapped the presents. Gwylithin said she and Arwen did their best to protect the girls from the stress they were both feeling. Alau smiled a lot, and mothered the two younger girls, but she hung around the edges of Gwylithin's conversations the way eldest children often do, and I was sure she knew exactly what was happening to the farm. And beyond the farm there were plenty of pointers to decline that an observant child could pick up.

Alau and her sister Maly went to the village school in Cerrigydrudion. Gwylithin's aunty Nan taught there. There had been four schools in the area until the 1980s. But there was no longer the farming population to support that number. Now there was one school.

Once, on a rainy day, I stopped at Ivor Jones's farm-supply store in Cerrig to buy wellingtons. The shop sold a bewildering mixture of clothes and fertilizers and small farming implements. An old lady behind the counter told me business was quiet. She spent a good fifteen minutes advising me on which wellingtons would be best suited to my feet; it was old-fashioned customer service, but I suspected too that she was glad of the company. Three months later, and again blasted by the wind and rain, I was back visiting Gwylithin and Arwen when I drove over to the shop, intending to buy a scarf. There was a notice in the window announcing that Ivor Jones was closing down. He was moving to Bangor for work. Ivor himself came out, a short young man with sandy hair. He said there just wasn't the business any more.

I left Ivor and walked up the road past the Lion Inn and the war memorial to the school. Aunty Nan was in her early fifties, a big warm woman who spoke in passionate, rolling phrases. She too was married to a struggling tenant farmer. There were eighty-six children in the school, boys and girls, and most of the boys she taught wanted to be farmers. As I walked in, I heard the sound of children singing. It was a Welsh hymn, 'Dim ond Seren' ('The Last Star'), and the fingers on the piano were those of Nan Owen. I've always believed you could tell fairly quickly if a school was a happy place or not. Riotous, frantic schools are not happy. They are places where weaker children get singled out and bullied; nor are schools happy places if kids walk around with their heads bowed and try to melt into the wall to allow you to pass. Nan Owen's school was neither of these. There was a sense of order, but they were lively and, for the most part, smiling children. Most came from farming families, a fact that presented Nan with difficulties when it came to the issue of career guidance.

'A lot of these children want to be farmers, like their parents and their grandparents. And you don't just tell them no, you can't be a farmer. You tell them that farmers need to be educated these days, that they must go on and get qualifications, a farmer needs to be a scholar with all these forms to fill in and so on. And in that way you hope they will be ready.'

But was that telling them the truth about the future?

'Oh no. But what should I say? Should I tell them that there won't be a farming community at Cerrigydrudion? Don't even think about farming, children? I couldn't break their little hearts like that. No.'

Nan Owen could see the bigger picture. She watched what was happening to young couples like Arwen and Gwylithin and then tried to look ahead a decade or so. What she saw was the vanishing of a community: the hills and valleys where her people had given generations of their labour would no longer be able to sustain them.

'It saddens me. Along with the farming there is a culture. There is our Welsh language and our sense of community. That is dwindling now. You see, children in a school like this get a special identity. They get a sense that they belong. They say "yes", I'm part of something. And if there are no children here, there will be no school. No school' – and here she pauses – 'at Cerrigydrudion.'

I met Nan again the following Sunday at the Methodist chapel. The tenant farmers of the valley had worshipped here for more than a hundred years. It was a small congregation, mostly the older people and Gwylithin and her three girls. Arwen and the majority of the men were out working on the mountain. The service was held in one of the side rooms normally used for Sunday School. There was a table on which the preacher had placed his Bible. In front of that were two small heaters. The preacher was a visitor, a genial[10] young man with curly hair and thick glasses whose voice rose and fell in the style

---

[10]**genial**   kindly and cheerful

of an old-fashioned revivalist.[11] He spoke for an hour, the preaching punctuated by hymns. Gwylithin's youngest daughter became bored and took out a small comb, stroking her mother's red hair. The service was in Welsh, and so I couldn't follow what was being said. I was told later that he had asked the people to have courage in their times of difficulty. Just beyond the preacher's head there was a window through which I could see sheep grazing on the mountainside. By the end of the service, the air in the room had thickened and covered the window in condensation, and it was no longer possible to see the valley or the animals.

Further reading

It's worth reading more of *A Stranger's Eye*. You could alternatively try *Letter to Daniel* (Penguin, 1995), also by Fergal Keane.

---

[11]**revivalist**   religious enthusiast

Activities

Coming to England

Before you read

1   What do you think are the most exciting and daunting aspects of moving from one country to live in another?

What's it about?

2   Floella Benjamin makes reference a number of times to the fact that she is seen as being different, an outsider. Make a list of these, then compare your list with a partner's. Have you picked out the same words and phrases?

3   From Floella Benjamin's point of view, what are the greatest contrasts between living in Trinidad and living in London?

4   Looking at her description of school life in London, in what ways was it both different from and similar to her experience in Trinidad? Discuss this in small groups.

Thinking about the text

5   Re-read Floella Benjamin's description of her school building (page 135). Write a similar 'first impression' description of your own school. Make it concise and descriptive. Share it with a partner.

6   You are putting together a radio programme about the experience of families from the West Indies moving to Britain in the 1960s. Script an interview with Floella Benjamin today, asking her to reflect on her arrival in London. Use ideas in the extract as the basis for your script, but adding her further reflections as she looks back over 40 years.

7   Write a short story entitled 'Settling in'. It might be based on your own real experiences, or an imaginary tale rooted in your moving to live in another town or country.

Refugee Boy

Before you read

1   Refugees around the world are often in the news. Which countries have you recently read or heard about in which the issue of refugees is presenting challenges?

2   Enter the word 'Campsfield' into an Internet search engine. Make notes on what it is and some of the controversial issues linked to it. Present a short talk to your group on the subject.

What's it about?

3   From reading this chapter, what picture do you have of Alem's foster family? What images do you have of Mr and Mrs Fitzgerald and Ruth?

4   Do Mariam and Sheila come across as sympathetic characters? Discuss this in small groups.

5   'He felt as if his life was a roller-coaster going from one extreme to the other.' What evidence is there in this extract that Alem is experiencing many ups and downs? Talk about these with a partner.

Thinking about the text

6   Why does the present of the CDs mean so much to Alem? Script this as a conversation with Ruth.

7   Alem has arrived in England, without his parents. His father has come over from Ethiopia to join him – and is then arrested. Alem has started a new school and lives with a foster family. Put yourself in Alem's shoes and write a series of journal entries about his first weeks in England.

8   Using www.refugeecouncil.org.uk as source material, write an account of the work the Refugee Council does in this country.

9   From the viewpoint of a refugee recently arrived in England, write a poem that reflects both on what you have left behind and your fears and hopes for the future. You might like to read the last short chapter of *Refugee Boy* to help you with this task.

What's Your Problem?

Before you read

1   Talk with a partner about the advantages and disadvantages of living in a city and living in a village.

What's it about?

2   The family members receive a number of threats – obvious and less obvious – in the course of this extract. Make a list of these. With a partner, discuss which you think the family members would find the most upsetting or threatening.

3   What would you say are the key themes of this chapter (and the novel)? Debate these statements in your groups.

This is a story about:
● city life versus country life
● parents versus children
● tolerance and intolerance
● a clash of cultures
● bullying.

Thinking about the text

4   What impressions do you form of Jas and his family? What do you think has motivated Jas's father to move his business from the city to the village? Talk with your partner about how you see them.

5   Climb inside the shoes of Jas's father. What do you think is going through his mind as he deals with the two men who come to the shop? Write this up as an entry in his diary.

6   The novel is dedicated to the memory of Stephen Lawrence and to his family. Using www.stephenlawrence.org.uk for source material, prepare a short presentation on Stephen and how his tragic story links to this extract.

7   What do you think happens next? Write the next chapter and explore 'the next warning' – the phrase at the end of this extract. You could write this using either Jas or his father as the first-person narrator.

A Boy Called 'Grenade'

Before you read

1   Nicknames have always been a part of life, whether amongst children or adults. Why do we use them? Can they sometimes be hurtful? Can they also be fun?

What's it about?

2   Why does Fergal Keane use the phrase 'the long hour I spent with him'?

3   Talk in your groups about what Fergal Keane learns from his encounter with Placide. Think carefully about the final sentence of the passage. In what ways might either of them be seen as an 'outsider'?

Thinking about the text

4   'Reporters like me arrive in a place like Rwanda or Belfast or Dunblane'. These are all places Fergal Keane has reported from. Based on some library or Internet research, what do they have in common that will have made them a focus for reporters?

5   Fergal Keane writes in such a way that the reader will feel sympathy both with him and with Placide. Pick out those words and phrases in the essay which
    a   make you sympathise with the journalist
    b   make you feel sorry for Placide.

6   Retell this encounter from Placide's point of view. Try to capture his feelings and attitudes towards the reporter.

7   'But the people whose grief we disinter are left to their lives and memories.' Should journalists interview people, and particularly children, who have experienced tragedy? What are your views? Hold a class debate in which you present the arguments for and against this kind of journalism.

8   Write your own short story or drama script that explores a number of characters learning about something tragic that has happened in the past and that continues to haunt them.

Mirad, a Boy from Bosnia

Before you read

1   One famous playwright said that it was his job always to entertain and educate at the same time. If you wrote a play for stage or television and wanted to get a particular message across to your audience, what subject would you choose to write about, and why?

What's it about?

2   Construct a timeline showing the main events covered in this extract. Use a highlighter pen to colour-code the main events and themes which the writer is exploring.

3   Write your own short character descriptions of Fazila and Djuka, piecing together clues about them from the text.

4   What do you learn in this extract about what happened to different members of Mirad's family during the civil war?

5   Write 'Mirad' at the centre of a spider diagram and note down any words or phrases that describe his appearance and character. Now create another spider diagram around 'Mirad', this time listing some of the incidents that happened to him. Use these notes to write an article about Mirad for a magazine which is featuring the experiences of children caught up in wars.

Thinking about the text

6   What do you imagine you would have done at different points in Mirad's adventures? Try to put yourself in his place. In small groups, talk about how you might have reacted to some of the scenes he confronted.

7   Imagine you met up with Mirad today. Script or role-play a conversation with him in which he reminisces about his family and his terrible experiences during the civil war. Think carefully about what might be his most vivid memories.

8   The playwright Ad de Bont has observed, 'I wanted to explore the question, "How do you go on living after the kind of experiences Mirad and his mother had been through?"' Script an interview with Ad de Bont in which you try to find out more about why he came to write this play.

Zlata's Diary

Before you read

1   In small groups, discuss why you think people keep diaries and why other people might want to read them.

What's it about?

2   In your groups, talk about the kind of person you imagine Zlata to be. What are her ambitions, her thoughts about the war and her family, and her hopes for the future?

3   What picture do you have of Zlata's family and friends? Draw quick sketches or cartoons of them. Note down words and phrases that describe them and annotate your pictures.

4   Make a list of those phrases that you think bring alive the horrors of the civil war, when looked at from Zlata's perspective.

5   From your close reading of the text, which aspects of her experience do you think Zlata found most difficult? What are your thoughts on how *you* might have reacted in similar circumstances?

Thinking about the text

6   In telling this kind of story about real-life events, what are the advantages and disadvantages of the diary format, compared say with a series of newspaper articles or a straight piece of autobiographical writing? Talk about this with a partner.

7   You are a war correspondent for a national newspaper. Using ideas and images from these extracts, write an account of life and death in Sarajevo in 1992.

8   You may already have read *The Diary of Anne Frank*. If not, dip into her diary, rooted in a different, earlier war. What are the similarities and differences between the two diaries? (See www.anne.frank.com)

Shooting an Elephant

Before you read

1   Talk with a partner about a time when you were pushed into doing something by someone else that you really didn't want to do. How did it happen? How did you feel?

What's it about?

2   George Orwell uses some quite challenging vocabulary, some of which has been explained for you. Choose ten other words and check their precise meaning in the dictionary.

3   Talk in your groups about what ideas Orwell is exploring in the sentence beginning, 'It was a tiny incident in itself . . . ' (page 172).

Thinking about the text

4   What do you like or dislike about Orwell's style of writing? Look carefully at how he structures his paragraphs and particular techniques he employs. Discuss in groups.

5   As a first-person narrator, Orwell tells the reader what *he* sees. Take any point in the text and write a short paragraph which could be added to this passage, written from the viewpoint of an interested onlooker – either one of Orwell's colleagues or a local Burman.

6   'Afterwards, of course, there were endless discussions about the shooting of the elephant.' Script and role-play two or three of these conversations.

7   You are the editor of the local newspaper. Write up this incident in such a way that you attack the way Orwell as an 'outsider' behaved. Think of a provocative headline and sub-headings.

8   Imagine you are making a short TV drama based on this incident. Draft out with a partner:
   ● how you'll direct the crowd scenes
   ● how you'll convey what the main character is feeling
   ● the key visual scenes
   ● how you'll prepare for the climax
   ● what you want the viewers to see, hear and feel.

A Stranger's Eye

Before you read

1 It is often said that we live in a fast-changing world. Do you enjoy changes and new challenges or not? Give your reasons.

What's it about?

2 Make a list of the words and phrases that the writer uses to emphasise the sense of tradition and history in the farmers' way of life.

3 Talk with a partner about how the Fergal Keane emphasises how hard life on the land is for Gwylithin, Arwen and their family.

4 What motivates Arwen and Gwylithin to farm in the area they do? What picture do you have of the location? Talk about this in groups.

5 Why does Fergal Keane end this passage with a description of the service at the Methodist chapel? And what is the particular impact of his final sentence?

Thinking about the text

6 You are putting together a feature article on the family for *Farmers Weekly* magazine. You are trying to present the challenges the family faces. Include short interviews with members of the family which best present your case. Think about two or three photos you will include.

7 'It was the law of supply and demand all right, and the big chains held all the power.' (page 181)
Use this sentence as the focus for a debate for and against the power of the supermarkets. You need two speakers on each side of the motion, one to propose and one to second. The audience decides who has put forward the most convincing case!

8 Imagine you are the local MP who represents this rural area of Wales. Write a speech to give in a parliamentary debate on the plight of the Welsh farming community. Try to persuade your colleagues in parliament that something has to be done to help this way of life survive.

Compare and contrast

1   Based on your readings in this section, write a short essay in which you compare the similar and different experiences of young people as 'outsiders' arriving in a foreign country.

2   Script an imaginary dialogue between Jas (*What's Your Problem?*) and Floella Benjamin (*Coming to England*) about how they cope with the prejudice and racism they encounter.

3   How successful are the writers in this section in describing the experiences of children and young people caught up in war? Talk about this in groups, with close reference to the texts. In your opinion, which writer captures most vividly the feelings of the characters?

4   Imagine that Mirad (*Mirad, a Boy from Bosnia*) and Zlata (*Zlata's Diary*) meet up some years after the civil war. Improvise a meeting between them in which they share their memories of the war. Try to bring out how they considered themselves to be 'outsiders' caught up in someone else's warfare.

5   At the end of this section we are left with a series of images, snapshots of people's lives – some real, some imaginary. Imagine you could invite any of the characters to take part in a televised discussion with a live studio audience. Choose three volunteers to take on the role of the different people and a chairperson to direct the discussion. As the audience, the rest of the class should prepare questions that ask them to reflect on what has happened to them – and how their lives have unfolded. Aim to explore, in part, the theme of being an 'outsider'. You may want to prepare for this in groups before holding the full discussion.

6   Imagine you are a reviewer for a national newspaper. Write a review of the two extracts by Fergal Keane. Talk about his different subject matter, his attitudes towards those he interviews, and his style of writing. What is it about his use of language and his sharp eye for detail that makes his writing convincing and persuasive?

4 Feeling different

This is an important section because it will help you think carefully about how we all relate to those around us, those whom we meet every day but might be tempted to treat a little differently for one reason or another. Gervase Phinn's and D. J. Enright's poems remind us we all have individual abilities, skills and ways of looking at the world, while *Face* and *The Bus People* have some striking things to say about disability.

Activities

1 Which novels, plays or short stories have your read which you think present a thoughtful exploration of the difficult subject of bullying? Why and how were the authors successful? Can you think of television programmes or films that have covered the topic in a sensitive way? What does your school do well in the way it addresses any incidents of bullying?

2 Writers in this section write about different kinds of disability. What other books or films have you come across in which you think disability is written about or filmed in ways that promote good understanding of the subject?

3 From your own experiences, from talking with others, and from your wider reading, do adults and children approach the subject of 'feeling different' in similar or different ways?

The Rebel

by D. J. Enright

▮ This is a poem about rebels and how they are viewed as 'outsiders'.

When everybody has short hair,
The rebel lets his hair grow long.

When everybody has long hair,
The rebel cuts his hair short.

When everybody talks during the lesson,
The rebel doesn't say a word.

When nobody talks during the lesson,
The rebel creates a disturbance.

When everybody wears a uniform,
The rebel dresses in fantastic clothes.

When everybody wears fantastic clothes,
The rebel dresses soberly.

In the company of dog lovers,
The rebel expresses a preference for cats.

In the company of cat lovers,
The rebel puts in a good word for dogs.

When everybody is praising the sun,
The rebel remarks on the need for rain.

When everybody is greeting the rain,
The rebel regrets the absence of sun.

When everybody goes to the meeting,
The rebel stays at home and reads a book.

When everybody stays at home and reads a book,
The rebel goes to the meeting.

When everybody says, Yes please,
The rebel says, No thank you.

When everybody says, No thank you,
The rebel says, Yes please.

It is very good that we have rebels.
You may not find it very good to be one.

Further reading

If you liked this, try dipping into the book *Poems with Attitude* by Andrew
Peters and Polly Peters, published by Hodder Wayland in 2000.

Less Able

by Gervase Phinn

Here is another poem about being different, although of course it has something very interesting to say about how we define the word 'ability'.

(*A poem for Claire Stainthorpe, Headteacher of St Hilda's C. E. School, Ampleforth*)

He could not describe the beauty that surrounded him:
The soft green dale and craggy hills.
He could not spell the names
Of those mysterious places which he knew so well.
But he could snare a rabbit, ride a horse,
Repair a fence and dig a dyke,
Drive a tractor, plough a field,
Milk a cow and lamb a ewe,
Name a bird by a faded feather,
Smell the seasons and predict the weather,
That less able child could.

Further reading

There are some other great poems and stories by Gervase Phinn. See if you can read *Classroom Creatures* or *What's the Matter, Royston Knapper?*

Dear Aunty

by Patricia Borlenghi

Growing up, families, relationships, friends – all are issues young people have to deal with which can make them feel as though they are on their own, on the outside. This extract is taken from a book that offers advice on such problems.

Dear Aunty

My parents are getting a divorce. They have talked about what will happen after the divorce. I will be living with my mum and my brother, and we are staying in our house, and my dad is moving to a new job in a new town. I am scared that I won't see my dad any more.

Kylie, aged 12

Dear Kylie

Divorce can be very stressful, especially for the children involved. It can be a very distressing experience, I'm afraid. Children are always stuck in the middle through no fault of their own. Divorce can affect many people, and it is most likely that some of your schoolfriends are in the same position as yourself. Do try to talk to them about it if you can.

Hopefully, your parents will come to an amicable arrangement about your dad's parental contact. Even if they cannot agree about this between themselves, your feelings and your opinion will be taken into account. Sometimes parental contact is decided by a court, and the judge should ensure you and your father's views are taken into account. If he is moving a long way away, the most likely thing will be that you will see him at prearranged times, for instance during holidays, and maybe for some weekends. And don't forget you can telephone him, write to him, or e-mail him any time you wish. Make sure he has an e-mail address when he moves to his new home. The likelihood is that he may be on e-mail at his new job, but it would be better to contact him at home, and you can keep him up to date with your life, and even confide in him about any worries you may have.

Best wishes
Aunty

Dear Aunty

My parents are divorced. Every weekend I go and stay with my dad but I hate my stepmother. I can't bear her, and it's not just because I think she's not as nice or as pretty as my mum is. She's always sucking up to my dad, but she's just pretending. Underneath it all she makes him do exactly what she wants.

And he's always buying her presents. I hate her so much, I don't want to spend my weekends with her.

Briony, aged 10

Dear Briony

Lots of people will sympathise with you. It is difficult to form a good relationship with your step-parents. Unfortunately step-mothers traditionally do get rather a bad press. However, there are lots of girls in a similar boat to you, and basically, you just have to take a deep breath and try to get on with her.

Your feelings of jealousy towards your stepmother are understandable, but what about your dad? She must have some redeeming qualities or your dad wouldn't have married her, and he does love her, obviously. Notice I use the word 'love'. If you love your dad, and want to keep seeing him, then for his sake, try at least to make an effort. In this life I am afraid nothing is clear-cut, and you obviously feel very protective towards your mother. Your feelings for your stepmother may never be warm, but you will have to learn how to act in a civilised manner towards her. Show you are mature and try to get on with her. You may even end up liking her, so try to give it a go at least.

If you find things don't improve, then have a word with your dad. See if there are any other solutions, but don't give him an ultimatum – you'll probably lose out.

Best wishes
Aunty

Dear Aunty

I never got on with my dad, and when he started hitting my mum, that was the end as far as I was concerned. Now he and mum are divorced. I don't really want to see him any more, but when my parents got divorced, the court judge said my dad had to have contact. When he comes to see me, once a month, I don't really know what to say to him. I can't forgive him for hitting my mum.

Nadia, aged 12

Dear Nadia

This is very difficult for you. Maybe you could try to approach your dad and discuss the way you feel with him. If you have the courage, try to ask him why he used to hit your mum. Some men hit women and truly regret it later. It might help if you could talk about it with him. You many never forgive him for hitting your mum but there may be good things about him you are too angry to see at the moment.

If you still find you're not getting on better with him, it might be possible to go back to court and get the contact reduced. When you are older it will be up to you whether you want to continue to see him or not. You need to think long and hard about this. Do you really want a life where you will never see him again? It might help if you had some legal advice on this troublesome matter.

Best wishes
Aunty

Further reading

For any problems or issues you want to know more about, have a look at the websites www.childline.co.uk and www.bbc.co.uk/health/kids

Face

by Benjamin Zephaniah

> Martin, Matthew and Mark make up a Gang of Three, accompanied by Martin's girlfriend Natalie. One day, Martin is horribly burnt in a car accident and faces a future of being looked at very differently by his friends. He becomes an 'outsider' within his school.

One day in school had taught Martin a lot. That evening he listened to no music, and he spent no time looking at pictures of footballers. Instead he spent the whole evening in his room in quiet contemplation.[1] He was now beginning to look at *himself* in before and after terms. Ever since he had first woken up in hospital after the accident, he had begun to listen to a voice of reason in his head. It was an honest voice, a voice that had nothing to gain by taking sides. Back then it had started as a whisper but now the voice was loud.

Knowing that he had hundreds of days left to attend school, he began his meditation by asking himself one question. *How can I improve on today?* He considered the Simon Hill affair and promised himself not to lose his temper if he ever got into a similar situation. He thought about what Mrs Powell had said in morning assembly and what Mr Lincoln had said in registration, then he promised himself that he wouldn't read too much into people's words. He thought, *maybe they weren't talking about me.* And *maybe*, he thought, *all those people in the streets and their cars, and on the buses, maybe they weren't all looking at me.* He walked over to the full-length mirror on his wardrobe and looked at himself. *So what if they were looking at me?* he asked himself. *Two months ago, if I'd seen me looking like I look now, I would have had a good look. Be honest, Mr Martin Turner, you would have probably made some remark, or even cracked a joke with your friends.*

---

[1]**contemplation** thinking

The next day Martin went back to school with a sense of purpose. At lunch time he found the girl who had given him the get well card and told her as she was eating, 'I'm sure you didn't want to offend me, so thanks for the card but you should know that I am well'.

'I'm sorry,' she said. 'I read about you in the papers, I really felt for you.'

'OK. I just want you to know that I'm not sick.'

'Point taken. I'm sorry. Are we friends?' she enquired.

'Yeah, friends are cool.'

He chose not to speak to Simon Hill but he also decided not to make him an enemy. Rumours were continuing to spread about the role of drugs in the accident but Martin displayed a positive attitude and carried on regardless.

The days felt much longer than they used to. Martin counted the hours and the lessons as they passed. He was less self-conscious about his face but he made sure it wasn't going to stop him doing what he wanted to do, including his favourite pastime at school – gymnastics. He hardly felt any pain now. Most of the time he was only reminded of his new face when he touched it or when others stared.

On Wednesday the whole school was talking about him for something completely different. That morning he took Year 10 by storm with a stunning gymnastics display, first on the trampoline and then on the floor mat, his speciality. Some of the old fun-loving Martin appeared when, at the end of a fantastic floor mat routine, he entertained the crowd with a mixture of comical dance and gymnastics. Martin left school that day high-spirited. When he told his parents about his display that evening, they began to feel that Martin was quickly and happily adjusting to life in school.

Thursday morning went well for Martin. He was beginning to enjoy lessons like never before. Teachers and many of his fellow pupils could see that he was now keen to learn. He was showing a genuine interest in subjects and although he was not the prankster he used to be he was beginning to relax.

At lunch time Martin made his way to the dining room and collected his meal. After picking up his drink, he looked for his friends but Natalie was sitting with a group of her girlfriends. She waved to him but he could see that there was no room there. Certainly there was no room for a boy. On the other side of the hall he could see Mark and Matthew. He began to walk in their direction but as he reached them he could see there were no free seats there either.

'Where have you been?' Matthew asked.

'I had to go and check something out in the library,' Martin replied.

Matthew looked around and, seeing spare seats elsewhere, said, 'Well, we're almost finished. Find a seat somewhere and we'll see you afterwards.'

Martin looked around. He saw a group of boys and girls from his class sitting close, so he went over and sat down. 'All right,' Martin said to them as he sat down.

There was a collective 'All right' from everyone on the table and they all continued to eat. All seemed to be going well until Margaret Knight, the girl sitting opposite him, threw down her knife and fork and exclaimed, 'Why did you sit here?'

Martin's response was quick. 'Because it's a seat and I wanna eat me dinner. This is the dining hall, isn't it? What's your problem?'

'You're my problem,' she replied. 'You're putting me off my food.'

Martin could feel his temperature rising but the voice in his head reminded him of his promise to stay cool. Instead of all out war, Martin began a war of words with her.

'You put lots of people off their food with your smelly breath but we've all got to eat to live.'

'Why don't you sit with your friends? They're used to you.'

'Why don't you sit on your own?' Martin replied with a grin.

'I was here before you. Look, there's lots of empty seats. Why did you come to spoil my dinner?'

'I can sit anywhere I want. Ain't no rules about where people sit as long as it's on a chair with a table in front of it. So if you've got a problem, go and get advice – I'm not moving.'

Margaret picked up her tray and stood up. 'I was going anyway. I don't have to sit here and let you talk to me like that.' She walked off, emptied her tray and left the hall.

Martin didn't eat much. He remembered promising himself not to lose his temper in times like these, but he was really upset by what had just happened. Only the scraping of plates and chewing of gum could be heard. Nobody knew what to say.

After the meal, outside in the playground, Martin was approached by Najma Khan. 'Can I have a word with you, Martin?' she asked.

'Yeah, but I'm warning you, if you want to go raving tomorrow night – I'm busy – I'm washing me hair.'

Najma smiled. 'Oh what a shame. Seriously now – I just wanted to say that Margaret didn't really mean what she said earlier. She asked me to say sorry for her.'

Martin was not convinced. 'If she's that sorry, why didn't she say sorry herself?'

'She's not very good at talking, so she sent me.'

'She had lots of mouth in the dinner hall,' Martin said. 'She's what I call a facialist. She's dealing in facial discrimination.'

'Well, she told me that she has nothing against you personally and that she just gets put off her food easily.'

'And what do you think about that, Najma?'

'I think she's being stupid,' Najma replied, 'but that's the way she is. I'm always telling her how silly she can be.'

'Well, you tell her some more,' Martin said as he walked away. 'Tell her I said she's a facialist and if she's got anything else she wants to tell me – tell her to tell me herself. By the way, I'm sorry about tomorrow night – maybe some other time.'

For the rest of the day, every time Margaret Knight saw Martin, she hid herself or turned around and went another way.

The next day was trouble-free, a day of Maths, History, Geography and Biology. It was Friday, and Martin had had a week of ups and downs. He was very much looking forward to the weekend. At the end of the day, the Gang of Three and Natalie met at the school gate and began to make their way to Martin's house. The other three felt protective towards Martin and, although it was never planned, each one felt that the least they could do in the early days of the term was to make sure he got home all right. Martin was aware of this trend and he easily guessed why they escorted him every afternoon. He also realised that walking home on those first few days would have been very different without them.

As they walked down the High Street, Natalie made an announcement. 'Right, you three,' she said, stopping suddenly and taking the gang by surprise. 'I've got something to tell you.'

'I know what it is,' Martin said jokingly. 'You're gonna buy us all a present for being your friend.'

'No,' Natalie replied laughing.

Mark thought that he should have a go. 'I know . . . you're . . . you're . . . you're gonna be rich.'

'No, almost.'

'Come on,' Martin insisted. 'Tell us.'

'Well,' Natalie said. 'You remember that hair shampoo commercial that I done?'

The boys all nodded frantically.

'The company that I did the commercial for want me to do another one. I am playing the same person – just a bit older. Do you know what that means?'

Matthew tried to be funny. 'Yes it means you're playing the same person – just a bit older.'

Natalie was almost jumping with excitement. 'Yes, but what's more important is that if they want me to play the same person that's a bit older, then they'll probably want me to do it again and again and again. I'll become known as the Nulocks girl.'

'So you *will* be rich,' Mark interrupted.

'Maybe, I don't know. The money goes into a trust and I get it when I am eighteen or something like that.'

Matthew and Mark congratulated her. Martin wasn't so sure. 'Do you really want to be known as the Nulocks girl?'

'That will only be for a time,' Natalie replied. 'The agent said that the main thing is that it's a high profile commercial, shown all over the world, and it'll get me even better work in the future.'

'I suppose that's not bad,' Martin replied half-heartedly. 'The problem is, I've heard of a thing called typecasting. It's where you get known for only one type of thing and no one wants you to work for them unless you're doing that one thing.'

'Now look who's not being supportive!' Natalie snapped. 'What did you say friends were for again? You know this is a good chance for me and all you can do is criticise. Stop thinking about yourself for once, Martin. Why don't you try wishing me good luck?'

'I do wish you good luck but I'm just trying to warn you about the business.'

'What do you know about the business? You don't know anything,' she said angrily. She took a breath and continued, 'I'm young, so as long as I don't do too much of one thing I'll have time to change. That's what my agent said and she should know.'

'Yeah, she should know,' Matthew interjected in an effort to calm things down.

'That's right,' Natalie agreed.

'Forget it. Just make sure that you remember us when you're rich and famous,' Mark added as they continued their journey home.

After their evening meal, Martin's parents asked him how his week had been. He told them about the fight he had had with Simon Hill, only to discover that they already knew about it. At this point Martin realised that, during the week, many eyes had been watching him.

'I've been speaking to the headmistress,' his father said. 'She told me that if you need some more time off, you should take it.'

'I'm OK,' Martin replied. 'I'm not ill, my brain's working OK and I can hold a pen in my hand and write. So I don't see no reason why I should not go to school.'

As Martin's father was leaving the dinner table he placed his hand on Martin's head and asked, 'What are you doing over the weekend, son?'

Martin stood up and replied, 'Homework,' and then he went up to his room.

Further reading

Have a look at www.benjaminzephaniah.com for more information about the author.

The Rescue of Karen Arscott

by Gene Kemp

> Harriet Carter arrives in a new school, quickly to encounter the bullying of Karen Arscott. This short story has some powerful messages about how a school community may or may not succeed in dealing with a bully.

Amongst us lot she stuck out like a sore thumb. Or rather an orchid on a rubbish tip. Not that I know what an orchid looks like but you get the idea. She first appeared at our Wednesday morning Assembly, stuck there in line between Lindy Brown and Karen Arscott and there couldn't have been any place to do more for her – talk about a rose between two thorns. Lindy is knee high to a corgi, but thin with it, pipe cleaner shape, with a drippy nose and straggly hair. Her main hobby is weeping in corners. Mrs Conway, that's our class teacher, keeps leading us aside in turn, asking us to be *kind*, telling us to try to get her to join in. Poor Lindy had problems, she says. Who doesn't, asks my friend Angie, rolling her big eyes.

Now Karen is different. Worse. Worse than anything you can imagine. She looks like that creature from the Black Lagoon, or out of the depths of the Id or whatever it was in those old movies. Get out of my way, she snarls. So I do. We all do. I've been getting out of her way for the past ten years since she flattened me in the Infants' playground and took my lunch and my new pencil case. Next day I brought my Mum into the playground. After she'd gone, Karen flattened me again. After that I gave up saying anything about Karen – just learnt to move very fast in the opposite direction whenever I saw her. And the boys learnt to move even faster. On one of her bad days she could clear the playground quicker than the school dentist arriving. When we left the Primary we hoped she'd go to a different Comprehensive. We kept saying all the good things we knew about the others very loudly when she was about. But it was hopeless, as we realized when we heard her Mum telling our teacher that Karen didn't want to leave her form mates. Her Mum looked like Giant Haystacks, the wrestler, so our teacher agreed, nodding up and down a lot.

But practice had made me very nippy, and there was a good crowd of us – Angie, Tamsin, Jackie and Pat. So we managed without too much aggro even when she turned up in our class despite there being four streams to each year.

No, the one who copped it all was Lindy, fresh from another school and a born loser from the start. We did try to stop it, to help, but Lindy was so wet and Karen so tough that by our year it was more or less the thing that those two paired off and Karen was The Boss.

And then, there in the hall one gloomy February morning, stood this girl in between the two of them. And she was beautiful. Her hair was long and black, her face was pale, her eyes misty. Even Angie looked ordinary beside her. The rest of us like Rejects United.

Back in the classroom everyone crowded round her as they always do with anyone new till the novelty wears off. I tried to join in but there was no room so I thought I might just as well get on with the homework I hadn't finished the night before.

Then I made out a beauty programme wondering if Mum would let me dye my hair. It would be smashing not to be a natural born mouse, and to be slim. Not that I'm really very fat, and a thirty-six bra sounds all right except if you're only five foot tall you look more as if you're wearing a bolster than the Dawson Comprehensive answer to Miss World. Then I chucked the list away. Why bother? Never, never in a million light years was I going to look like that new girl. What was her name? Harriet, Mrs Conway was saying, Harriet Carter. Just look at Darren Carr making shapes with his hands in the air. He would, the cheeky so and so.

'Lisa, pay attention, please. Lisa!'

I sat up. 'Yes Miss.'

Back to basics.

She turned out to be a very quiet girl. Her work was good and she didn't put a foot wrong with the teachers or anyone, being friendly to everyone but not too friendly and going straight home after school. She seemed to live some distance away, no one knew where. In fact Harriet was a bit of a mystery, and rumours soon ran round the school that a) she was a South American millionairess in hiding because of kidnapping threats, b) she was a refugee from Eastern Europe, c) her mother was dead and she had to get home to cook for her Dad. Somehow the last seemed the most likely. So, said Angie, she's got problems, too.

In the end she just became another one of the class. The boys gave up chasing her when they saw she really wasn't interested, and focus switched back to Angie who was now going out with the captain of the soccer team, who (they said) had never been out with a girl before. What will she make of him, we wondered. Also, we were doing a bit of work, since the teachers mostly came in saying, There's only so many weeks left now till the exams, filling us with terror – well some of us.

It was a very wet spring term. Every day it rained. Karen developed boils on her face which didn't do much for her looks and even less for her temper. Lindy actually appeared in new PE kit. Miss Johnson had gone on at her so much I suppose she was driven to it. Karen threw it down the loo so that it was soaking wet for the lesson. For once Lindy complained and for once we backed her, and Karen caught it in the neck, detentions for a week, etc. But Lindy appeared with a bruise on her face. Walked into a door she said quietly, my own silly fault, I ought to wear my glasses.

We stayed indoors at lunchtime, it was always so wet, and we had access to the library, to the hall for badminton, and to other rooms for things like chess, stamp club and so on. I went to the Art Room, where I was painting Harriet. I'd asked if I could for my Art continuous assessment.

'Might be a good idea,' said old Hamby, grinning. He's a joker, that guy. 'Your work's jolly good, Lisa,' I started to beam like the Cheshire Cat, 'but there isn't enough of it, haha.' And he went away chuckling to himself.

'Some people are getting senile,'[1] I said. So I painted Harriet. I got to know her face well, but what went on behind it was still a mystery.

Someone who also came to the Art Room was Lindy. And without Karen, who was forbidden to go in there because she'd wrecked it on three occasions.

This day we came out together, Harriet, Lindy and me, and Lindy was quite pink and human and chatty. Her leaf and tree prints were really good and she was always better when she was doing something Arty, seemed to have more confidence. Besides, Harriet, though she hardly said anything herself, always got Lindy to chat away merrily.

Karen Arscott sat in the middle of the corridor blocking the way to the classroom. Lindy turned pale, the bruise on her face showing up clearly.

'Whatcher bin doing, then?' said Karen to Lindy.

Without a word Lindy handed over her folder.

---

[1]**senile**   confused and forgetful because of old age

'Load o' crap, ain't it?' said Karen and threw Lindy's collection on the floor and stamped on it.

'Any objections?' she went on.

Like a shadow Harriet slipped between her and Lindy, pushed Karen back on to the chair then tipped the chair and Karen up. A bellow of rage echoed down the corridor as Karen lumbered to her feet. A crowd gathered. They were all coming but no one was going to interfere, least of all the boys, though cries of, 'Let her have it, Harriet,' were heard. Karen charged at Harriet, who waited almost carelessly till the last possible minute, then moved to one side, and Karen crashed heavily into the wall, the picture on the rail above descending on to her head and putting paid to her. A cheer went up. Until,

'Just what is going on here?' said Mr Keithley, the Headmaster.

But Lindy went on her knees beside Karen and lifted her head on to her lap. Harriet, paler than ever, looked at them, then turned and walked through the crowd, who just melted away before her.

I never saw her again.

Mr Keithley, who always seemed to know everything that went on in the school, said Karen had got her deserts at last, and would we please pack up Harriet's things for her as she would be moving on. So we did. Lindy looked after Karen like a mother hen with its chick, and there was no more trouble in that direction. Karen was a changed person. She depended on Lindy a lot.

The weather improved. The sun shone at last. After a time I stopped resenting the dullness of school without Harriet. And, after a longer time, I forgot her and to my surprise found a boyfriend. The portrait? Well, I kept that, though I didn't hand it in for assessment. For one thing it wasn't finished. Besides, I didn't want people looking at it and marking it B or C or lower.

About three years later I went to Art School, and moved my gear into a bedsit for term time. As I was clearing out a drawer, a photo in the old newspaper-lining caught my eye, I don't know why. I looked more closely and saw that it resembled Harriet. But an older Harriet with shorter hair. I realized it was her mother.

Underneath, the caption read: *Mrs Adrienne Carter was today convicted of the manslaughter of her husband, Frederick Herbert Carter. She attacked and killed him with a heavy stick after he had severely beaten their daughter, Harriet, aged nine years.*

Oh, Harriet, Harriet.

Further reading

If you liked this, it's worth having a look at *The Mink War* (Faber & Faber, 1992) or *Snaggletooth's Mystery* (Faber & Faber, 2002) by Gene Kemp. Another recommended read is *School's OK*, edited by Roy Blatchford.

Red Sky in the Morning
by Elizabeth Laird

Anna is living with a secret. She doesn't want her friends at school to know that her baby brother is severely disabled. Katy is her sister. The opening sentence of the extract neatly sums up Anna's plight.

For the next two years I lived what they call a double life. It sounds romantic when you put it like that, but it was really an awful worry. Home and school were completely separated, or as separated as I could make them. If I ever become an actress, I shall owe my talent to the training of those years. I used to shut the front door every morning playing the part of Dad's Hosanna, and the light of Ben's life, and somewhere between the garden gate and the bus stop, I'd become spotty Anna Peacock (Pee-wit the Pea-brain), the dummy of the second year.

For a long time I didn't mind too much about school. I lived in a dream world, divorced from the realities of everyday life. The awful truth is that I was madly in love with Miss Winter. She had a whip-lash body, and short curly hair, and when she slammed the ball over the net in tennis lessons, her shorts sort of flipped up and settled down again on her iron-hard thighs, and I used to feel a dreadful yearning to be saved from a man-eating shark by her. Too embarrassing to remember, really. Having a crush on Miss Winter didn't do me any good, either. I went all numb, and I just let myself in for unnecessary suffering. I still wince at the memory of her shouting at me, '*Run*, Anna! Where are your arms? For heaven's sake, girl! Hit the ball! Harder! Are you paralysed or something?'

It would have been much more sensible to fall in love with Miss Penny, because English is my best subject, and she liked me as well. But there you are. Love is blind. And it's hard to take a person seriously when their nickname is Spenda. Spenda Penny. Geddit? Anyway, all that kind of thing is far behind me now, I'm thankful to say. I grew out of it months ago.

At home, I was a different person. I belonged to Ben. By the time he was two, he had grown quite big, and his head, of course, was enormous. I knew he wasn't developing in the way that most babies do. I mean, he didn't learn to sit up till he was nearly a year old, and he was only just crawling on his second birthday. I could remember Katy, when she was two, posting shapes into a plastic letter-box thing, and stacking up a tower of plastic pots. Mum hadn't even got them out for Ben. I went up to the attic, and fetched them down one day. I didn't see why he shouldn't have normal toys, same as any other kid. Mum looked a bit funny when she saw them.

'Look, Anna,' she said, in the voice of one trying hard to be patient but finding it rather difficult, 'You've got to accept facts. Benny's not like other babies. He's not going to be able to pile up those beakers. He can't even pick things up and hold them properly. And it's no good wishing that he could.'

I was really annoyed with Mum when she said that. Of course I knew Ben was different. What did she take me for? And what did she take Ben for, too? Even if he wasn't normal, he could learn to do some things. He might even get some fun out of it.

'I know, Mum,' I said, in the voice of one trying hard to be polite but finding it rather difficult, 'but I don't see why he can't just look at them, and chew them a bit if he wants to.'

I picked Ben up and he snuggled his great big head down onto my shoulder. He couldn't talk or anything like that, but at long last he'd learned to kiss. I'd spent ages teaching him. You wouldn't believe that learning a little thing like kissing would be so difficult. It took nearly a week getting him to purse his lips, then another week to put them against my cheek, then two to make the actual kiss. One month of solid hard work. But when he did it for the first time, I felt so proud and happy it was like stars exploding inside my head. And Ben went mad with joy. He knew he'd been clever. He laughed and laughed, and beat his weak little arms up and down in the air. Dr Randall had been right about one thing, the night that Ben was born. Laughing was no problem. He could laugh all right.

Mind you, I had second thoughts about teaching Ben to kiss. I began to wish I'd taught him something else. The problem was that once he'd learned how to do it, he wouldn't stop. He never seemed to get bored with it. And no one else, except Mum, and sometimes Dad, seemed quite so keen to be kissed by Ben. Even I had to admit that his mouth was wetter than most people's.

'I think it's disgusting,' Katy used to say, looking all prissy, and stuck-up. 'I don't know how you can stand it, getting dribbled all over like that.'

A few weeks earlier, I'd have pinched Katy good and hard for saying that, but I was growing too big for childish squabbles. Anyway, I'd realised that the poor child was suffering from the pangs of jealousy. They were no stranger to me. I knew how it felt to see one's best friend go off with a snotty little sycophant.[1] That was one of my best descriptions of Emma. I'd thought up lots of them, especially last thing at night, but 'snotty sycophant' combined, I thought, strict truthfulness and a neat elegance of phrasing. It was exquisitely crushing. I'd never dared say it to her face, but I was holding it in reserve. One day, I knew, my time for annihilating Emma would come.

I'd realised that Katy was jealous the day she shrieked at me, 'You never play with me like you do with Ben. What have I got to do? Get myself handicapped or something?'

I was just about to tear her limb from limb when I suddenly understood, and a calm feeling of superiority came over me. I felt about fifty years old. So I smiled at her, and said very kindly, 'Now now, Katy, don't be jealous. Of course I'm really very fond of you.'

But the wretched child just got madder than ever. After that I tried to ignore her. I promised myself that one day I'd do something really stunning for Katy, like taking her out for a hamburger, or letting her listen to my golden oldie Beatles record. But I kept putting it off. The trouble was, she made me feel

---

[1]**sycophant**   creep

guilty. I really did like Ben much better than her. But did that mean I actually preferred him to be handicapped? That would be twisted and selfish. Still, when I thought about it, I decided it was OK. It was best to love Ben just for himself. Wishing couldn't make him any better, but loving him would make him happy. Perhaps that was what Mum had been trying to tell me.

Mum minded much more than I did about him being different. She avoided other babies. She never looked at them, or tickled their tummies in the supermarket like she had done before Ben was born. I suppose she didn't want to think about what he might have been like. She just marched grimly on with him in his push chair, trying not to see the expressions on people's faces when they caught sight of him.

I didn't mind about the handicap as much as Mum, but I did mind about the way people looked at him. They'd see him, take one long, horrified stare, then their faces would kind of freeze up, and they'd gaze into the distance trying to pretend they hadn't noticed anything. But the minute your back was turned, and you were hunting round the shelves for the cheapest jar of marmalade, you could practically feel their eyes boring into poor, innocent old Ben. He didn't care, mind you. He only went on holding his feet and trying to stuff them into his mouth, just like tiny babies do, only he was two years old.

I used to feel like a gladiator in ancient Rome, girding himself up for battle, before I went to the shops with him. I used to avoid the high street, and walk on a bit further, to the parade furthest away from the school. I'd never met anyone from school there, so I was lulled into a false sense of security. I used to put on his little coat, pull on his mittens, and get ready to stare down anyone who was rude. Actually, I had a worse time than Mum on these expeditions. People didn't dare say anything to her, but just because I looked younger than my age, more like an early thirteen than a middle fourteen, they took all kinds of liberties with me. Once a woman stopped me, and said, 'Do you mind, dear?' and got right down to really stare at Ben, and then said, 'What on earth's the matter with him? I've never seen one as bad as that before.' She gave me a funny look as if she thought I must be mental or something. I didn't mind children so much. They used to say what they thought right out loud, without trying to pretend. Things like, 'Oh look, Mummy. That baby's got such a funny head.' But I did mind the mothers who would look round and say *'Shh,'* and pull the kids away. Why didn't they smile, and say something nice? They could have said, 'Yes, but he's got lovely curls,' which was perfectly true. The worst time was when one horrible old woman with a beard muttered, 'It's a shame letting a child like that out where a pregnant woman might see it. Oughtn't to be allowed.'

I was so dumbstruck I couldn't think of a thing to say. I mean, what would you have done? But luckily I was in the newsagent's, and Mrs Chapman, who runs it, is a really nice person. She'd always been good about Ben.

'Silly old bat,' she said. 'Don't you take any notice of her, Anna. Ben's lovely, aren't you, my duck?' and she leaned over her rack of Twixes and Mars bars so far that her great bosoms got tangled up in them, and she pulled a funny face at him. Ben went wild. He always laughed at Mrs Chapman.

I loved her for that. Going to her shop, and seeing her nice fat body squeeze between the shelves of sweets and newspapers, and watching her wobble when she bent over Ben to give him a kiss made up for everyone else being funny about us.

'It's kids like this that teach us what loving's all about,' she used to say. 'You mark my words, Anna, they're special. I had a little cousin like this you know. Ray of sunshine, she was.'

In the end, though, it was Mrs Chapman who led to my downfall. I'd gone to the parade on Saturday morning, and was in her shop trying to choose a birthday card for Dad. Men are so difficult to buy things for, I find. One never knows what kind of thing will appeal. Ben was up near the counter, in his push chair, flapping his hands at Mrs Chapman. I had rejected a joke card with a drunk trying to smoke forty cigarettes at once (it was Dad's fortieth birthday), because I didn't want to encourage him to take up bad habits at his time of life, and I was hesitating over an arty one of a lonely fisherman by a misty lake, when I heard a familiar voice.

'Oh stop it, Greg. Oh, you are awful.'

I froze. It was Miranda. She was the one in my class who was always twined round a boy. She had that kind of tight, bulgy body that seems about to burst out of its clothes, and she knew everything there was to know about sex. I tried not to listen when she got going in the cloakroom. Call me a prig if you like, but I have my standards, and I draw the line at pornography. It degrades women.

My only hope was that Miranda and her horrible Greg would be so wrapped up in each other that they wouldn't notice me, or Ben. But I'd reckoned without Mrs Chapman.

'Here, you two, mind the baby!' she called down the shop, seeing them about to trip over the push chair. Miranda must have looked at Ben then, because I heard her say,

'Oh my Gawd,' in that silly way she does, and then giggle. I just hoped desperately that they wouldn't see me. I didn't even dare go on looking at the birthday cards. I bent my head right down and looked at the floor. To this day, I could draw you a perfect sketch of the dusty floorboards, complete with all the cracks and knots in the wood. But I didn't get away with it. No such luck.

'Get Ben out of the way, Anna,' Mrs Chapman called to me, really loudly. 'You don't want these love-birds here to do him a mischief.'

There was no help for it then. I had to come out from behind the card stand. I felt my face flush flaming red, and my hands go all wet with sweat. Miranda gasped when she saw me. If I hadn't been so upset I'd have burst out laughing at her. She was so done up she looked ridiculous. I mean, down at the shops on a Saturday morning in our town isn't exactly the same as a Saturday night in Monte Carlo. And green lurex tights on one end of her, and a plunging neck line at the other were too crude for words. But I was too flustered to think up anything witty that would give me the advantage. I wanted to turn tail and run.

'Is this Ben, your brother?' said Miranda, when she'd finally got her bright orange mouth working again.

'Yes it is, actually,' I said, 'and if you've got any questions, comments, sick jokes or wisecracks, now's your chance, Miranda.'

She looked at me then, and I was sorry I'd been so hasty. She didn't look as if she wanted to laugh at all. She just shook her head a bit, and said, 'Knock it off, pea-brain,' in a quiet sort of voice, and trailed out of the shop, towing the deplorable Greg behind her.

I stood there trembling. I didn't know where I was for a moment. The floorboards heaved. Then I felt Mrs Chapman's enormous soft arm round my shoulder.

'Hey,' she said, 'don't your schoolfriends know about Ben, then?'

I shook my head.

'They didn't,' I said. 'They will now.'

Mrs Chapman gave me a shake.

'Well,' she said, 'you may be a bit upset with me for letting the cat out of the bag, but I'm not going to say I'm sorry. You're a little idiot, Anna. You can't keep something like this a secret. It's high time your schoolfriends knew about it. You're not ashamed of Benny, are you?'

'Course not,' I said, but I knew I was really.

Mrs Chapman did something she'd never done before. She took a Milky Way off the rack, tore off the paper, and gave it to me.

'It's on the house,' she said. 'First, last and only time. Now come on, tell me. Why don't you want your friends to know? What are you so frightened of?'

It isn't easy having a really deep conversation with a newsagent on a Saturday morning. People keep coming in to buy cigarettes, or to ask in husky voices for rude magazines from the top shelves, or to demand sympathy cards suitable for an old person whose goldfish has died. I vowed then and there never to become a shopkeeper. You have to have a butterfly mind. Mine is flighty enough, without giving it any unnecessary encouragement.

Anyway, we managed all right. Mrs Chapman got it all out of me, about how the girls at school didn't like me much, and why I'd kept quiet about Ben because I didn't want to let myself down, and I was afraid of being teased. Then she gave me a good talking to. The funny thing is, I didn't mind. She was so kind, and I knew she was talking sense. I trusted her. It was partly because she'd known and loved a handicapped child herself, but it was more than that. Mrs Chapman was wise. She could look into the human heart and plumb its murky depths.

'What are you afraid of, then?' she said. 'Sympathy? Don't be daft, Anna. You can't have too much sympathy in this life. You need it. We all need it. But you've got to learn how to accept it. It's harder to be on the receiving end than the giving end sometimes. And you're not really afraid they'll laugh at you, are you? They're decent kids, deep down. Even that Marina, or Miranda or whatever her name is, she's got a heart, you know. They'll only tease you if you're silly enough to go all proud and prickly, like you did just now, because then you're rejecting them. If you're honest, and open, and say, "Look, it's true, my brother's severely handicapped and I never told you because I felt too miserable about it," I bet you a packet of bacon and onion crisps they'll be very nice about it.

'Why don't you tell them how you're trying to teach Ben things, and show them how much he's learned? He can clap his hands now, can't you, my precious?' and she leaned down, wheezing a bit, and prodded Ben's tummy. He squirmed with pleasure. Then she straightened up again, putting one hand on her back to help herself.

'People are only scared of handicaps because they're not used to them,' she went on. 'You let them get to know Ben, and see how you're so good at looking after him, and I bet they'll be all over him like bees round a honey pot, wanting to love him too.'

Mrs Chapman talked a long time, in between selling pencil sharpeners and tubes of Smarties, but she didn't quite convince me. I could just imagine the sly digs Emma would make, and hear Debbie's cool, unconcerned voice saying rather grandly, 'Well, you fooled us all, didn't you Pee-wit? What made you think we'd be interested anyway?'

But Mrs Chapman was right about one thing. The day after tomorrow I'd have to face them all at school. There was no getting away from that. And being frank and forthright was my only hope. There was no point in being stiff and starchy.

It was an awful long wait until Monday.

Further reading

If you liked Elizabeth Laird's style, try reading one of her other books. *Jake's Tower* (Macmillan, 2001) and *Kiss the Dust* (Puffin, 2007) are good reads.

The Curious Incident of the Dog in the Night-time

by Mark Haddon

The boy at the centre of this novel – 15-year-old Christopher – has a photographic memory and is brilliant at maths, but he finds relating to human beings difficult. This extract is taken from the opening pages of the novel. Mrs Shears is a neighbour with a dog. Mr Jeavons is the psychologist who, together with Siobhan, supports Chris at school.

It was 7 minutes after midnight. The dog was lying on the grass in the middle of the lawn in front of Mrs Shears' house. Its eyes were closed. It looked as if it was running on its side, the way dogs run when they think they are chasing a cat in a dream. But the dog was not running or asleep. The dog was dead. There was a garden fork sticking out of the dog. The points of the fork must have gone all the way through the dog and into the ground because the fork had not fallen over. I decided that the dog was probably killed with the fork because I could not see any other wounds in the dog and I do not think you would stick a garden fork into a dog after it had died for some other reason, like cancer for example, or a road accident. But I could not be certain about this.

I went through Mrs Shears' gate, closing it behind me. I walked onto her lawn and knelt beside the dog. I put my hand on the muzzle of the dog. It was still warm.

The dog was called Wellington. It belonged to Mrs Shears who was our friend. She lived on the opposite side of the road, two houses to the left.

Wellington was a poodle. Not one of the small poodles that have hairstyles, but a big poodle. It had curly black fur, but when you got close you could see that the skin underneath the fur was a very pale yellow, like chicken.

I stroked Wellington and wondered who had killed him, and why.

My name is Christopher John Francis Boone. I know all the countries of the world and their capital cities and every prime number up to 7,507.

Eight years ago, when I first met Siobhan, she showed me this picture

and I knew that it meant 'sad', which is what I felt when I found the dead dog.

Then she showed me this picture

and I knew that it meant 'happy', like when I'm reading about the Apollo space missions, or when I am still awake at three or four in the morning and I can walk up and down the street and pretend that I am the only person in the whole world.

Then she drew some other pictures

but I was unable to say what these meant.

I got Siobhan to draw lots of these faces and then write down next to them exactly what they meant. I kept the piece of paper in my pocket and took it out when I didn't understand what someone was saying. But it was very difficult to decide which of the diagrams was most like the face they were making because people's faces move very quickly.

When I told Siobhan that I was doing this, she got out a pencil and another piece of paper and said it probably made people feel very

and then she laughed. So I tore the original piece of paper up and threw it away. And Siobhan apologised. And now if I don't know what someone is saying I ask them what they mean or I walk away.

I pulled the fork out of the dog and lifted him into my arms and hugged him. He was leaking blood from the fork-holes.

I like dogs. You always know what a dog is thinking. It has four moods. Happy, sad, cross and concentrating. Also, dogs are faithful and they do not tell lies because they cannot talk.

I had been hugging the dog for 4 minutes when I heard screaming. I looked up and saw Mrs Shears running towards me from the patio. She was wearing pyjamas and a housecoat. Her toenails were painted bright pink and she had no shoes on.

She was shouting, 'What the hell have you done to my dog?'

I do not like people shouting at me. It makes me scared that they are going to hit me or touch me and I do not know what is going to happen.

'Let go of the dog,' she shouted. 'Let go of the dog for Christ's sake.'

I put the dog down on the lawn and moved back 2 metres.

She bent down. I thought she was going to pick the dog up herself, but she didn't. Perhaps she noticed how much blood there was and didn't want to get dirty. Instead, she started screaming again.

I put my hands over my ears and closed my eyes and rolled forward till I was hunched up with my forehead pressed onto the grass. The grass was wet and cold. It was nice.

This is a murder mystery novel.

Siobhan said that I should write something I would want to read myself. Mostly I read books about science and maths. I do not like proper novels. In proper novels people say things like, 'I am veined with iron, with silver and with streaks of common mud. I cannot contract into the firm fist which those clench who do not depend on stimulus.'[1] What does this mean? I do not know. Nor does Father. Nor do Siobhan or Mr Jeavons. I have asked them.

Siobhan has long blonde hair and wears glasses which are made of green plastic. And Mr Jeavons smells of soap and wears brown shoes that have approximately 60 tiny circular holes in each of them.

But I do like murder mystery novels. So I am writing a murder mystery novel.

In a murder mystery novel someone has to work out who the murderer is and then catch them. It is a puzzle. If it is a good puzzle you can sometimes work out the answer before the end of the book.

Siobhan said that the book should begin with something to grab people's attention. That is why I started with the dog. I also started with the dog because it happened to me and I find it hard to imagine things which did not happen to me.

---

[1] I found this book in the library in town when Mother took me into town once.

Siobhan read the first page and said that it was different. She put this word into inverted commas by making the wiggly quotation sign with her first and second fingers. She said that it was usually people who were killed in murder mystery novels. I said that two dogs were killed in *The Hound of the Baskervilles*, the hound itself and James Mortimer's spaniel, but Siobhan said they weren't the victims of the murder, Sir Charles Baskerville was. She said that this was because readers cared more about people than dogs, so if a person was killed in the book readers would want to carry on reading.

I said that I wanted to write about something real and I knew people who had died but I did not know any people who had been killed, except Edward's father from school, Mr Paulson, and that was a gliding accident, not murder, and I didn't really know him. I also said that I cared about dogs because they were faithful and honest, and some dogs were cleverer and more interesting than some people. Steve, for example, who comes to school on Thursdays, needs help to eat his food and could not even fetch a stick. Siobhan asked me not to say this to Steve's mother.

Then the police arrived. I like the police. They have uniforms and numbers and you know what they are meant to be doing. There was a policewoman and a policeman. The policewoman had a little hole in her tights on her left ankle and a red scratch in the middle of the hole. The policeman had a big orange leaf stuck to the bottom of his shoe which was poking out from one side.

The policewoman put her arms round Mrs Shears and led her back towards the house.

I lifted my head off the grass.

The policeman squatted down beside me and said, 'Would you like to tell me what's going on here, young man?'

I sat up and said, 'The dog is dead.'

'I'd got that far,' he said.

I said, 'I think someone killed the dog.'

'How old are you?' he asked.

I replied, 'I am 15 years and 3 months and 2 days.'

'And what, precisely, were you doing in the garden?' he asked.

'I was holding the dog,' I replied.

'And why were you holding the dog?' he asked.

This was a difficult question. It was something I wanted to do. I like dogs. It made me sad to see that the dog was dead.

I like policemen, too, and I wanted to answer the question properly, but the policeman did not give me enough time to work out the correct answer.

'Why were you holding the dog?' he asked again.

'I like dogs,' I said.

'Did you kill the dog?' he asked.

I said, 'I did not kill the dog.'

'Is this your fork?' he asked.

I said, 'No.'

'You seem very upset about this,' he said.

He was asking too many questions and he was asking them too quickly. They were stacking up in my head like loaves in the factory where Uncle Terry works. The factory is a bakery and he operates the slicing machines. And sometimes the slicer is not working fast enough but the bread keeps coming and there is a blockage. I sometimes think of my mind as a machine, but not always as a bread-slicing machine. It makes it easier to explain to other people what is going on inside it.

The policeman said, 'I am going to ask you once again . . .'

I rolled back onto the lawn and pressed my forehead to the ground again and made the noise that Father calls groaning. I make this noise when there is too much information coming into my head from the outside world. It is like when you are upset and you hold the radio against your ear and you tune it halfway between two stations so that all you get is white noise and then you turn the volume right up so that this is all you can hear and then you know you are safe because you cannot hear anything else.

The policeman took hold of my arm and lifted me onto my feet.

I didn't like him touching me like this.

And this is when I hit him.

Further reading

If you enjoyed this, you could read *A Spot of Bother,* also by Mark Haddon published by Vintage in 2007. Have a look at his website (www.markhaddon.com) which shows many of his unique illustrations.

The Fifth Child

by Doris Lessing

> Ben is the fifth child born to David and Harriet. Theirs is a happy
> and comfortable family. But as Ben grows as a baby and young
> child, they realise he has a character that is altogether different from
> that of their other children. His behaviour gradually becomes more
> and more dangerous to those around him. Dorothy is Ben's grand-
> mother and Alice is his cousin, who both help look after the
> children.

Then something bad happened. Just after all the family had
gone away, as the school term began, Paul went into Ben's room
by himself. Of all the children, he was the most fascinated by
Ben. Dorothy and Alice, who were together in the kitchen,
Harriet having gone off to take the older ones to school, heard
screams. They ran upstairs to find that Paul had put his hand
in to Ben through the cot bars, and Ben had grabbed the hand
and pulled Paul hard against the bars, bending the arm deliberately backwards. The two women freed Paul. They did not
bother to scold Ben, who was crowing with pleasure and
achievement. Paul's arm was badly sprained.

No one felt like saying to the children, 'Be careful of Ben.'
But there was no need after the incident with Paul's arm. That
evening the children heard what had happened, but did not
look at their parents and Dorothy and Alice. They did not look
at each other. They stood silent, heads bent. This told the
adults that the children's attitudes to Ben were already formed:
they had discussed Ben and knew what to think about him.
Luke, Helen, and Jane went away upstairs silently, and it was a
bad moment for the parents.

Alice said, watching them, 'Poor little things.'

Dorothy said, 'It's a shame.'

Harriet felt that these two women, these two elderly, tough,
seasoned survivors, were condemning her, Harriet, out of their vast

experience of life. She glanced at David, and saw he felt the same. Condemnation, and criticism, and dislike: Ben seemed to cause these emotions, bring them forth out of people into the light . . .

The day after this incident, Alice announced that she felt she was no longer needed in this house, she would go back to her own life: she was sure Dorothy could manage. After all, Jane was going to school now. Jane would not have gone to school this year, a proper school, all day, for another year: they had sent her early. Precisely because of Ben, though no one had said it. Alice left, with no suggestion it was because of Ben. But she had told Dorothy, who had told the parents, that Ben gave her the horrors. He must be a changeling.[1] Dorothy, always sensible, calm, matter-of-fact, had laughed at her. 'Yes, I laughed at her,' she reported. Then, grim, 'But why did I?'

David and Harriet conferred, in the low, almost guilty, incredulous[2] voices that Ben seemed to impose. This baby was not six months old yet . . . he was going to destroy their family life. He was already destroying it. They would have to make sure that he was in his room at mealtimes and when the children were downstairs with the adults. Family times, in short.

Now Ben was almost always in his room, like a prisoner. He outgrew his barred cot at nine months: Harriet caught him just as he was about to fall over the top. A small bed, an ordinary one, was put into his room. He walked easily, holding on to the walls, or a chair. He had never crawled, had pulled himself straight up on to his feet. There were toys all over the floor – or, rather, the fragments of them. He did not play with them: he banged them on the floor or the walls until they broke. The day he stood alone, by himself, without holding on, he roared out his triumph. All the other children had laughed, chuckled, and wanted to be loved, admired, praised, on reaching this moment of achievement. This one did not. It was a cold triumph, and he staggered about, eyes

---

[1]**changeling**   in folklore, the child of a fairy or troll that has been substituted for a human child
[2]**incredulous**   not believing

gleaming with hard pleasure, while he ignored his mother. Harriet often wondered what he saw when he looked at her: nothing in his touch or his look ever seemed to say, This is my mother.

One early morning, something took Harriet quickly out of her bed into the baby's room, and there she saw Ben balanced on the window-sill. It was high – heaven only knew how he had got up there! The window was open. In a moment he would have fallen out of it. Harriet was thinking, What a pity I came in . . . and refused to be shocked at herself. Heavy bars were put in, and there Ben would stand on the sill, gripping the bars and shaking them, and surveying the outside world, letting out his thick, raucous cries. All the Christmas holidays he was kept in that room. It was extraordinary how people, asking – cautiously – 'How is Ben?' and hearing, 'Oh, he's all right,' did not ask again. Sometimes a yell from Ben loud enough to reach downstairs silenced a conversation. Then the frown appeared on their faces that Harriet dreaded, waiting for it: she knew it masked some comment or thought that could not be voiced.

And so the house was not the same; there was a constraint and a wariness in everybody. Harriet knew that sometimes people went up to look at Ben, out of the fearful, uneasy curiosity he evoked, when she was out of the way. She knew when they had seen him, because of the way they looked at her afterwards. As if I were a criminal! she raged to herself. She spent far too much of her time quietly seething, but did not seem able to stop. Even David, she believed, condemned her. She said to him, 'I suppose in the old times, in primitive societies, this was how they treated a woman who'd given birth to a freak. As if it was her fault. But we are supposed to be civilised!'

He said, in the patient, watchful way he now had with her, 'You exaggerate everything!'

'That's a good word – for this situation! Congratulations! Exaggerate!'

'Oh God, Harriet,' he said differently, helplessly, 'don't let's do this – if we don't stand together, then . . . '

It was at Easter that the schoolgirl Bridget, who had returned to see if this miraculous kingdom of everyday life was perhaps still there, enquired, 'What is wrong with him? Is he a mongol?'

'Down's syndrome,' said Harriet. 'No one calls it mongol now. But no, he's not.'

'What's wrong with him, then?'

'Nothing at all,' said Harriet airily. 'As you can see for yourself.'

Bridget went away, and never came back.

The summer holidays again. It was 1975. There were fewer guests: some had written or rung to say they could not afford the train fare, or the petrol. 'Any excuse is better than none,' remarked Dorothy.

'But people are hard up,' said David.

'They weren't so hard up before that they couldn't afford to come and live here for weeks at a time at your expense.'

Ben was over a year old now. He had not said one word yet, but in other ways he was more normal. Now it was difficult to keep him in his room. Children playing in the garden heard his thick, angry cries, and saw him up on the sill trying to push aside his bars.

So he came out of his little prison and joined them downstairs. He seemed to know that he ought to be like them. He would stand, head lowered, watching how everyone talked, and laughed, sitting around the big table; or sat talking in the living-room, while the children ran in and out. His eyes were on one face, then another: whomever he was looking at became conscious of that insistent gaze and stopped talking; or turned a back, or a shoulder, so as not to have to see him. He could silence a room full of people just by being there, or disperse them: they went off making excuses.

Towards the end of the holidays, someone came bringing a dog, a little terrier. Ben could not leave it alone. Wherever the dog was, Ben followed. He did not pet it, or stroke it: he stood staring. One morning when Harriet came down to start breakfast for the children, the dog was lying dead on the kitchen floor. It had had a heart attack? Suddenly sick with suspicion, she rushed up to see if Ben was in his room: he was squatting on his bed, and when she came in, he looked up and laughed, but soundlessly, in his way, which was like a baring of the teeth. He had opened his door, gone quietly past his sleeping parents, down the stairs, found the dog, killed it, and gone back up again, quietly, into his room, and shut the door . . . all that, by himself! She locked Ben in: if he could kill a dog, then why not a child?

When she went down again, the children were crowding around the dead dog. And then the adults came, and it was obvious what they thought.

Of course it was impossible – a small child killing a lively dog. But officially the dog's death remained a mystery; the vet said it had been strangled. This business of the dog spoiled what was left of the holidays, and people went off home early.

Dorothy said, 'People are going to think twice about coming again.'

Three months later, Mr McGregor, the old grey cat, was killed in the same way. He had always been afraid of Ben, and kept out of reach. But Ben must have stalked him, or found him sleeping.

At Christmas the house was half empty.

It was the worst year of Harriet's life, and she was not able to care that people avoided them. Every day was a long nightmare. She woke in the morning unable to believe she would ever get through to the evening. Ben was always on his feet, and had to be watched every second. He slept very little. He spent most of the night standing on his window-sill, staring into the garden, and if Harriet looked in on him, he would turn and give her a long stare, alien, chilling: in the half dark of the room he really did look like a little troll or a hobgoblin crouching there. If he was locked in during the day, he screamed and bellowed so that the whole house resounded with it, and they were all afraid the police would arrive. He would suddenly, for no reason she could see, take off and run into the garden, and then out the gate and into the street. One day, she ran a mile or more after him, seeing only that stubby squat little figure going through traffic lights, ignoring cars that hooted and people who screamed warnings at him. She was weeping, panting, half crazed, desperate to get to him before something terrible happened, but she was praying, Oh, do run him over, do, yes, *please* . . . She caught up with him just before a main road, grabbed him, and held the fighting child with all her strength. He was spitting and hissing, while he jerked like a monster fish in her arms. A taxi went by; she called to it, she pushed the child in, and got in after him, holding him fast by an arm that seemed would break with his flailing about and fighting.

What could be done? Again she went to Dr Brett, who examined him and said he was physically in order.

Harriet described his behaviour and the doctor listened.

From time to time, a well-controlled incredulity appeared on his face, and he kept his eyes down, fiddling with pencils.

'You can ask David, ask my mother,' said Harriet.

'He's a hyperactive child – that's how they are described these days, I believe,' said old-fashioned Dr Brett. She went to him because he was old-fashioned.

At last he did look at her, not evading her.

'What do you expect me to do, Harriet? Drug him silly? Well, I am against it.'

She was crying inwardly, Yes, yes, yes, that's exactly what I want! But she said, 'No, of course not.'

'He's physically normal for eighteen months. He's very strong and active of course, but he's always been that. You say he's not talking? But that's not unusual. Wasn't Helen a late talker? I believe she was?'

'Yes,' said Harriet.

She took Ben home. Now he was locked into his room each night, and there were heavy bars on the door as well. Every second of his waking hours, he was watched. Harriet watched him while her mother managed everything else.

David said, 'What is the point of thanking you, Dorothy? It seems everything has gone a long way beyond thank-yous.'

'Everything has gone a long way beyond. Period.' Said Dorothy.

Harriet was thin, red-eyed, haggard. Once again she was bursting into tears over nothing at all. The children kept out of her way. Tact? Were they afraid of her? Dorothy suggested staying alone with Ben for a week in August while the family went off together somewhere.

Neither Harriet nor David would normally have wanted to go anywhere, for they loved their home. And what about the family coming for the summer?

'I haven't noticed any rush to book themselves in,' said Dorothy.

They went to France, with the car. For Harriet it was all happiness: she felt she had been given back her children. She could not get enough of them, nor they of her. And Paul, her baby whom Ben had deprived her of, the wonderful three-year-old, enchanting, a charmer – was her baby again. They were a family still! Happiness . . . they could hardly believe, any of them, that Ben could have taken so much away from them.

When they got home, Dorothy was very tired and she had a bad bruise on her forearm and another on her cheek. She did not say what had happened. But when the children had gone to bed on the first evening, she said to Harriet and David, 'I have to talk – no, sit down and listen.'

They sat with her at the kitchen table.

'You two are going to have to face it. Ben has got to go into an institution.'

'But he's normal,' said Harriet, grim. 'The doctor says he is.'

'He may be normal for what he is. But he is not normal for what we are.'

'What kind of institution would take him?'

'There must be something,' said Dorothy, and began to cry.

Further reading

If this story had an impact on you, *Ben in the World* (HarperCollins, 2000) by Doris Lessing is a powerful sequel.

The Bus People

by Rachel Anderson

> This is one of a number of short stories collected in the volume *The Bus People*. Each story features a child who has some kind of disability, often severe and chronic. What unites the children is that they are collected by bus each morning to take them to school, before returning by the same bus in the afternoon.

Early each morning, there is a female slave who rouses me, who washes me, who oils my body, who dresses me. The slave prepares my food. The slave feeds me.

'Morning, Micky, love. Nice sleepies? Happy dreams?'

I dreamed of chocolate biscuits, and ice-cream, though I want to dream of something else which I can't yet understand.

'Time for wakey-wakies now, there's a good lad.'

She opens the curtains. There are blue bears and yellow stars on the curtains. I want something different which I haven't found. It is to do with the touch of flesh. The slave is a woman and she touches flesh. But it is more than that.

'Up you come. Tablet time, pet.'

That's her now, the slave come to rouse me.

'Schoolday, sleepyhead. Can't have our little lie-in today.'

Too brutally for a caring slave, the woman rouses the drowsy youth. So let us face some facts. There is no slave. I live with my mother. She loves me to suffocation. And this has always been the order of my day. I live imprisoned inside a cage for two from which the only escape is a bus ride to school in the morning and a bus ride home in the evening. She stifles me with her love.

She pulls back the bed covers and removes the leg splints. Each is moulded to the shape of a leg and held in place by black velcro straps. I find the sight of those short twisty legs encased in splints disturbing. I am glad when the splints are off.

'Tablet time, pet.'

A man desires a woman to call his own whom he may hold close to him. A hand to hold. I seek my own body-woman I can do what I want with behind closed curtains.

'Here we are, dear. Got your old mum to take care of you. Swallow it down nicely.'

She presses to my lips the spoonful of jam. In the jam are white chalky particles of bitter grit. The four tablets, crushed to powder, are disguised in raspberry conserve. No one is fooled by the sweet sticky lubrication of jam. These tablets inhibit the onset of the *status epilepticus*[1] when the world revolves with nauseous lights and sounds and I slide down into a state of continuous fitting from which even my slave cannot arouse me.

'There's my good boy. Down the hatch.'

That's what dad used to say. Now she says it.

Status epilepticus deprives me of oxygen, turns me purple, causes further brain damage. When I was younger, some mornings, I grinned and firmly clenched my teeth like a barred gate, forbidding entry to the spoon.

'Come on, dear. Don't be difficult today or we'll be all behind.'

Yet inside herself, she liked it when I resisted. When I made my boyish rebellion, pretending I did not want to take my medication, then it seemed as though there was communication between us. A battle of wills proves a relationship. For ten minutes she must leave me lying on the bed while the tablets and jam go down into my crooked system. She drinks her cup of milky tea standing by the window in her dressing gown, chatting about the coming day's events, the weather, what Mrs Thingy across the way is doing, whether the bus will be late or early.

The sameness of each day's conversation provides order and stability. She provides her own answers to her questions about the day, the weather, the neighbour, and the bus schedule. Bertram is always on time, like an automaton. And Mrs Thingy is always in position behind her lace curtain across the road so that she can

---

[1] *status epilepticus*   epilepsy

watch me, when the bus arrives, being wheeled out like the victim of some gross accident, and she can ask herself what sin my mum committed to have landed herself with such a son as this.

I do not want my mum to talk about the weather, and Mrs Thingy. I want to think about the curious new power I have between my legs. Two of my legs are short and feeble, requiring splints to hold them straight and firm. The third lower limb, once as small and helpless as the other pair, is growing in strength, taking on its own life of energy.

'Who's my wetty boy, then? Never mind. Mum'll clean you up, make you nice and sweet again.'

I am on the bed while she removes the pyjamas, the plastic pants, the disposable napkins. Dreams of bodies wilt and fade. She washes me, dries me, smears Johnson's baby oil into the creases, replaces the soiled garments with fresh.

'There we are, my lamb.'

Next, she stands me up from the bed, and leans me against the wall so that she can pull up my trousers, and fasten the flies. There is velcro fastening here too. She pats me on the head.

'Clean shirt for a clean boy.'

There is always the problem with dribbling so I must wear a clean sweatshirt every day. I do not sweat because I take no exercise. Right Guard is not for me.

'Nearly brekkies time. And what's a good baby going to have today?'

She places my hands round her waist for balance and tucks the upper garments into my trousers. She pulls down my clean sweatshirt. MAN CITY is now written across my chest. She bought it through her mail order catalogue. She spent a long time choosing it from the coloured pictures.

'Arsenal?' she read aloud. 'Everton? Nottingham Forest?'

What did she mean?

'Which one d'you want to support, pet?'

When she had chosen the right wording she filled in the boxes in the order form and sent it off. I am glad she chose for me MAN CITY. But what does it mean? Who is MAN CITY?

I did not attempt to ask her the meaning of the message, because she rarely tells me those things which she believes I do not need to know.

'Don't you go bothering your little head about all that, pet. You just let your old mum take care of the difficult things.'

As soon as MAN CITY is on, she grasps my hands in hers and we move from the room. She walks backwards, I forwards, like an elegantly dancing couple, one step, two step, slip step, slow step, along the landing, down the stairs. She should have been re-housed years ago. Dad used to carry me down over one shoulder. Men are stronger than women.

Weetabix, bran-flakes, and prunes in syrup are ready on the table. Constipation is the scourge of the crumpled torso. My constipation causes her more trouble than it does me. The record is five days, after which point she calls in the health visitor and the nurse who covers the bed in green rubber sheeting. Then it is enema time. Yee hah. Fun!

She flirts the spoon against my lips. My lips are closed. I neither like nor dislike prunes. But on principle I must refuse the first mouthful. Only when she has coaxed me enough, I part my lips and accept. In the end, I have no choice. I am enslaved to her care. My refusal is but a small step in the ritual dance into which we are both now locked.

Some people call her a saint. Year by year, she taught me to sit, to be quiet. That way, people liked me, or did not mind me.

'He's a bonny little chap, isn't it?' they said if I was still and silent, sitting like an egg in my wheelchair.

'Poor Mary. Fancy being left with a child like that,' they said when I beat my head on the back of the chair, growled in my throat, dribbled, and roared, before finally slipping into the oblivion of *status epilepticus*.

Dad left years ago. It was the continual strain of living with her. But that was no way out for me, so I withdrew instead behind the blue bears and yellow stars which is where she wanted me. But now the expectation of more ice-cream or an extra chocolate biscuit are no longer enough.

'There's the bus now, poppet. All ready, are we? On with your nice cosy jacket.'

And then, in the schoolyard as I was being lifted from the bus, I heard the bus escort speaking and I learned that there was another possibility available to me. I discovered that I could move on from blue bears into another world.

'If only he was in the right place,' said Mrs Lovegrove. 'He's so dependent on that mother of his. He could surely do more for himself.'

I overheard the teacher to whom she was speaking say, 'What about St John Chrysostom's College for the Disabled School-leaver?' And later they even tried to tell me about it, about how boys could live there during the term, sleep the nights there, not one night but many, so that, by day, they could learn the skills to help them become men and live in the world as men.

So a visit was arranged. When she heard about it, my mum didn't want to go.

'All that long way? I'd never manage the trains,' she said.

She didn't want me to go either.

'He's doing ever so well as he is. He likes it in Mrs Richards' group, don't you, pet?' When she calls me pet, she bends over and ruffles my hair. She stands behind me where I cannot see her face, and I imagine the milky pale hand of a hired woman from the market place caressing my ears and ruffling my hair.

'He'll have to leave special school eventually. It's as well to start looking around now.'

'I wouldn't want him far off. He needs me.'

They wondered at school what was planned for me when my mum grew old.

'He'll be stopping at home with me just so long as I can manage. I've always promised him that, and whatever you experts say to the contrary, I'm not going back on my word to him. If you have a boy like my Michael, he's got to have a lot more love than your ordinary kid. Some of you people don't seem to understand that. I'm sorry to speak my mind like this. But that's just how it is.'

However, she was persuaded that there was nothing to lose by going to look at St John Chrysostom's. We travelled by Local Authority taxi, me and my mum. Mrs Lovegrove from the bus came too, as escort. Mrs Lovegrove told my mum what a fine place St John Chrysostom's was. I didn't need to listen. I already guessed in my flesh that it would be just the place for me, away from raspberry jam and curtains with pastel bears.

It was a large house, in a park, with big trees. As soon as we arrived they separated us, me from my mum. I could not believe my luck. I had been there no more than five minutes and already I had gained my first hold on freedom.

My mum was led off for coffee and an interview with the principal while I was taken over by a ginger-bearded man in his shirt sleeves. He was a teacher but you'd never have known it. The other lads didn't call him Sir. They called him Bill.

Bill pushed my chair along the paths.

'You'd be better off with electric, wouldn't you, sonny?' he said. 'Some of the lads here use their mobility allowance to go electric. Then you could get around by yourself.'

He showed me into the workshops where they teach skills and vocations. I saw boys wiring things up with brightly coloured wires, hammering things of wood together. I saw boys stuffing cushions with kapok,[2] and sorting coloured pins into groups. I could do that if somebody showed me how.

Bill showed me the snooker room, the darts room, the gymnasium, the smoking area and the bar for the over-18s. He took me to the television room. But he won't ever catch me using that facility, not when there's so much other choice. I've watched more telly, side by side on the settee with my mum with a packet of chocolate digestives between us, than most people in a lifetime.

---

[2] **kapok**   soft, fibrous matter used for stuffing

Bill said, 'D'you do signing? Makaton? Bliss?[3] What signing do you use at home?'

'Yeerghaaarh,' I said. I shook my head. It went round and round like the moon revolving on a stick. My mum says she can understand perfectly well what I need without needing to go waving her arms about in the air like some madman. My mum never learned signing. I never learned. My mum was right in her way. In Makaton and Bliss where are those words for what I have to say? There is want and need and like and love and touch. Where is Man City and Manhood?

'Never mind,' said Bill. 'We'll manage.' He bumped me up the ramp into the dormitory block.

'You'd have to learn to use the lift on your own,' he said. 'Press the button. Number three.'

I have no numbers. I have colours.

'Top one. Blue.'

I commanded my hand to rise and to press the button, but today the hand would not obey. This end-of-limb was not my slave. Bill did not help. He was speaking to someone outside the lift. They were behind me and I could not see them. I cannot turn my own head.

I growled to the hand. Reluctantly, the hand obeyed, or perhaps it was only chance.

'That's it,' said Bill. 'Good.'

'Each student has his own cubicle,' said Bill. 'Nobody goes into anyone else's without permission. OK? We try to show respect for others' privacy.'

Bill knocked on a door which had a drawing of a black skull and crossbones pinned to it.

From inside a voice replied.

Bill opened the door a crack. 'May we come in?' he asked. 'Just showing round a new recruit.'

'*May* we,' he had asked. This respect was like a gift. No slave

---

[3]**Makaton; Bliss**   communication programmes

ever knocks on my door. At home, the door is always propped open with a chair.

'Just ajar, pet. Better that way. In case you need anything. You know I'm always there.'

She has not had a full night's sleep since the day that I was born. I know because she has said as much on several occasions.

'But that's what mother-love is all about, lambkins.'

He was a crumpled hunk, lounging across his bed, holding a picture postcard close to his eyes and smoking a thin black cheroot[4]. The postcard was of a woman showing pieces of misplaced flesh and rounded body. I had never seen such a picture before but I knew what it was. There was also music in his room, wham, bam, wham that man, and the air was thick with the aromatic smoke.

Bill said, 'Ashtray!' and chucked one onto the bed.

In that room, I saw things that I had been looking for all this time, but until this moment, I hadn't known what they were. There were posters on the wall and on the ceiling and on the door which showed people and guns and thighs and unexpected folds in the flesh. There were posters which showed toothpaste squirting from a tube, and suntan oil dribbling down warm shoulders. There were stallions running. And on the bedside locker, by his head, was a poster showing the cleft in the body where the legs meet inside the bushy curls.

These were the images I had been waiting to dream about. The boy on the bed had found them before me. I became excited on my chair and humped up and down. The strange sensation between my legs grew strong.

'Yeeeoorrgh!' I said.

'The rooms are mostly the same,' said Bill. 'You can do what you like. But you have to keep it tidy yourself. No one else does. Do they, Alid?'

The boy on the bed shrugged and flicked cheroot ash at the ashtray. He missed. It was his room. He could do as he pleased.

---

[4]**cheroot**   cigar

'You are coming here, you?' he said to me. Although his head swung as he spoke his eyes held contact with mine like magnets.

I waved my hands at him. I should've learned signing.

'Michael has got to do the assessment first,' said Bill. 'Like everybody else.'

'See you around then,' said the boy on the bed.

The assessment had been a worry. Yet it turned out to be perfectly feasible. I did OK. The hands obeyed. The coloured blocks balanced on other coloured blocks. The nuts screwed onto the bolts. The left hand and the right hand knew each other. The eyes recognized images on the page.

'Which picture is the saucepan, Michael?'

At the image the head nodded.

'Well done. And which is the saucer?'

'Good. Now this one, Michael. Michael? Michael, can you hear? Flower, plant, pot or garden?'

Next, recognize printed words. I can't do printed words. But can he recognize his own written name? Yes, I know my own written name.

I am Man City.

'So you can write your own name too? Why, that *is* good. Really good.'

I became inflated by my success. I grabbed the crayon and wrote everything I knew. I wrote the zigs and the zags, the running lines and the straight. I wrote the gun shooting, the legs stretching, and the soft sheen on the sunburned body-flesh.

And then it was time for lunch. Bill reappeared and wheeled me to the dining-block. In the dining-hall they had separate tables just like a restaurant. We could sit four to a table. Bill wheeled me to the serving-hatch and left me to sort out for myself. A serving lady carried my tray but there was nobody to feed me. I had to manage. Everyone else did.

I saw the cheroot boy from upstairs. He waved and his eyes saw mine. I waved. He came over to my table. He placed himself near me, so that when his elbow touched the frame of my wheelchair I could feel the warmth of him running through the cold metal tubing to reach my hand.

He had chosen rice and curried meat. I had chosen beans with chips. We smiled. I liked him. At St John Chrysostom's we can choose our own meal.

He asked me, 'You are coming here?'

I shook my head up and round and down.

'What you name then, you boy?'

'Mer. Mer,' I said and then became angry that lips and throat and tongue would not obey and pronounce my name to my friend.

'Mermer?' he said. And then he saw my sweatshirt and he could read. 'You mean Mermer Man City? That is a good name.' And he laughed and touched the words on my shirt with his hand.

I laughed too and I nodded.

'I call you Man City then. That's OK?'

It was OK.

After lunch, Bill returned for me and wheeled me to the toilets. He did nothing to assist. He left me to attend to it while he was occupied with his own pee. He seemed to ignore me. I wetted myself. I could not unfasten the velcro flies. I put myself into a wet mess. But I did not ask Bill for help. It was good to be alone like a man in the toilets. I do not like being pushed into the Ladies toilets by my mum. She says not to be a silly billy.

When we were back in the taxi with Mrs Lovegrove and the driver, she kicked up a fuss.

'Oh really! They should've called me. Look at the state of you. I knew I shouldn't have let you go off on your own with that young man.'

'Bill,' I said and waved my hands. Does Bill keep pictures in his room?

It seemed such a long drive home. I was tired. So I was sick too. Mrs Lovegrove suggested we stop at a hotel for a break.

'Unless you have something you need to be back for?'

'Well no,' said my mum. 'Not exactly. But I never like to be away from home too long. With a boy like my Michael, you never know, do you? Sometimes during the morning while he's at school I nip out. But never for long. I don't like to be out long. Just in case the bus is back early and that.'

'Would you like a drink, Micky?' said Mrs Lovegrove.

Yes, I'd like to drink the drink that men drink. When I go to St John Chrysostom's they will teach me how to be a man and to drink like a man.

'He'll have a juice, if that's no trouble to you, Mrs Lovegrove,' said my mum. 'He likes orange. It's good for his little system too.'

My mum had the towelling bib round my neck in an instant. She had all the stuff I need in her carri-bag. When the drinks came, Mrs Lovegrove lifted the glass of juice to my mouth.

'No, dear,' said my mum. 'He likes his own drinking straw better, don't you, pet?' She decanted the juice from the hotel's glass into my plastic beaker, inserted the special articulated plastic straw and held it for me to drink.

'You'd be surprised,' said Mrs Lovegrove, 'how independent some of the lads become after only a term or two at St John's.'

'My Micky's never been away from me. I'm not sure he'd like it,' said my mum. 'There's all the little things he needs doing that only a mother knows.'

'Of course, I dare say you'd miss him at first. But the staff find they come on such a lot, it's really worth it. Still, you don't have to make up your mind yet, do you? Not till you get the letter. There's three school-leaving dates each year, once he's reached sixteen.'

So I waited for the letter to come, that letter from the college which will release me from the slave-woman who dominates, who cares and protects, who represses, who believes that she owns me by virtue of having given me life.

'Up with your arms, pet. So we can pop your vest over your head. There's my good chappie!'

They'll be sending off that letter any day now, the letter to say when I shall start.

In the mornings, I lay as usual, as immobile as a rolled pork roast in my leg splints, my eyes closed to the baby bears, listening to the slave shuffling downstairs as she made her cup of tea and crushed my tablets with the back of a spoon.

But these days, as I waited for her to come up to my room and begin the ritual that starts each day, I no longer dreamed insubstantial dreams of chocolate biscuits. I dreamed of the touch of flesh, of the comfort of a body near to mine, of pleasure girls chosen in a market place and taken to the privacy of my own cubicle. My world was stretching beyond the cotton curtains. The sun-bronzed youth, now reaching the peak of his development, has many desires which all should be fulfilled.

I listened, each day, for the arrival of post flopping through the letter box and onto the mat. A big flop was mum's mail order catalogue, huge and heavy as a tombstone. She buys everything by direct order.

'We can't go getting out to the shops, see,' she explained once to Mrs Thingy. 'Not like other people. Not with my little boy being the way he is. And all those stairs to go up. And all the people staring. Mind you, when I was younger, I was very fond of a spot of shopping.'

When I am away at St John's she will be able to go round the shops again, unencumbered. And while she shops, I will be learning skills. My slow mind will be taught to understand more quickly. My obstinate hands will be trained to obey, to whittle wood, to weave baskets. I will master the skill of dressing myself as other boys do, the skill of preparing my own medication. I will not mess around with childish concoctions of conserve. I will swallow down those tablets whole.

Downstairs, I ceased the ritual refusal of prunes and bran. Why resist what my body needs when the world of St John's is there waiting?

'There's my good boy.'

The slave can scarcely believe how co-operative I have become. She ruffled the long hair above my ears and I tolerated her treatment of me as an infant, knowing that it will not last much longer. When I am at St John's I will have it short-cropped and manly, with a close-shaven neck, like the boy who smoked a cheroot and held a postcard of pieces of a woman.

Now I have so much. I have the future. I can afford to be compliant, gentle, tolerant with my carer.

Slavery is degrading to both slave and master. She too will surely be glad to be free of her bondage.

But waiting for the letter, time hangs suspended. I am waiting in the space between my life as a child, and my life as a man. And when the letter did not come I feared that perhaps they had forgotten me.

I knew she was anxious too. And then, at last it came. That morning, there were some brown envelopes, a brightly coloured letter telling her about French windows, and a plain white typed envelope. That was the one. I knew it because she never receives white typed envelopes.

She was upstairs, fetching my muffler. I was in my chair, positioned beside the breakfast table. I know now how to make myself fall from my wheelchair. Head first from the chair is painful but I had to get to the letter, which I could see down the hallway and lying on the doormat. I propelled myself, worm-like, along the floor. My nodding head knocks against the wall. The carpet is rough as wirewool on the palms of my soft hands. I love the pain. I am Man City. I am worming wriggling free.

'Micky dear!' she called to me from upstairs. 'What are you doing, pet?'

Instinctively, she knew that I was not where she had left me, not silent and still beside the empty cereal dishes. Does she know too how I have been practising the carpet crawl?

'Micky pet!' she called from the top of the stairs. Then, 'Oh no no!' for she saw me sprawling along the hall. She thought I had fallen. I left the other mail on the mat. I had the white typed envelope between my teeth. It was mine.

She rushed downstairs to me with her dressing gown flying like wings, and she gathered me up.

No, mum. No, leave me. Even squirming worms need freedom.

She doesn't leave me. She never leaves me. She enfolded me in the wings of her gown and I smell the strange smell of old worn-out woman.

'There's a kind boy. Trying to help your poor old ma. You needn't bother dear. I'll see to it after you've left for school.'

She took it from me, and walked me back, one step, two step, to the sitting room. She did not open the envelope. Her hand was trembling as she held it, just like my hands tremble before *status epilepticus*. She carried the dishes across the kitchen to the sink. She flushed the tea-leaves from the teapot down the sink while the envelope lay out of reach on the table beside the branflakes.

Come along now, slave. Open it. Read it. Shout out the good news. Freedom. When do I start? The woodwork room. Body posters on the walls of my private cubicle. The cookery classes.

At long last she got around to reading it out loud for me to hear. At St John Chrysostom's they teach many skills. Reading is a skill they may teach me. Hurry slave, before Bertram gets here.

'*Dear Mrs Graham,*' she reads. '*We regret to inform you that a place is not available at this unit for your son Michael. After very careful consideration of his case, and of his particular needs, as well as close observation of him during his visit here, we feel that this unit is not able to offer him the high degree of supervision which he currently needs.* Well, thank goodness for that!'

I felt my face contort into a grimace. I wanted to cry, but instead I heard myself laughing like a hyena.

'Why Micky, pet, you're crying. What is it? Don't worry, pet, I wouldn't have let you go there. I won't ever let anyone take you away from me.'

'Yeeerughaaah!' I cried out. Transplant me a new body so that they can see how I am Man City. Transplant me a voice so she can hear me cry for what I want. 'Yeeraghuuh!' She puts her arms around me to re-enfold me in her suffocating embrace.

'It was a dustbin place, that dump. I'd never let them put you in a place like that. My own baby. I'll look after you always. That's mummy's promise.'

Out in the street, the bus hooter sounded. Mrs Thingy took up her post behind her lace curtain. The world revolved and the noise of the horn shrieked and resounded inside my head.

'There's Bertram now.'

The gaoler put on my jacket, and wheeled me to the door where Mrs Lovegrove was ready to receive me. I am out on parole till four, and back in by nightfall. So it will be every day every day for the rest of my life. My experience of the other kind of outer life out there was too fragile for me to be able to hold on.

'And what's up with our Micky Sunshine then?' said Bertram as Mrs Lovegrove folded and loaded on board my chair. 'Something really eating you up today, eh?'

'Don't take any notice of him,' my mum called from the front step. 'He just had a bit of a fright earlier on. Thought they'd come to take him away. Now he's just putting it on. Being an old silly billy. You know how he suffers from his bowels. He'll be right as rain once the prunes have done their work.'

Further reading

If you found this story interesting, try reading other stories from *The Bus People*. You could also have a look at *The Poacher's Son* by Rachel Anderson published by Barn Owl Books, 2006.

Activities

The Rebel

Before you read

1   Discuss in small groups: do you think of yourself as a rebel who likes to shock other people, or as someone who mostly follows the rules and enjoys a quiet life?

What's it about?

2   Mount a dramatised reading of the poem and record it. This could involve a single reader, a pair or a group of readers. Try to bring out the rebellion that lies at the heart of the poem. Think of some suitable background music to your reading.

Thinking about the text

3   In groups, talk about which of the couplets you like best. What do you enjoy about the rhythm, the repetition and the construction of the poem? What is the effect of the final couplet?

4   Take one of the couplets as the starting point for writing your own short story.

5   Write five or six couplets of your own, in a similar style, which could be inserted before the final couplet in the original.

6   'It is very good that we have rebels.
  You may not find it very good to be one.'

Use this as the starting point for a short piece of drama showing a rebel making a stance and the consequences for him/her. The setting could be either a familiar one, like your school or youth club, or an extraordinary one like a different planet. The consequences could be funny or very serious!

Less Able

Before you read

1 If you were a school inspector (as this author has been for many years), what would you most enjoy about going into lots of different schools?

What's it about?

2 What do you think inspired the poet to write this poem? Look for evidence in the text (e.g. words that show you that the poet has thought a lot about the 'less able' child).

3 How does the poet persuade us that the boy he is writing about is not 'less able' as schools often define the term? Does he use certain words or phrases to show the reader his opinions? Talk about this in pairs.

Thinking about the text

4 As a group, discuss how your school and your teachers use the word 'ability'. Would you say it is narrowly or broadly defined and interpreted? Give examples.

5 Write a short persuasive essay in which you argue that society tends to promote rather narrow definitions of 'ability'.

Dear Aunty

Before you read

1   Which magazines or newspapers do you read? Do you read 'agony aunt' columns? Talk with a partner about why some people enjoy reading these kinds of articles and why some people find them dull and boring.

What's it about?

2   In what ways do Kylie, Briony and Nadia feel 'outsiders' in their families?

3   Does the advice given by Aunty seem good advice to you? If not, discuss with a partner how you would rephrase some of it.

Thinking about the text

4   Rather than just write an advice book, the author has chosen to present advice in the form of questions and answers. Do you find this style of presentation effective? Talk with a partner about why or why not.

5   Make a list of what you think are the most difficult things facing a young person whose parents are divorcing. Turn these into a 'top tips' list as part of a feature in a teenage magazine.

6   Think of another issue that commonly concerns teenagers and that often features in 'Agony Aunt' columns. Devise your own scenarios and advice around this issue, trying to capture the style and tone of these extracts.

Face

Before you read

1   It is said that you can read a person's thoughts and character just by looking at their face. What do you think?

What's it about?

2   What state of mind is Martin in as this chapter opens? And how is he feeling at the end of the chapter? Talk about this in groups. Do you sympathise with him?

3   Listing the names of everyone Martin meets at school, create a spider diagram on which you note down different people's attitudes towards him.

Thinking about the text

4   What do you think 'the Simon Hill affair' was? Write a short account of it, told from Martin's viewpoint; use clues in the text. Think what might have happened, where it took place, who was involved and what Martin learned from it.

5   What signs are there in this chapter that Martin is coming to terms with the accident that has left him disfigured? Write up your thoughts in a series of diary entries, from Martin's viewpoint.

6   Write a short sequel chapter to the one you have read here. Try to capture the author's style, writing with the same third-person narrator.

7   The following is a verse from the poem *Faceless*, which appears at the end of the Benjamin Zephaniah novel.

> *You have to look beyond the face*
> *To see the person true,*
> *Deep down within my inner space*
> *I am the same as you;*
> *I've counted since that fire burnt*
> *The many lessons I have learnt.*

Either continue the poem or use these thoughts as a starting point for your own story or non-fiction writing. You might also like to read the original poem in full.

The Rescue of Karen Arscott

Before you read

1   Debate the following topic in your class: 'Bullies always win'.

What's it about?

2   'Amongst us lot she stuck out like a sore thumb. Or rather an orchid on a rubbish tip.' On reading this opening, what kind of story did you expect to be reading? Were your expectations met? Why does Gene Kemp use these two images?

3   Draw quick sketches or cartoons of both Karen and Harriet. Note down words and phrases that describe the two girls and annotate your pictures. Use your notes to write character descriptions (up to 100 words) on each of them.

4   'Karen was a changed person' (page 218). Talk with a partner about how this came about. What exactly do you think caused Karen to change?

5   What effect does the final section of the story have on the narrative that has gone before? How did it change your thoughts towards both Karen and Harriet?

Thinking about the text

6   Retell the action of this story through a series of diary entries:
   a   from Karen's point of view
   b   from Harriet's point of view.

7   'I got to know her face well, but what went on behind it was still a mystery.' Write your own short story entitled 'Outsider', using this sentence as either your starting or finishing point.

8   'A short story succeeds when it has the aspect of *verisimilitude* – the appearance of being true.' Write a review of this story, concentrating on its verisimilitude. Use quotations from the text to support your commentary.

Red Sky in the Morning

Before you read

1   'Everyday society is getting better all the time in how it responds to disability issues.' Talk with a partner about examples you have come across which support or oppose this statement.

What's it about?

2   Talk with a partner about the way the author draws the reader's attention to Anna's 'double life'. Which phrases and sentences would you highlight?

3   Ben is severely disabled. Give examples from the text of where Anna feels he makes small but important progress with physical skills.

4   Discuss in small groups how you see the personalities and dynamics of Anna's family. Give thumbnail sketches of her parents and sister Katy.

5   Why is Mrs Chapman an important person in this extract? Write a short commentary on her role in helping Anna be more open about Ben's disability.

Thinking about the text

6   'People are only scared of handicaps because they're not used to them.' Use this as a starting point for your own piece of persuasive writing.

7   Imagine Anna is writing a letter to a close friend telling her about the next few weeks at school, following on from this extract. How do events unfold? Write Anna's letter.

8   Based on her experiences, Anna is asked to create a podcast for a website which offers advice to young people who are living with disabled brothers and sisters. With a partner, brainstorm some of the key things you think she will want to say. Draft a text for the recording, aiming for about two minutes in length. Then record.

The Curious Incident of the Dog in the Night-time

Before you read

1   Sometimes incidents that seem small to some people feel incredibly important to others. Talk with a partner about an example of this – perhaps a car breaking down, someone having something stolen or someone's pet dying. Discuss why you think people have different *emotional* reactions to events.

What's it about?

2   Under the headings 'personality', 'interests', 'attitudes' and 'feelings' note down any words or short phrases that apply to C. J. F. Boone. Use these notes to write a short character description.

Thinking about the text

3   Trying to capture how you think Christopher would write about a typical school day, draft out a few entries in his diary in which he talks about friends and teachers – and one particular incident that happens to him in school.

4   'And this is when I hit him.' Write the next chapter, involving Christopher and his father at the police station. Add a few off-beat illustrations, in the Mark Haddon style, like this one:

5   Look at Mark Haddon's website www.markhaddon.com. Use it to put together a short press release on the author and *The Curious Incident of the Dog in the Night-time*.

The Fifth Child

Before you read

1   Families come in all shapes and forms today. Discuss in groups why families are an important part of the way we live.

What's it about?

2   Create two spider diagrams. Make one which gathers together all the words and phrases that describe Ben's personality. Draft another which lists his *actions* in this extract.

3   Imagine you are Harriet. Draft a series of letters that she writes to a friend, which cover the period of this extract and a few weeks before and afterwards. Focus on your thoughts and feelings about what is happening to Ben. Look carefully at the text to see how the novelist describes Harriet's state of mind.

4   Talk in your groups about how the reactions of the children and the adults to Ben's behaviour are similar and different.

Thinking about the text

5   Hot-seat the author. Draft some questions about where her sympathies lie in this book and how and why she came to write it. Role-play your interview with her. Then write it up, in the style of a feature article for a magazine of your choosing.

6   Write a short story in which you take the family and Ben's life forwards a few years. What has happened to Ben? Where is he living? Who is looking after him? How are the rest of the family?

7   Put yourself in the shoes of Ben's parents. Imagine that, despite his strange behaviour, they want him to be educated in a mainstream school. But the doctors think he needs a special school. Rehearse and role-play the discussions which follow. How are matters resolved?

The Bus People

Before you read

1   Picture some passengers travelling on a bus:
    - a student on the way to sit an exam
    - an old man going to visit his daughter
    - a mother and her young child travelling to hospital
    - a young person setting off at the beginning of a journey to South America.

    Write a paragraph or two about each one, describing their thoughts and feelings and what sort of a day they are expecting to have.

What's it about?

2   Re-read the first 20 lines of the story. Why does the writer open the tale in the way she does? What picture do you form of the relationship between mother and son? Talk about these questions with a partner.

3   Why does Micky want to go to live at St John Chrysostom's? Which words and phrases does the author use to show this?

4   Why does Rachel Anderson end the story in the way she does? Where do the author's sympathies lie in this story? Think about the specific language and the techniques she uses.

Thinking about the text

5   Rewrite this extract as a short story either with a third-person narrator or as told from the mother's viewpoint. Preparing for this task, make a list of words and phrases that Micky uses which emphasise his anger, helplessness and dependency on his mother.

6   Imagine that the letter from St John's invites Micky to go and live there. Write a follow-on short story about Micky's move, exploring who he meets there and how life is, his thoughts and feelings and those of his mother.

7   You have been commissioned to produce some material for the website of a national charity which aims to promote disabled people living independently. Using this story and any other resources you can gather, work in a group to compile some interesting and challenging material for this website. This could also include a scripted interview with the author as a podcast.

Compare and contrast

1   Represent some of the ideas, issues and themes in this section for
    a particular purpose and audience:
    ● enacting a public inquiry or tribunal
    ● giving an eye-witness report to the police
    ● writing a campaigning letter to an organisation
    ● producing a short documentary video.

2   Which of the passages or poems that you have read in this section
    has most affected your feelings and opinions? Did you identify
    with any of the situations or characters? Has an author changed
    your views?

3   The *Dear Aunty* extract is in the form of a letter about a problem
    followed by some advice. Take any two of the characters you have
    read about in this section. Write a letter to them, in which you
    offer them sensitive advice about how to feel less of an 'outsider'
    and perhaps how they might overcome their problems.

4   Both Elizabeth Laird and Doris Lessing write about a character
    called Ben. Write your own short story or play in which these two
    characters come together in some chance encounter when they are
    older; both they and their families meet up. What happens?

5   Most of the extracts deal with children and young people facing
    difficult challenges. Write a short essay in which you analyse how
    successful two or three of the writers are in presenting a convinc-
    ing picture of how children think and feel. What writing techniques
    do they use to good effect?

Notes on authors

Tim Adams has been a literary editor and is a full-time journalist.

Rachel Anderson, born in 1943, has written widely for children and young people, with her novels *The War Orphan*, *The Poacher's Son* and *Joe's Story* being among the most popular.

Lance Armstrong, born in Texas, USA, in 1971, is an extraordinary sportsman who dominated competitive cycling for a decade between 1996 and 2006. He won the Tour de France seven times, having overcome an amazing battle with severe cancer. He now spends much of his time raising awareness about cancer around the world. He is author (co-written with Sally Jenkins) of *It's Not about the Bike* and *Every Second Counts*.

Floella Benjamin moved from Trinidad to Britain with her family as a child in 1960. She has worked in television as an actress and as a presenter of BBC children's programmes. She has written several children's books including *Skip across the Ocean* and *Coming to England*.

Ad de Bont, born in 1949, is artistic director of the Dutch theatre company Wederzijds, which works extensively in schools. He wrote *Mirad* in 1993, stirred by the number of young refugees from wars whom he had come across in Holland.

Patricia Borlenghi is a writer for children and young people. *Chaucer the Cat and the Animal Pilgrims* is one of her popular titles.

Robert Browning (1812–1889) was an English poet and playwright who spent much of his life in Italy. He was married to Elizabeth Barrett and together they became a celebrated writing partnership. *The Ring and the Book* is the long blank-verse poem that finally made Browning rich and successful.

Charles Dickens (1812–1870) is one of Britain's most celebrated writers. Born into a poor family, his is a 'rags to riches' story, earning his fortune with an inexhaustible output of novels. Characters in *Oliver Twist*,

Great Expectations, Hard Times, A Christmas Carol and many other books have become household names.

George Eliot (1819–1880) was born Mary Ann Evans but assumed a male pen-name. Her long novels are challenging to read but contain wonderful descriptions of people's lives and relationships, and the landscapes in which they lived. *Silas Marner* was published in 1861.

D. J. Enright (1920–2002) was a British academic, poet, novelist and man of letters. He served as Professor of English in the University of Singapore and later as Honorary Professor of English at Warwick University. He published many collections of poetry throughout his working life and often wrote on the theme of inequality.

Zlata Filipovic was born in 1980 and began writing her diary shortly before her 11th birthday. It was originally published in Croat by UNICEF. Just before Christmas 1993, a few days after her diary's first publication in France, Zlata and her parents were allowed to leave Sarajevo and flew to France on a UN plane.

Jean Giono (1895–1970) was a distinguished French writer, born in humble circumstances. His work is full of the values of simple country life and is shaped by his pacifism that grew out of the experience of two world wars. He travelled little and rarely left his native village in Provence.

Graham Greene (1904–1991) came from a distinguished family; his Catholic beliefs remained important to him throughout his life and writings. He was a prolific novelist, playwright, short story writer and critic. Among his best-known novels are *The Third Man*, *Brighton Rock*, *The Quiet American* and *The Power and the Glory*.

Mark Haddon, born in 1962, lives and writes in Oxford and has enjoyed best-selling success with *The Curious Incident of the Dog in the Night-time*. He has written a number of books for children including the *Agent Z* series. *A Spot of Bother* is his latest novel.

Conn and Hal Iggulden are the authors of the best-selling title *The Dangerous Book for Boys*. In its introduction, they write: 'In this age of video games and mobile phones, there must still be a place for knots, tree-houses and stories of incredible courage.'

Fergal Keane was born in Ireland in 1961 and is well known for his broadcast journalism from around the world with the BBC. He has written two very powerful collections of essays: *Letter to Daniel* and *Letters Home*.

Gene Kemp, born in 1926, has been a major author for children since the seventies, and also writes for TV and radio. Amongst her most widely read books are *The Turbulent Term of Tyke Tiler* and *Zowie Corby Plays Chicken*.

Elizabeth Laird was born in New Zealand and has lived and written in different parts of the world. She has been a prolific writer for children, with *Red Sky in the Morning* being one of a number that have received awards. She writes: 'My starting point is themes such as courage, endurance, forgiveness and love.'

Harper Lee, born in 1926, is an American novelist best known for her award-winning novel *To Kill a Mockingbird*, published in 1960. She has not published any other major writings. In a recent interview she observed: 'Now . . . in an abundant society where people have laptops, cell phones, iPods and minds like empty rooms, I still plod along with books.'

Doris Lessing was born in 1919 and has written about her life in different parts of the world, notably Africa. She is one of the greatest living British novelists. Many of her books address challenging political as well as difficult social issues, as with *The Fifth Child*, and her short stories are well worth exploring.

Michael Morpurgo was born in 1943 and is one of Britain's most popular children's authors, with a number of award-winning titles to his name. He has written over 100 novels and has been the nation's Children's Laureate, a recognition of his major contribution to children's literature.

Alfred Noyes lived from 1880 to 1958 and was the author of around 60 books. Titles included poetry, novels and short stories, and he is best known for his ballads like *The Highwayman*.

George Orwell (1903–1950) occupies a special place in 20th-century English literature and politics. He lived and worked in different parts of the world, including fighting in the Spanish Civil War in the 1930s. He is probably best known for his books *Animal Farm* and *Nineteen Eighty-Four*.

Gervase Phinn was born in Yorkshire in 1946. He spent many years as a teacher and inspector of schools before becoming a full-time writer and broadcaster. In his novels and poetry, which are full of humour, he draws heavily on his experiences in schools. Amongst his best-sellers are *Wayne in a Manger*, *The Other Side of the Dale* and *Over Hill and Dale*.

Stephen Pile is the compiler of *The Book of Heroic Failures*. The book's dedication reads: 'To all those who have written terrible books on how to be a success, I dedicate this terrible book on how it's perfectly all right to be incompetent for hours on end, because I am and so is everyone else I know.'

Bali Rai was born in Leicester in 1971 and is a full-time writer, making many visits to schools and libraries. Among his best-known books are *What's Up?*, *Concrete Chips*, *Dream On* and *(Un)arranged Marriage*.

Andrew Smith is English, although was born in New York and lived in California until his early teens. He is a journalist and writer.

Benjamin Zephaniah was born in England in 1958 and spent some of his childhood in his family's home in Jamaica. He is a well-known performance poet, recording artist and writer, whose work includes *Face*, *Refugee Boy* and *Gangsta Rap*.